New Perspectives on

Microsoft®

Internet
Explorer 4

INTRODUCTORY

The New Perspectives Series

The New Perspectives Series consists of texts and technology that teach computer concepts and microcomputer applications (listed below). You can order these New Perspectives texts in many different lengths, software releases, custom-bound combinations, CourseKits™ and Custom Editions®. Contact your Course Technology sales representative or customer service representative for the most up-to-date details.

The New Perspectives Series

Computer Concepts

Borland® dBASE®

Borland® Paradox®

Corel® Presentations™

Corel® Quattro Pro®

Corel® WordPerfect®

DOS

HTML

Lotus® 1-2-3®

Microsoft® Access

Microsoft® Excel

Microsoft® FrontPage™

Microsoft® Internet Explorer

Microsoft® Office Professional

Microsoft® PowerPoint®

Microsoft® Windows® 3.1

Microsoft® Windows® 95

Microsoft® Windows 98

Microsoft® Windows NT® Server 4.0

Microsoft® Windows NT® Workstation 4.0

Microsoft® Word

Microsoft® Works

Microsoft® Visual Basic® 4 and 5

Netscape Communicator™

Netscape Navigator™

Netscape Navigator™ Gold

New Perspectives on
Microsoft®
Internet Explorer 4

INTRODUCTORY

Sandra E. Poindexter
Northern Michigan University

Joan and Patrick Carey
Carey Associates, Inc.

COURSE
TECHNOLOGY

ONE MAIN STREET, CAMBRIDGE, MA 02142

an International Thomson Publishing company I(T)P®

Cambridge • Albany • Bonn • Boston • Cincinnati • London • Madrid • Melbourne • Mexico City
New York • Paris • San Francisco • Singapore • Tokyo • Toronto • Washington

New Perspectives on Microsoft® Internet Explorer 4 — Introductory is published by Course Technology.

Associate Publisher	Mac Mendelsohn
Series Consulting Editor	Susan Solomon
Product Manager	Rachel Crapser
Developmental Editor	Joan Carey
Production Editor	Daphne Barbas
Text and Cover Designer	Ella Hanna
Cover Illustrator	Douglas Goodman

© 1998 by Course Technology—I(T)P®

For more information contact:

Course Technology
One Main Street
Cambridge, MA 02142

ITP Europe
Berkshire House 168-173
High Holborn
London WCIV 7AA
England

Nelson ITP, Australia
102 Dodds Street
South Melbourne, 3205
Victoria, Australia

ITP Nelson Canada
1120 Birchmount Road
Scarborough, Ontario
Canada M1K 5G4

International Thomson Editores
Seneca, 53
Colonia Polanco
11560 Mexico D.F. Mexico

ITP GmbH
Königswinterer Strasse 418
53227 Bonn
Germany

ITP Asia
60 Albert Street, #15-01
Albert Complex
Singapore 189969

ITP Japan
Hirakawacho Kyowa Building, 3F
2-2-1 Hirakawacho
Chiyoda-ku, Tokyo 102
Japan

Trademarks
Course Technology and the Open Book logo are registered trademarks and CourseKits is a trademark of Course Technology. Custom Editions is a registered trademark of International Thomson Publishing.

I(T)P® The ITP logo is a registered trademark of International Thomson Publishing.

Some of the product names and company names used in this book have been used for identification purposes only and may be trademarks or registered trademarks of their respective manufacturers and sellers.

Disclaimer
Course Technology reserves the right to revise this publication and make changes from time to time in its content without notice.

ISBN 0-7600-5785-0

Printed in the United States of America

1 2 3 4 5 6 7 8 9 10 BM 02 01 00 99 98

At **Course Technology** we have one foot in education and the other in technology. We believe that technology is transforming the way people teach and learn, and we are excited about providing instructors and students with materials that use technology to teach about technology.

Our development process is unparalleled in the higher education publishing industry. Every product we create goes through an exacting process of design, development, review, and testing.

Reviewers give us direction and insight that shape our manuscripts and bring them up to the latest standards. Every manuscript is quality tested. Students whose backgrounds match the intended audience work through every keystroke, carefully checking for clarity and pointing out errors in logic and sequence. Together with our own technical reviewers, these testers help us ensure that everything that carries our name is error-free and easy to use.

We show both how and why technology is critical to solving problems in college and in whatever field you choose to teach or pursue. Our time-tested, step-by-step instructions provide unparalleled clarity. Examples and applications are chosen and crafted to motivate students.

As the New Perspectives Series team at Course Technology, our goal is to produce the most timely, accurate, creative, and technologically sound product in the entire college publishing industry. We strive for consistent high quality. This takes a lot of communication, coordination, and hard work. But we love what we do. We are determined to be the best. Write to us and let us know what you think. You can also e-mail us at *newperspectives@course.com*.

The New Perspectives Series Team

Joseph J. Adamski	Jessica Evans	Mac Mendelsohn
Judy Adamski	Kathy Finnegan	William Newman
Roy Ageloff	Marilyn Freedman	Dan Oja
Tim Ashe	Robin Geller	David Paradice
David Auer	Kate Habib	June Parsons
Daphne Barbas	Donna Gridley	Harry Phillips
Dirk Baldwin	Roger Hayen	Sandra Poindexter
Rachel Bunin	Cindy Johnson	Kim Rivers
Joan Carey	Charles Hommel	Ann Shaffer
Patrick Carey	Janice Jutras	Karen Shortill
Sharon Caswell	Chris Kelly	Susan Solomon
Barbara Clemens	Mary Kemper	Susanne Walker
Rachel Crapser	Stacy Klein	John Zeanchock
Kim Crowley	Terry Ann Kremer	Beverly Zimmerman
Melissa Dezotell	John Leschke	Scott Zimmerman
Michael Ekedahl	Scott MacDonald	

Preface The New Perspectives Series

What is the New Perspectives Series?

Course Technology's **New Perspectives Series** is an integrated system of instruction that combines text and technology products to teach computer concepts and microcomputer applications. Users consistently praise this series for innovative pedagogy, creativity, supportive and engaging style, accuracy, and use of interactive technology. The first New Perspectives text was published in January of 1993. Since then, the series has grown to more than 100 titles and has become the best-selling series on computer concepts and microcomputer applications. Others have imitated the New Perspectives features, design, and technologies, but none have replicated its quality and its ability to consistently anticipate and meet the needs of instructors and students.

What is the Integrated System of Instruction?

New Perspectives textbooks are part of a truly Integrated System of Instruction: text, graphics, video, sound, animation, and simulations that are linked and that provide a flexible, unified, and interactive system to help you teach and help your students learn. Specifically, the *New Perspectives Integrated System of Instruction* includes a Course Technology textbook in addition to some or all of the following items: Course Labs, Course Test Manager, Online Companions, and Figures on CD-ROM. These components—shown in the graphic on the back cover of this book—have been developed to work together to provide a complete, integrative teaching and learning experience.

How is the New Perspectives Series different from other microcomputer concepts and applications series?

The **New Perspectives Series** distinguishes itself from other series in at least four substantial ways: sound instructional design, consistent quality, innovative technology, and proven pedagogy. The applications texts in this series consist of two or more tutorials, which are based on sound instructional design. Each tutorial is motivated by a realistic case that is meaningful to students. Rather than learn a laundry list of features, students learn the features in the context of solving a problem. This process motivates all concepts and skills by demonstrating to students *why* they would want to know them.

Instructors and students have come to rely on the high quality of the **New Perspectives Series** and to consistently praise its accuracy. This accuracy is a result of Course Technology's unique multi-step quality assurance process that incorporates student testing at at least two stages of development, using hardware and software configurations appropriate to the product. All solutions, test questions, and other supplements are tested using similar procedures. Instructors who adopt this series report that students can work through the tutorials independently with minimum intervention or "damage control" by instructors or staff. This consistent quality has meant that if instructors are pleased with one product from the series, they can rely on the same quality with any other New Perspectives product.

The **New Perspectives Series** also distinguishes itself by its innovative technology. This series innovated Course Labs, truly *interactive* learning applications. These have set the standard for interactive learning.

How do I know that the New Perspectives Series will work?

Some instructors who use this series report a significant difference between how much their students learn and retain with this series as compared to other series. With other series, instructors often find that students can work through the book and do well on homework and tests, but still not demonstrate competency when asked to perform particular tasks outside the context of the text's sample case or project. With the **New Perspectives Series,** however, instructors report that students have a complete, integrative learning experience that stays with them. They credit this high retention and competency to the fact that this series incorporates critical thinking and problem-solving with computer skills mastery.

How does this book I'm holding fit into the New Perspectives Series?

New Perspectives applications books are available in the following categories:

Brief books are typically about 150 pages long, contain two to four tutorials, and are intended to teach the basics of an application.

Introductory books are typically about 300 pages long and consist of four to seven tutorials that go beyond the basics. These books often build out of the Brief editions by providing two or three additional tutorials. The book you are holding is an Introductory book.

Comprehensive books are typically about 600 pages long and consist of all of the tutorials in the Introductory books, plus a few more tutorials covering higher-level topics. Comprehensive books typically also include two Windows tutorials and three or four Additional Cases.

Advanced books cover topics similar to those in the Comprehensive books, but go into more depth. Advanced books present the most high-level coverage in the series.

Office books are typically 800 pages long and include coverage of each of the major components of the Office suite. These books often include tutorials introducing the suite, exploring the operating system, and integrating the programs in the suite.

Custom Books The New Perspectives Series offers you two ways to customize a New Perspectives text to fit your course exactly: *CourseKits*™, two or more texts packaged together in a box, and *Custom Editions*®, your choice of books bound together. Custom Editions offer you unparalleled flexibility in designing your concepts and applications courses. You can build your own book by ordering a combination of titles bound together to cover only the topics you want. Your students save because they buy only the materials they need. There is no minimum order, and books are spiral bound. Both CourseKits and Custom Editions offer significant price discounts. Contact your Course Technology sales representative for more information.

New Perspectives Series Microcomputer Applications				
■ **Brief Titles or Modules**	■ **Introductory Titles or Modules**	■ **Intermediate Tutorials**	■ **Advanced Titles or Modules**	■ **Other Modules**
Brief	**Introductory**	**Comprehensive**	**Advanced**	**Custom Editions**
2 to 4 tutorials	6 or 7 tutorials, or Brief + 2 or 3 more tutorials	Introductory + 4 or 5 more tutorials. Includes Brief Windows tutorials and Additional Cases	Quick Review of basics + in-depth, high-level coverage	Choose from any of the above to build your own Custom Editions® or CourseKits™

In what kind of course could I use this book?

This book can be used in any course in which you want students to learn all the most important topics of Internet Explorer 4, including Web browsing and searching with Internet Explorer, e-mail and newsgroup management with Outlook Express, and Web page composition with FrontPage Express. It is particularly recommended for a short course on Internet Explorer or as part of a full-semester course on the Internet. This book assumes that students have learned basic Windows 95 or Windows NT navigation and file management skills from Course Technology's *New Perspectives on Microsoft Windows 95—Brief, New Perspectives on Microsoft Windows NT Workstation 4.0—Introductory*, or an *equivalent* book.

How do the Windows 95/NT/98 editions differ from the Windows 3.1 editions?

Sessions We've divided the tutorials into sessions. Each session is designed to be completed in about 45 minutes to an hour (depending, of course, upon student needs and the speed of your lab equipment). With sessions, learning is broken up into more easily assimilated portions. You can more accurately allocate time in your syllabus, and students can better manage the available lab time. Each session begins with a "session box," which quickly describes the skills students will learn in the session. Furthermore, each session is numbered, which makes it easier for you and your students to navigate and communicate about the tutorial. Look on page IE 1.5 for the session box that opens Session 1.1.

Quick Checks Each session concludes with meaningful, conceptual Quick Check questions that test students' understanding of what they learned in the session. Answers to the Quick Check questions in this book are provided on pages IE 3.41 through IE 3.42 and IE 5.36 through 5.38.

New Design We have retained the best of the old design to help students differentiate between what they are to *do* and what they are to *read*. The steps are clearly identified by their shaded background and numbered steps. This text also features easier to follow page numbering and colored tabs, so students can always find their place in a text. Furthermore, this new design presents steps and screen shots in a larger, easier to read format. Some good examples of our new design are pages IE 1.14 and IE 1.30.

What features are retained in the Windows 95 editions of the New Perspectives Series?

"Read This Before You Begin" Page This page is consistent with Course Technology's unequaled commitment to helping instructors introduce technology into the classroom. Technical considerations and assumptions about software are listed to help instructors save time and eliminate unnecessary aggravation. See pages IE 1.2 and IE 4.2 for the "Read This Before You Begin" pages in this book.

Tutorial Case Each tutorial begins with a problem presented in a case that is meaningful to students. The problem turns the task of learning how to use an application into a problem-solving process. The problems increase in complexity with each tutorial. These cases touch on multicultural, international, and ethical issues—so important to today's business curriculum. See page IE 1.3 for the case that begins Tutorial 1.

Step-by-Step Methodology This unique Course Technology methodology keeps students on track. They enter data, click buttons, or press keys always within the context of solving the problem posed in the tutorial case. The text constantly guides students, letting them know where they are in the course of solving the problem. In addition, the numerous screen shots include labels that direct students' attention to what they should look at on the screen. On almost every page in this book, you can find an example of how steps, screen shots, and labels work together.

TROUBLE?

TROUBLE? Paragraphs These paragraphs anticipate the mistakes or problems that students are likely to have and help them recover and continue with the tutorial. By putting these paragraphs in the book, rather than in the Instructor's Manual, we facilitate independent learning and free the instructor to focus on substantive conceptual issues rather than on common procedural errors. Some representative examples of TROUBLE? paragraphs appear on page IE 1.12.

REFERENCE window

Reference Windows Reference Windows appear throughout the text. They are succinct summaries of the most important tasks covered in the tutorials. Reference Windows are specially designed and written so students can refer to them when doing the Tutorial Assignments and Case Problems, and after completing the course. Page IE 1.30 contains the Reference Window for viewing images on demand.

Task Reference The Task Reference contains a summary of how to perform common tasks using the most efficient method, as well as references to pages where the task is discussed in more detail. It appears as a table at the end of the book.

Tutorial Assignments, Case Problems, and Lab Assignments Each tutorial concludes with Tutorial Assignments, which provide students with additional hands-on practice of the skills they learned in the tutorial. See page IE 1.35 for examples of Tutorial Assignments. The Tutorial Assignments are followed by four Case Problems that have approximately the same scope as the tutorial case. In the Windows 95 applications texts, the last Case Problem of each tutorial typically requires students to solve the problem independently, either "from scratch" or with minimum guidance. See page IE 1.36 for examples of Case Problems. Finally, if a Course Lab accompanies a tutorial, Lab Assignments are included after the Case Problems. See page IE 1.38 for examples of Lab Assignments.

Exploration Exercises The Windows environment allows students to learn by exploring and discovering what they can do. Exploration Exercises can be Tutorial Assignments or Case Problems that challenge students, encourage them to explore the capabilities of the program they are using, and extend their knowledge using the Help facility and other reference materials. Page IE 1.37 contains Exploration Exercises for Tutorial 1.

What supplements are available with this textbook?

Course Labs: Now, Concepts Come to Life Computer skills and concepts come to life with the New Perspectives Course Labs—highly-interactive tutorials that combine illustrations, animations, digital images, and simulations. The Labs guide students step-by-step, present them with Quick Check questions, let them explore on their own, test their comprehension, and provide printed feedback. Lab icons at the beginning of the tutorial and in the tutorial margins indicate when a topic has a corresponding Lab. Lab Assignments are included at the end of each relevant tutorial. The Labs available with this book and the tutorials in which they appear are:

TUTORIAL 1

The Internet
World Wide Web

TUTORIAL 3

E-Mail

Course Test Manager: Testing and Practice at the Computer or on Paper
Course Test Manager is cutting-edge, Windows-based testing software that helps instructors design and administer practice tests and actual examinations. This full-featured program allows students to randomly generate practice tests that provide immediate on-screen feedback and detailed study guides. Instructors can also use Course Test Manager to produce printed tests. Course Test Manager can automatically grade the tests students take at the computer and can generate statistical information on individual as well as group performance.

Figures on CD-ROM: This lecture presentation tool allows instructors to create electronic slide shows or traditional overhead transparencies using the figure files from the book. Instructors can customize, edit, save, and display figures from the text in order to illustrate key topics or concepts in class.

Online Companions: Dedicated to Keeping You and Your Students Up-To-Date When you use a New Perspectives product, you can access Course Technology's faculty sites and student sites on the World Wide Web. You can browse this text's password-protected Faculty Online Companion to obtain an online Instructor's Manual, Solution Files, Student Files, and more by visiting Course Technology's Online Resource Center at http://www.course.com. Please see your Instructor's Manual or call your Course Technology customer service representative for more information.

Instructor's Manual New Perspectives Series Instructor's Manuals contain instructor's notes and solutions for each tutorial. Instructor's notes provide tutorial overviews and outlines, technical notes, lecture notes, and extra Case Problems. Solutions include answers to Tutorial Assignments, Case Problems, and Lab Assignments.

Student Files Student Files contain all of the data that students will use to complete the tutorials, Tutorial Assignments, and Case Problems. A Readme file includes technical tips for lab management. See the inside covers of this book and the "Read This Before You Begin" pages for more information on Student Files.

Solution Files Solution Files contain every file students are asked to create or modify in the tutorials, Tutorial Assignments, and Case Problems.

The following supplements are included in the Instructor's Resource Kit that accompanies this textbook:

- Electronic Instructor's Manual
- Solution Files
- Student Files

- Course Labs
- Course Test Manager Testbank
- Course Test Manager Engine
- Figures on CD-ROM

Some of the supplements listed above are also available over the World Wide Web through Course Technology's password-protected Faculty Online Companion for this text. Please see your Instructor's Manual or call your Course Technology customer service representative for more information.

Acknowledgments

We wish to thank Inge Schmitt, Notre Dame College of Ohio, and Bob Dahlen, Century College, for their suggestions for improving the tutorials. Many thanks to the New Perspectives team at Course Technology, particularly Mac Mendelsohn, Associate Vice-President, Associate Publisher; Rachel Crapser, Product Manager; Chris Greacen and Nancy Ludlow, Online Development Group; Greg Bigelow, Manager of Quality; Brian McCooey, Quality Assurance Project Leader; Seth Freeman, Alex White, Chris Hall, and Jessica Sisak, Quality Assurance Testers; and Daphne Barbas, Production Editor.

Joan Carey, Patrick Carey, and Sandra Poindexter

Without the assistance of Martin Eskelinen, Helen Heck, Jane Phillips, Mike Bradley, and Steve and Anna Poindexter this book could not have been written. Finally, my thanks to Peter Heck who gave me the drive not just to finish, but to succeed.

Sandra Poindexter

Thanks also to our four little sons, Michael, Peter, Thomas, and John Paul, whose many little sacrifices made it possible for us to work on this book.

Joan & Patrick Carey

Microsoft® Internet Explorer 4

LEVEL I

TUTORIALS

Read This **Before You Begin**

Navigating the Web with Internet Explorer

Conducting Teacher Workshops at Northern University

In this tutorial you will:

- Understand the structure of the Internet and the World Wide Web

- Identify Internet Explorer components

- Start and exit Internet Explorer and view and hide Explorer toolbars

- Open a Web page from your Student Disk

- Navigate links and frames

- Open a Web page with its URL

- Move among Web pages

- Load images

- Print a Web page

- Get online help

LABS

The Internet
World Wide Web

CASE

Northern University

Michelle Pine, an education student at Northern University, is researching the use of the Internet as a teaching tool in the classroom and as an aid for preparing class lessons. She uses the Northern University Internet connection regularly to keep in contact with her friends and professors. She also uses an online service at home to communicate with her family, who live in New Mexico.

Michelle has been amazed at the wealth and variety of information she has found freely available on the Internet, especially the amount geared toward educators. At forums, educators can share ideas, advice, and encouragement. Teachers can find current information about every subject that can be incorporated into the curriculum. Geography and history, for example, come alive with multimedia travel through various time periods and lands. Science is no longer limited by physical equipment, and students can conduct experiments in virtual labs that would be impossible in many classrooms. Humanity studies become more vibrant through tours of world-famous museums, music, and video clips from particular artists, styles, or times. The more Michelle looks, the more resources she finds. What's more, she has discovered that information is updated and added daily.

As a special project for one of her education courses, Michelle is planning a two-hour workshop for teachers on Internet basics and Internet Explorer. The 25 educators enrolled in the workshop have little working knowledge of the Internet and Internet Explorer but are interested in its possibilities.

Michelle asks you to help her facilitate the workshop. She'd like to give the talk while you help out at the computer keyboard. Michelle wants to begin by giving the educators an overview of the Internet and the World Wide Web. Then she'll teach them Internet Explorer basics using a presentation she created especially for the workshop. Finally, she'll demonstrate how to connect to and navigate through pages on the Web.

Using the Tutorials Effectively

These tutorials will help you learn about Internet Explorer. They are designed to be used at a computer. Each tutorial is divided into sessions designed to be completed in about 45 minutes, but take as much time as you need. Watch for the session headings, such as Session 1.1 and Session 1.2. It's also a good idea to take a break between sessions.

Before you begin, read the following questions and answers, which are designed to help you use the tutorials effectively.

Where do I start?

Each tutorial begins with a case, which sets the scene and gives you background information to clarify what you will be doing in the tutorial. Ideally, you should read the case before you go to the lab. In the lab, begin with the first session.

How do I know what to do on the computer?

Each session contains steps that you will perform on a computer to learn how to use Internet Explorer. Read the text that introduces each series of steps. The steps you need to perform at a computer are numbered and set against a colored background. Read each step carefully and completely before you try it.

How do I know if I did the step correctly?

As you work, compare your computer screen with the corresponding figure in the tutorial. Don't worry if your screen display is somewhat different from the figure. The important parts of the screen display are labeled in each figure. Check to make sure these parts are on your screen.

What if I make a mistake?

Don't worry about making mistakes; they are part of the learning process. Paragraphs labeled "TROUBLE?" identify common problems and explain how to get back on track. Follow the steps in a TROUBLE? paragraph only if you are having the problem described. If you run into other problems, carefully consider the current state of your system, the position of the pointer, and any messages on the screen.

How do I use the Reference Windows?

Reference Windows summarize the procedures you learn in the tutorial steps. Do not complete the actions in the Reference Windows when you are working through each tutorial. Instead, refer to the Reference Windows while you are working on the assignments at the end of each tutorial.

How can I test my understanding of the material I learned in the tutorial?

At the end of each session, answer the Quick Check questions. The answers for the Quick Check questions are at the end of the tutorials. After you have completed the entire tutorial, complete the Tutorial Assignments and Case Problems. They are carefully structured so you will review what you have learned and then apply your knowledge to new situations.

What if I can't remember how to do something?

Refer to the Task Reference at the end of each tutorial; it summarizes how to accomplish tasks using the mouse, the menus, and the keyboard.

What are the Interactive Labs, and how should I use them?

Interactive Labs help you review concepts and practice skills that you learn in each tutorial. Lab icons at the beginning and in the margins of the tutorials indicate topics that have corresponding Labs. The Lab Assignments section includes instructions for how to use each Lab.

Now that you've seen how to use the tutorials effectively, you are ready to begin.

SESSION

1.1

In this session, you will learn about the Internet, the World Wide Web, and the Internet Explorer suite. You will also learn how to start and exit Internet Explorer, identify components of the Internet Explorer window, work with Internet Explorer toolbars, view Web pages, activate and abort a link, and work with frames.

The Internet World Wide Web

The Internet

Michelle wants to begin her talk by giving an overview of the technology that makes it possible for people to communicate with each other using their computers. She also wants to familiarize her audience with common network terms that will make it possible for them to understand how the Internet operates. When two or more computers are linked together so that they can exchange information and resources, they create a structure known as a **network**. Networks facilitate the sharing of data and resources among multiple users. Some computers, called **servers**, provide specific resources to the network, such as print capabilities or stored files. Figure 1-1 shows a small network consisting of a single server, a shared printer, and a handful of computers.

Figure 1-1 ◀
Small network

cable connects
network computers
together →

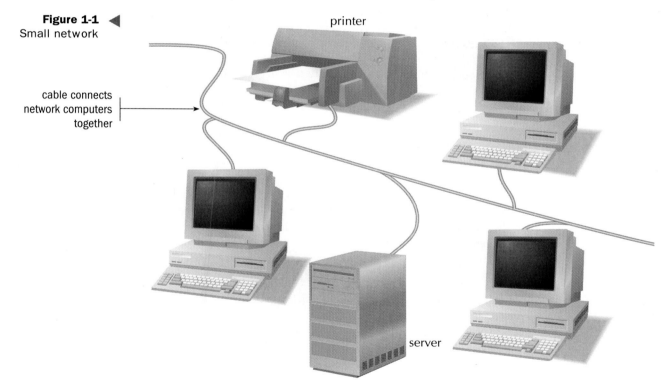

printer

server

Networks can also be connected to each other to allow information to be shared between computers on different networks. The **Internet**, the largest and most famous example of a "network of networks," is made up of millions of computers linked to networks all over the world. Computers and networks on the Internet are connected by fiber optic cables, satellites, phone lines, and other communication systems, as shown in Figure 1-2.

Figure 1-2 ◀
Structure of
the Internet

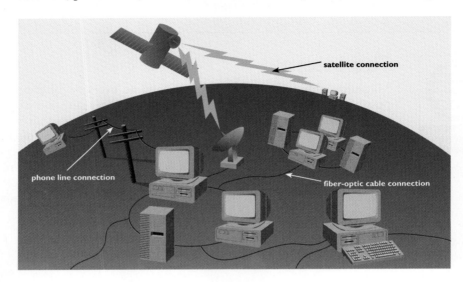

Computers on a network are often called **hosts**, and thus a computer with Internet access is sometimes called an **Internet host**.

The Internet, by design, is a decentralized structure. There is no Internet "company." Instead, the Internet is a collection of different organizations, such as universities and companies, that organize their own information. There are no rules about where information is stored, and no one regulates the quality of information available on the Internet. Even though the lack of central control can make it hard for beginners to find their way through the resources on the Internet, there are some advantages. The Internet is open to innovation and rapid growth as different organizations and individuals have the freedom to test new products and services and make them quickly available to a global audience. One such service developed in recent years is the **World Wide Web**, an Internet service that makes finding information and moving around the Internet easy.

The World Wide Web

The foundation of the World Wide Web was laid in 1989 by Timothy Berners-Lee and other researchers at the CERN research facility near Geneva, Switzerland. They wanted to make it easy for researchers to share data with a minimum of training and support. They created a system of **hypertext documents**—electronic files that contain elements known as **links**, which you can select, usually by clicking a mouse, to move to another part of the document or another document altogether. A link can be a word or phrase or a graphic image.

The system of hypertext documents developed at CERN proved to be easily adaptable to other information sources on the Internet. Within the space of a few years, hypertext documents were being created by numerous organizations for a large variety of topics. Because it was easy to link these different hypertext documents together, a single user could jump from one set of hypertext documents to another without much effort. This interconnected structure of hypertext documents became known as the World Wide Web or simply the Web.

Each hypertext document on the Web is called a **Web page** and is stored on a computer on the Internet called a **Web server**. A Web page can contain links to other Web pages located anywhere on the Internet—on the same computer as the original Web page or on an entirely different computer halfway across the world. The ability to cross-reference other Web pages with links is one of the most important features of the Web.

Figure 1-3 shows how when you click a link on one Web page you move to another Web page.

Web page on
rock climbing

Figure 1-3
Link in one
hypertext
document
opens another

click this link
to jump to a
different document

this Web page
appears when you
click the Tour link

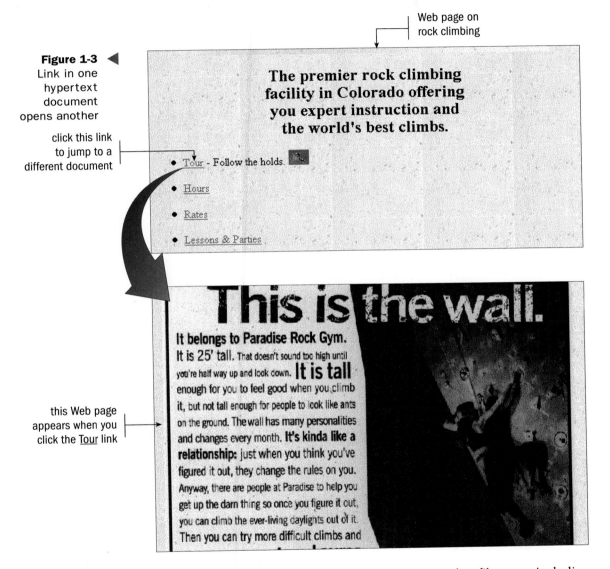

When you click a link, you can also connect to other file types, including scanned photographs, graphic images, film clips, sounds, and computer programs. A link could lead you into a discussion group called a **forum** or **newsgroup** where users share information on topics of common interest. Another link might point to the e-mail address of an individual (should you want to send a message).

Navigating Web pages using hypertext is an efficient way of accessing information. Michelle points out that when you read a book you follow a linear progression, reading one page after another. With hypertext, you progress through the pages in whatever order you want. Hypertext allows you to skip from one topic to another, following the information path that interests you, as shown in Figure 1-4.

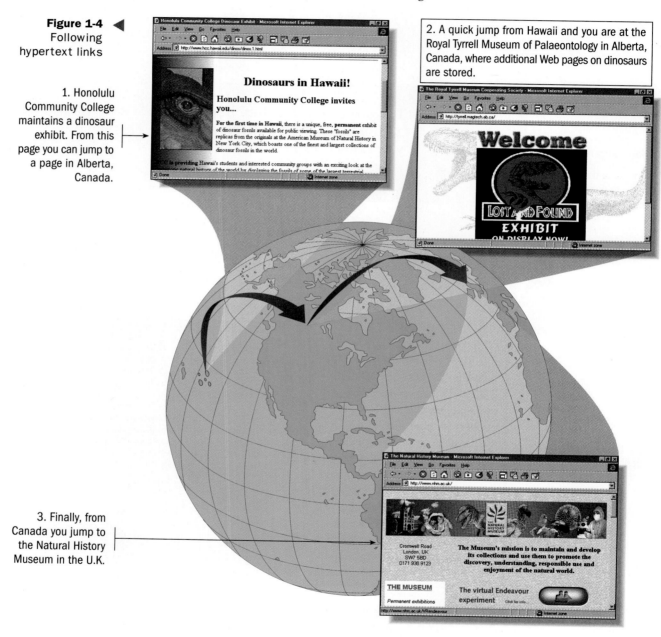

Figure 1-4 ◀
Following
hypertext links

1. Honolulu Community College maintains a dinosaur exhibit. From this page you can jump to a page in Alberta, Canada.

2. A quick jump from Hawaii and you are at the Royal Tyrrell Museum of Palaeontology in Alberta, Canada, where additional Web pages on dinosaurs are stored.

3. Finally, from Canada you jump to the Natural History Museum in the U.K.

Hypertext has great appeal because a single Internet user can jump from one set of hypertext documents to another set without much effort. Perhaps the greatest source of the Web's popularity, however, lies in the ease with which users can create their own Web pages. All you need is an account on a computer connected to the Internet that allows you to store your Web page and make it available for others to read. Many companies that sell access to the Internet, called **Internet Service Providers** or **ISPs**, include Web pages as part of their service.

Internet Explorer

To access the documents available on the Web, to communicate with others, and to publish your own Web page, you need special software. Until recently, you needed to purchase one program, called a **browser**, to view and work with Web pages, another to communicate with e-mail or participate in group discussions, and yet another to create and publish a Web page. Software developers are now producing **suites**, or groups of products, that allow you to be active on the Web with a single, seamlessly integrated package. **Internet Explorer** is Microsoft Corporation's Web software suite. It provides all the tools you need to communicate, share, and access information on the World Wide Web, and for this reason it is Northern University's product of choice. Michelle plans to use Internet Explorer at the workshop because it is easy to use and understand.

Michelle provides the following overview of the tools available in various installations and versions of Internet Explorer. She emphasizes that you shouldn't worry if you don't understand the functions of each component right now. You'll learn more about the individual Internet Explorer tools later.

You can obtain either the Browser Only, Standard, or Full installation of Internet Explorer. The Browser Only installation features browsing capabilities. The Standard installation adds e-mail and newsgroup capabilities. The Full installation adds conferencing, presentation, Web page creation, and additional functions to the Standard installation. This book assumes a Full installation. See Appendix A for information on downloading the Internet Explorer software over the Web. Figure 1-5 lists the most significant services Internet Explorer provides for each installation.

Figure 1-5 ◄
Internet
Explorer
components

Service	Description
Browser Only	
Internet Explorer	Browser that retrieves, displays, and organizes documents. These documents are retrieved from Web servers and displayed on your computer.
Standard adds the following:	
Outlook Express	E-mail and newsgroup manager that allows you to send, receive, compose, edit, search, and sort e-mail. **E-mail**, or electronic mail, is a note you write and send across the Internet. Outlook Express can handle e-mail containing practically any file type—graphics, sounds, videos and so on. Outlook Express also functions as a newsgroup manager that helps you participate in a discussion group.
Full adds the following:	
NetMeeting	Video, audio, and data conferencing software that allows you to meet and collaborate with others in real time.
NetShow	Online application software that helps you integrate audio and video into online presentations.
FrontPage Express	Web page editor that you use to create and edit Web pages.

You can also obtain additional components, useful **add-ons**, or software programs that extend the capabilities of the Internet Explorer suite, from Microsoft's Web site. You install add-ons using instructions that come with them; once an add-on is installed, Internet Explorer uses the add-on's capabilities just like other built-in Internet Explorer features. Appendix A contains information on using Microsoft's add-ons.

Michelle wants to keep the workshop simple, focusing only on navigating the Web rather than on e-mail, newsgroups, and Web page publishing. Thus, she will use only the browser component of Internet Explorer in her presentation.

What Is Internet Explorer?

With Internet Explorer, you can visit sites around the world; view multimedia documents; transfer files, images, and sounds to your computer; conduct searches for specific topics; and run software on other computers. Underneath the surface, Internet Explorer is running a variety of Internet services, but because Internet Explorer handles the commands for you, you can be blissfully unaware of the complexity of what really happens when you navigate the Web.

When a user tries to view a Web page, the user's browser, in this case Internet Explorer, locates and retrieves the document from the Web server and displays its contents on the user's computer. As shown in Figure 1-6, the server stores the Web page in one location, and browsers anywhere in the world can view it.

Figure 1-6 ◄
Using a browser to view a Web document on a server

Internet Explorer browser

browser in California locates and displays document stored on server in Florida

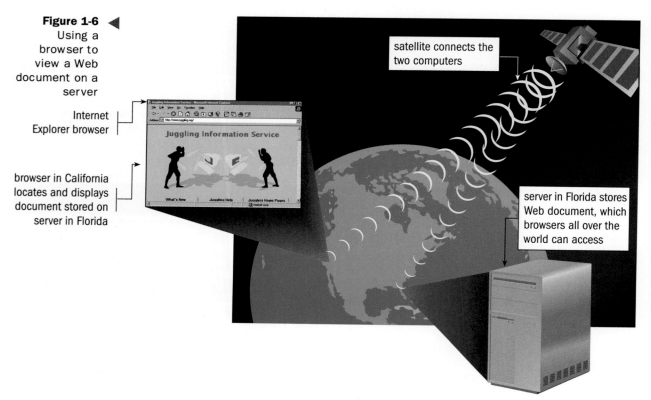

satellite connects the two computers

Juggling Information Service

What's New | Juggling Help | Jugglers Home Pages |

server in Florida stores Web document, which browsers all over the world can access

Here, a browser in California is accessing a document stored on a Web server in Florida. You might retrieve such a page without knowing or caring on which Web server it is stored. The wonder of the World Wide Web is that you can view a document stored on a Web server across the room or across the world using the same technique. Information stored on a server in Cairo is just as accessible as is one in Cleveland. Is there any doubt why the Web has been called the "Information Superhighway"?

Starting Internet Explorer

Before you can start using Internet Explorer to explore the Web, you must have an Internet connection. In a university setting your connection might come from the campus network on which you have an account. If you are working on a home computer, your connection might come over the phone line from an account with an Internet Service Provider. How you connect to the Internet depends on what service you have, but at a university you will most likely already be connected to the Internet and can start Internet Explorer and immediately begin to browse the Web.

Michelle explains that, unlike many other software applications, Internet Explorer does not open with a standard start-up screen. Instead, you see a document called the **home page**—the Web page that appears when you start Internet Explorer. Internet Explorer allows each computer installation to specify what home page users will see when they start Internet Explorer. When you launch Internet Explorer, you might see:

- The Microsoft Corporation home page

- Your school's or institution's home page

- A page your technical support person sets as the default

- A blank page

A home page can also refer to the Web page that a person, organization, or business has created to give information about itself. A home page might include information about the host, links to other sites, or relevant graphics and sounds. When Michelle starts Internet Explorer from home, she connects to the Microsoft Corporation home page, which provides fundamental information about Microsoft and its software. When she starts it in the university's lab, she sees Northern University's home page, stored on a Web server at Northern University.

REFERENCE window

STARTING INTERNET EXPLORER

- Click the Start button, point to Programs, point to the Internet Explorer program group, then click Internet Explorer.
or
- If your desktop displays an Internet icon that starts Internet Explorer, click or double-click that icon, depending on your operating system's configuration.
or
- If the Quick Launch toolbar appears on your taskbar with icons for different Internet Explorer components, click the Internet Explorer button 🅔 right from your taskbar to launch Internet Explorer.

These instructions show you how to start Internet Explorer from the Start menu.

To start Internet Explorer:

1. If necessary, connect to your Internet account.

   TROUBLE? If you are in a university setting you are probably already connected and can skip Step 1. If you don't know how to connect to your Internet account, ask your technical support person for help or call your Internet Service Provider's technical support line.

2. Click the **Start** button 🏁Start on the Windows taskbar.

3. Point at **Programs** with the mouse pointer. After a short pause, the Programs menu opens with a list of the programs available on your computer.

4. Point at **Internet Explorer** on the Programs menu, then point at **Internet Explorer** on the Internet Explorer menu. See Figure 1-7.

Figure 1-7 ◀
Starting
Internet
Explorer

your menus and
desktop might
look different

point here to open
Programs menu

Start button

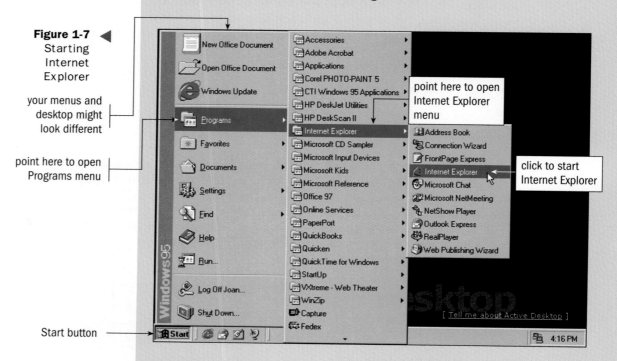

point here to open
Internet Explorer
menu

click to start
Internet Explorer

TROUBLE? If you don't see Internet Explorer on the Programs menu, ask your instructor or technical support person for assistance. If you are using your own computer, make sure Internet Explorer is installed.

TROUBLE? If your Internet Explorer menu shows different entries, don't worry. You just have a different version of Internet Explorer.

5. Click **Internet Explorer** to start Internet Explorer. The home page specified by your site's installation will open.

TROUBLE? If this is the first time Internet Explorer has been used on your computer, you might be prompted to establish a connection or to set other settings. If you are using a computer that is not your own, ask your technical support person for assistance. If you are using your own computer, read the instructions, proceed through the dialog boxes that appear, providing information where requested (such as your e-mail address), then click Next when you finish each step. If you reach a dialog box that you don't understand, you might need to call your Internet Service Provider's technical support line for assistance.

6. Click the **Maximize** button 🗖 in the upper-right corner of the Microsoft Internet Explorer window if the window is not already maximized. See Figure 1-8, which shows the Microsoft Corporation home page.

TROUBLE? If your screen shows a different home page, don't worry.

TROUBLE? If your window looks different, don't worry. You'll soon learn how to customize the Internet Explorer window so that it matches the figures.

Internet
Explorer

Figure 1-8
Internet
Explorer
window

title bar

menu bar

Standard toolbar

Address bar

document window;
yours will be different

Quick Launch bar

status bar

Regardless of which page appears when you first start Internet Explorer—the Microsoft home page, your university's home page, or a different home page—your window should share some common components with the one in Figure 1-8. Michelle points out the most important parts of the Internet Explorer window, shown in Figure 1-9. Don't worry if you don't see all these components. You'll soon learn how to make them appear.

Figure 1-9
Internet
Explorer window
components

Window component	Description
Title bar	Identifies the active Web page.
Menu bar	Groups Internet Explorer commands by menu name. You click a menu name to open a menu, and then click the command you want.
Standard toolbar	Offers single-click access to the more common menu commands.
Address bar	Identifies the address of the active Web page—the one currently displayed in the Internet Explorer document window. The address of a Web page is called its **uniform resource locator**, or **URL**. You'll learn more about URLs in the next session.
Links toolbar	Displays buttons that you can click to jump immediately to individual Web pages. You can add buttons for your personal favorites.
Quick Launch bar	Displays buttons that you can click to access different components of Internet Explorer.
Document window	Displays the active Web page.
Scroll bars	Allows you to move through the active page content. Click the up and down arrows on the vertical scroll bar to move the page up and down, or less frequently, the left and right arrows on the horizontal scroll bar to move the page left and right. You can also drag the scroll box or click above and below it to move through a page.
Activity indicator	Displays the Internet Explorer logo, which appears as a rotating globe [image] when a page is loading and [image] when the browser is idle. If the activity indicator is idle but the page doesn't seem to have been successfully retrieved, you know there is a problem with the connection.
Status bar	Indicates the status of the document you are retrieving from the Web server, as well as security information about the site.

Controlling the Internet Explorer Display

The Internet Explorer window looks different depending on what objects are displayed, such as the Address or Links bars, Standard toolbar, or an Explorer bar. You can easily drag toolbars to different locations so that more of the document window is available, or you can hide toolbars if you aren't likely to use them. You can also display the buttons with only icons instead of icons with text labels—again, to make more space available in the document window. For now, you want to display only the Standard toolbar with icons (not text labels) and the Address bar.

To control the Internet Explorer display:

1. Click **View** to open the View menu and then point to **Toolbar**. The commands you see control the presence or absence of objects and their features in the Internet Explorer window. The presence of a checkmark indicates whether that object or feature is enabled. For example, if the second command in the View menu, Status Bar, has a checkmark next to it, the Status Bar is visible. Figure 1-10 shows a screen whose Status Bar is visible, whose Standard, Address, and Links toolbars are all visible, and whose buttons show Text Labels. Notice on the menu that all these commands have checkmarks next to them.

   TROUBLE? If fewer toolbars are displayed on your screen or if they are organized differently, don't worry. You'll learn to control the position of the toolbars in the next steps.

Figure 1-10 ◀
Viewing status of Internet Explorer display

Standard toolbar is visible, with text labels

Address bar is visible

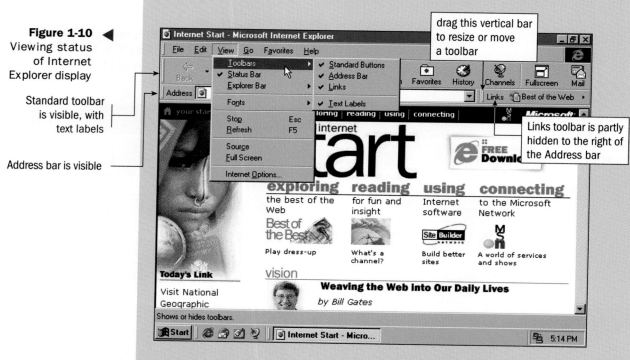

2. Now you'll experiment with hiding a toolbar. Look at the Toolbars submenu, which should still be open and note whether Links has a checkmark next to it. If it does, click **Links**. The Links toolbar disappears.

3. Click **View**, point at **Toolbar**, and then click **Links**, which should not have a checkmark next to it, again. The Links toolbar reappears in its previous position.

Internet
Explorer

4. Now practice dragging the Links toolbar to a new location. To drag a toolbar, drag the vertical bar that precedes it, as shown in Figure 1-10. Point at the vertical bar in front of the Links toolbar. The pointer changes from ↕ to ↔. Now drag the Links toolbar below the Address bar. As you drag, the pointer changes to ┤├.

TROUBLE? If the Links toolbar is already below the Address bar, drag it above the Address bar.

TROUBLE? If your Address bar isn't visible, click View, point to Toolbars, click Address Bar, and then repeat Step 4.

5. Drag the Links toolbar to the right of the Address bar.

6. Now resize the Links toolbar. Point at the vertical bar preceding the Links toolbar. Drag the vertical bar to the left. The Links toolbar is enlarged. The Address bar shrinks.

7. Now hide the Links toolbar, because you don't need it in this tutorial. Click **View**, point to **Toolbars**, and then click **Links**. The Links toolbar disappears and the Address bar enlarges to the entire width of the window.

8. Click **View** and then point to **Toolbars**. If there is a checkmark next to the Text Labels command in the Toolbar submenu, click **Text Labels** to remove the checkmark. The toolbar buttons now appear without Text Labels.

9. Click **View** once more, point to **Explorer Bar**, and click **None** to ensure no Explorer bars are visible. Compare your screen to Figure 1-11.

Figure 1-11 ◄
Final display

only Standard and
Address bars
are visible

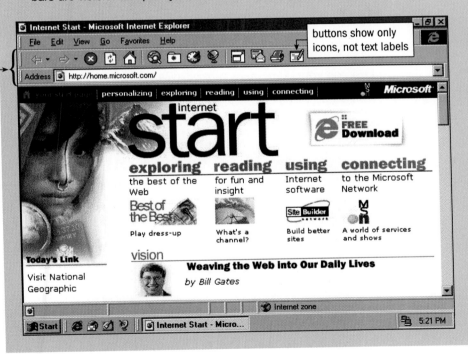

The components of your Internet Explorer window should now match the figures. Michelle can now begin demonstrating how to navigate the Web.

Navigating the Web

Once you are connected to the Internet and you have started the Internet Explorer browser, you can view Web pages using several different methods. If you have a Web page in the form of a file on a disk, you can simply open that page in your browser. If you are currently viewing a page with links, you can also click a link to activate it and jump to that page. You'll practice both methods now.

Opening a Web Page

Michelle has prepared a Web page that she will use at the workshop because she wants to be able to start from the same point from any computer, regardless of what home page appears in the document window. Michelle's Web page file is provided on your Student Disk. You'll open it in the Internet Explorer browser, and then you will be viewing the same page shown in the figures and you will be able to navigate the same links.

REFERENCE window	**OPENING A WEB PAGE INTO THE INTERNET EXPLORER BROWSER**
	■ Click File and then click Open.
	■ Type the page's full path or address, or click Browse, locate the file in the Open dialog box, and then click the Open button.
	■ Click the OK button.

Keep in mind that you are opening Michelle's file off your Student Disk, not off the Web. You can use the Internet Explorer browser to view Web page files on your Student Disk, on your computer's other drives, and on Web servers around the world. You'll learn how to view a file on the Web in Session 1.2.

To open a specific Web page:

1. Place your Student Disk in drive A. See the "Read This Before You Begin" page to make sure you are using the correct disk for this tutorial.

    TROUBLE? If you are using drive B, place your Student Disk in that drive instead, and for the rest of these tutorials substitute drive B wherever you see drive A.

2. Click **File** and then click **Open**.

3. Type **a:\Tutorial.01\michelle.htm** as shown in Figure 1-12.

    TROUBLE? If you are using drive B, type b:\Tutorial.01\Michelle.htm instead.

Figure 1-12 ◀
Opening a page

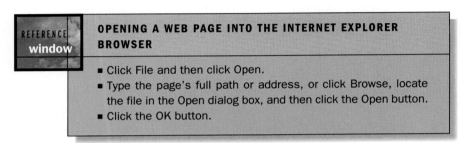

Internet
Explorer

4. Click the **OK** button. The Web page Michelle has prepared for the workshop opens. See Figure 1-13.

Figure 1-13 ◄
Michelle's
workshop page

A hypertext link on the Web, like a link in a chain, is a connector between two points. Links can appear in two ways: as text that you click or as a graphic that you click. A **text link** is a word or phrase that is underlined and often boldfaced or colored differently. A graphic link is a graphic image that you click to jump to another location. When you aren't sure whether a graphic image is a link, point to it with the mouse pointer. When you move the mouse pointer over a link—text or graphic—it changes shape from ⌖ to 🖑. The 🖑 pointer indicates that when you click, you will activate that link and jump to the new location. The destination of the link appears in the status bar, and for some graphic links a small identification box appears next to your pointer.

As you'll see, Michelle's workshop pages contain both text and graphic links. The text links are underlined and in color. Each link gives Internet Explorer the information it needs to locate the page. When you activate a link, you jump to a new location, called the **target** of the link, which can be another location on the active Web page (for example, often the bottom of a Web page contains a link that jumps you up to the top), a different document or file, or a Web page stored on a remote Web server anywhere in the world.

When you activate a link, there are three possible outcomes:

1. You successfully reach the target of the link. Internet Explorer contacts the site (host) you want, connects into the site, transfers the data from the host to your computer, and displays the data on your screen.

2. The link's target is busy, perhaps because the server storing the link's target is overwhelmed with too many requests. You'll have to try a different link, or try this link later.

3. The link points to a target that doesn't exist. Documents are often removed from Web servers as they become obsolete, or they are moved to new locations, and links that point to those documents are not updated.

The amount of time it takes to complete a link, called the **response time**, can vary, depending upon the number of people trying to connect to the same site, the number of people on the Internet at that time, and the site design.

Activating a Link

Activating a link starts a multi-step process. Although Internet Explorer does the work for you, it is important to follow the sequence of events so you can recognize problems when they occur and understand how to resolve them.

Figure 1-14 illustrates the string of events that occur when you link to a site. When you point to a link, the status bar displays a message that it is connecting to the address of the link's target, called its **Uniform Resource Locator** or **URL**. When you click a link, the activity indicator animates. The status bar displays a series of messages indicating that Internet Explorer is opening the host (or site) you want to visit and is waiting for a reply, is transferring data, and finally, is done.

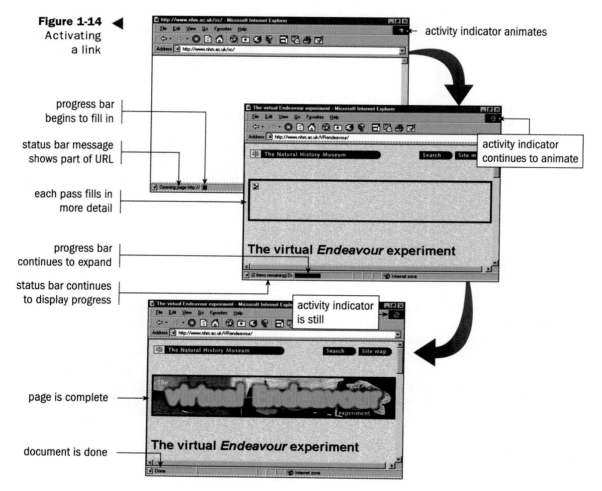

Figure 1-14
Activating
a link

activity indicator animates

progress bar
begins to fill in

status bar message
shows part of URL

activity indicator
continues to animate

each pass fills in
more detail

progress bar
continues to expand

status bar continues
to display progress

activity indicator
is still

The virtual *Endeavour* experiment

page is complete

document is done

The virtual *Endeavour* experiment

You can see the Web page build as Internet Explorer transfers information to your screen in multiple passes. The first wave brings a few pieces to the page, and with each subsequent pass, Internet Explorer fills in more detail until the material is complete. The progress bar fills in to indicate how much of the Web page has transferred. The vertical scroll box scrolls up as Internet Explorer adds more information and detail to the page. You don't have to wait until the page is complete before scrolling or clicking another link, but it might be difficult to determine links and other information until the page is mostly filled in.

Michelle's page contains links that let you experience each of the three outcomes mentioned earlier. First, you'll successfully activate a link.

To initiate a link to a Web page:

1. If necessary, scroll through Michelle's page until you find the "Click here for a Successful site link" sentence.

2. Point at the **Successful site** link. Notice that the pointer changes shape from ▷ to 🖑, indicating that you are pointing to a hypertext link. The status bar shows the URL for that link. See Figure 1-15.

Figure 1-15 ◀
Activating
a link

link's target appears
in status bar

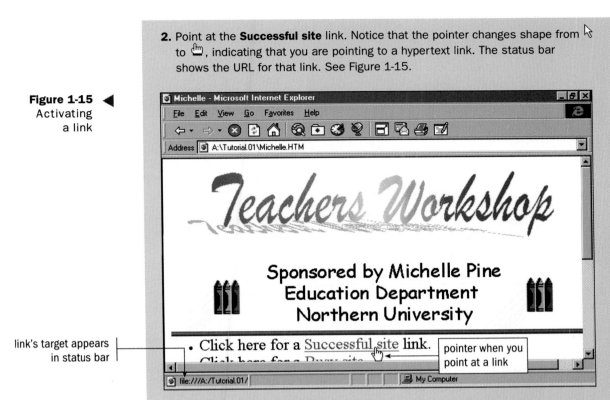

pointer when you
point at a link

TROUBLE? If the status message area does not contain a URL, slowly move your pointer over the underlined words. When you see the URL in the status message area, the pointer is positioned correctly.

3. Click the **Successful site** link to activate the link. The status bar notes the progress of the link. When the status bar displays, "Done," the link is complete and the Web page that is the target of the link appears. See Figure 1-16.

TROUBLE? If a message dialog box opens, the link was not successful. Click the OK button to close the dialog box, and repeat Steps 1 through 3. After you click the hypertext link, make sure you do not click anywhere else on the page until the link is complete.

Figure 1-16 ◀
Completed
link

graphic link

text link

status bar indicates
link is complete

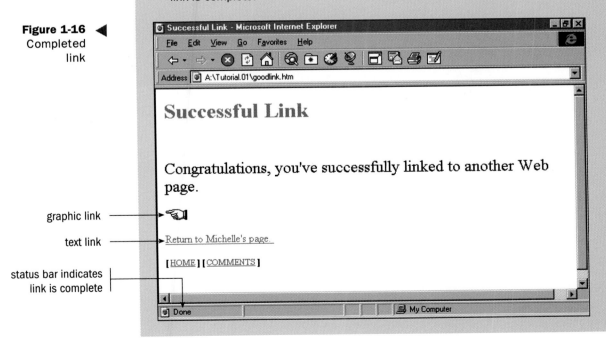

4. Move the pointer over the graphic image of a pointing hand. The pointer changes to 🖑 and the URL of Michelle's page appears in the status bar. This is a graphic link; to return to Michelle's page you could click it or the text link below it.

5. Click the **pointing hand** graphic link to return to Michelle's page.

You connected to a Web page with a single click, and then you used the graphic link in that page to return to Michelle's page. Using hypertext links is a simple way to move from one Web page to another. Notice that the Successful site link on Michelle's page has changed color (you might need to scroll down to see this). Internet Explorer displays text links you've already activated in a different color so you know which links you've already tried.

Aborting a Busy Link

Sometimes when you try to connect to a site, the link is not successful. Much like an expressway, the Internet can become so congested that the paths cannot support the number of users at peak times. When this happens, traffic backs up and slows to a halt, in effect closing the road. At these peak times, the load is too heavy for the Internet.

Aborting, or interrupting, a link is like taking the next exit ramp on the Internet. When the response time to a link seems too slow (longer than a few minutes) or nothing seems to be happening, you have no way of knowing how long it will take to complete a link. You can tell that a link is stalled when one of the following situations occurs:

1. the status message area does not change, but

2. the Stop button 🛑 on the toolbar is active, and

3. the activity indicator is animated 🌐

Rather than waiting for a site that has a long queue or is so busy it can't even respond to your request, you can abort the link.

Michelle wants to show the workshop how to stop an unsuccessful link. There is one site that she has tried to visit many times but has been unsuccessful. She asks you to try to link to that site.

To abort a delayed link:

1. Scroll down until you see the list of Busy site links on Michelle's page. The Busy site links target sites that are often busy—though they might not be when you perform Step 2.

2. Click the **Busy site** link to initiate the link. Watch the status message area; if the site is busy, it comes to a halt, although the activity indicator remains animated and the Stop button active. The link is stalled. See Figure 1-17. The line to visit this site might be very long, or many people might be using the Internet and you just can't get to the site. Either way, you'll want to abort the link rather than wait an interminable amount of time.

Figure 1-17
Stalled link

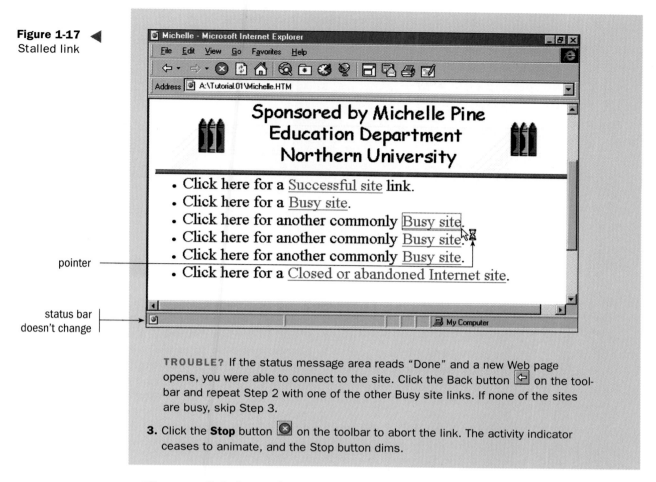

pointer

status bar
doesn't change

TROUBLE? If the status message area reads "Done" and a new Web page opens, you were able to connect to the site. Click the Back button on the toolbar and repeat Step 2 with one of the other Busy site links. If none of the sites are busy, skip Step 3.

3. Click the **Stop** button on the toolbar to abort the link. The activity indicator ceases to animate, and the Stop button dims.

Now try a link that no longer exists.

Activating a Defunct Link

Michelle wants to show the workshop that a link not only might complete successfully or stall, but that it might also be aborted by Internet Explorer. She explains that Internet Explorer terminates a link and displays an error message indicating the site was not found because:

- The URL specified by the hypertext link might no longer be active.

- The URL might be typed incorrectly.

- The server could not reach the site within the server's programmed wait time (for example, 90 seconds).

When such a message dialog box appears, you have no choice but to acknowledge the message and give up.

To end an Internet Explorer–terminated link:

1. If necessary, scroll down the page, then click the **Closed or abandoned Internet site** link to initiate a link to a nonexistent site. A message dialog box opens. See Figure 1-18. The dialog box indicates that Internet Explorer is unable to locate the server containing the target of the link.

Figure 1-18 ◀
Terminated link

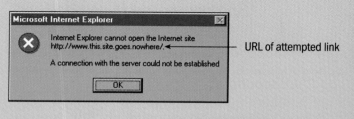

URL of attempted link

2. Click the **OK** button to close the dialog box.

In this case, Internet Explorer aborted the link because it could not establish a connection with the server. The server supposedly storing the target of the link does not have a proper domain name. Every host is part of a **domain**, or group, that has a unique name, similar to a family surname. Just as family members can share a surname yet live in separate households both nearby and far away, a domain contains one or more hosts that might be at the same physical location or spread great distances apart. Some domains are small and contain just a few hosts. Others are very large and contain hundreds of hosts. An educational institution or a government agency might each have its own domain name.

Each host can have a domain name registered with the **Domain Name Server (DNS)**. When you link to a site, Internet Explorer checks to see if the domain in its URL is registered with the DNS. If the site is not registered (similar to an unlisted telephone number in the phone book), Internet Explorer opens the message dialog box. Unless you know the correct URL for that site, you cannot link to it.

Working with Frames

Michelle wants to illustrate one more navigational concept. Web page designers often divide their pages into parts, called frames, to organize their information more effectively. A **frame** is a section of the document window. Each frame can have its own set of scroll bars and can display the contents of a different location. Many Web sites today employ frames because they allow the user to see different areas of information simultaneously. When you scroll through the contents of one frame, you do not affect the other frame or frames.

Michelle wants you to demonstrate frames using a page that she is designing for Northern University and the Education Department, listing available degree programs. She's included a link for this page on her main page.

To scroll through a frame:

1. Scroll to the bottom of Michelle's page until you see the "Click here to see how frames work" sentence.

2. Click the **frames** link. Figure 1-19 shows the page that opens. It contains three frames. The top frame identifies the page as that of the Education Department. The frame on the left identifies the two types of undergraduate programs—certification and noncertification—and the right frame displays information about the programs.

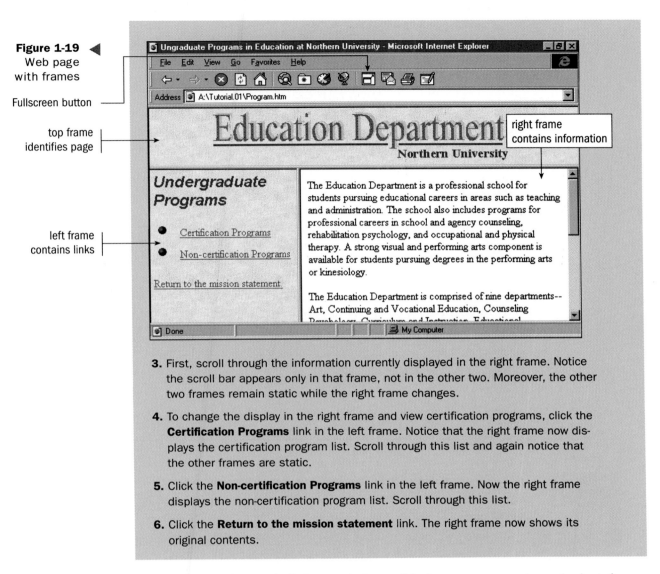

Figure 1-19
Web page
with frames

Fullscreen button

top frame
identifies page

left frame
contains links

right frame
contains information

3. First, scroll through the information currently displayed in the right frame. Notice the scroll bar appears only in that frame, not in the other two. Moreover, the other two frames remain static while the right frame changes.

4. To change the display in the right frame and view certification programs, click the **Certification Programs** link in the left frame. Notice that the right frame now displays the certification program list. Scroll through this list and again notice that the other frames are static.

5. Click the **Non-certification Programs** link in the left frame. Now the right frame displays the non-certification program list. Scroll through this list.

6. Click the **Return to the mission statement** link. The right frame now shows its original contents.

By using frames, Michelle has made it possible for users to examine only the information they are interested in. Knowing how to recognize and navigate frames is increasingly important because many Web pages now use them.

Pages with frames often contain a great deal of information, and you might want to display more of it on your screen. Internet Explorer offers a Fullscreen button on the Standard toolbar, which you can click, to make the active Web page take up the maximum amount of space on your screen.

To view the Education Department Web page at full screen capacity:

1. Click the **Fullscreen** button ⊟. The title, status, and menu bars disappear, the toolbars collapse, and you see as much of the Web page as possible.

2. Click ⊟ to restore the display.

Exiting Internet Explorer

Michelle decides to take a break in the workshop. Before you leave the computer, you need to close Internet Explorer. The next time you start Internet Explorer, the window will show the home page designated for your installation. To return to a site you visited in this session, you will need to reopen the Web page and link to the sites you want to see.

To exit Internet Explorer:

1. Click **File**.

2. Click **Close**. The Internet Explorer window closes.

You have completed Session 1.1. You have opened Internet Explorer, opened a Web page in the Internet Explorer browser, linked to a site successfully, aborted a stalled link, had Internet Explorer terminate a link for you, and experimented with frames.

Quick Check

1. True or False: When you start Internet Explorer, you will always see the same screen, no matter what computer you are using.

2. What is a home page?

3. The address of a Web page is called a(n) _____.

4. How does Internet Explorer display a text link that you've already activated?

5. When you try to link to a Web site but the page you want does not immediately appear, you might need to _____ the link because of congestion on the Internet.

6. What does Internet Explorer mean when it tells you, "The server does not have a DNS entry"?

SESSION

1.2

In this session, you will learn more about URLs and how to open a Web page using its URL, how to navigate the Web with Internet Explorer using toolbar buttons, how to speed up things by viewing images on demand, how to print Web pages, and how to use the online Help feature.

Opening a Location with a URL

Michelle now wants to show the instructors how to locate specific Web pages and how to use them in their classes. Some of the educators mention that they've read journal articles about integrating the Internet into the curricula for all age groups. These articles usually supply Internet addresses for helpful online resources. Michelle explains how to access these sites.

Clicking a hypertext link is just one way of jumping to a Web page. Clicking links, often called "surfing," is an easy way to navigate the Web when you don't have a specific destination in mind and just want to follow content links. Often, however, you want to visit a particular site. In order to get to that site, you need to know its address, which must be in a certain form. Entering the Uniform Resource Locator (URL) for a Web page is a direct route to get to a specific site.

A URL is composed of a protocol identifier, a server address, and a file pathname. For example, when Michelle saves the undergraduate program list she is creating for the Education Department, it will have the following URL:

http://www.northern.edu/education/program.html

protocol   server address   file pathname

Computers use standardized procedures, called **protocols**, to transmit files. Web documents travel between sites using **HyperText Transfer Protocol** or **HTTP**, so every URL for a

Web page begins with "http://" to identify its type. Another common protocol you might see is **File Transfer Protocol**, or **FTP**, a protocol that facilitates transferring files over the Web.

The server address contains the domain name and tells the exact location of the Internet server and the type of organization that owns and operates it. For example, in the domain name "www.northern.edu" the "www" indicates that the server is on the World Wide Web, "northern" indicates the name of the organization that owns the server (Northern University), and "edu" indicates that it's an educational site. The entire domain name tells you that Northern is an educational site on the Web. Figure 1-20 lists common domain name types. Outside the United States, domain name types include a two-letter country code. For example, "fi" indicates that the server is located in Finland.

Figure 1-20 ◀
Domain name
types

Domain	Description	Domain	Description	Domain	Description
au	Australia	fr	France	net	Networking organizations
ca	Canada	gov	Government agencies	org	Nonprofit organizations
com	Commercial sites	int	International organizations	uk	United Kingdom
de	Germany	jp	Japan		
edu	Educational institutions	mil	Military sites		

All files stored on a network server must have a unique pathname just as files on a disk do. The pathname includes the folder or folders the file is stored in, plus the filename and its extension. The filename and extension are always the last item in the pathname. The filename extension for Web pages is usually html (or just htm), which stands for hypertext markup language. Michelle's Education Department programs file, for example, is named program.html and is located in the education folder on the Northern server.

Sometimes when you try to go to a specific site, you might see an error message such as the one shown in Figure 1-21. If you see such an error message, you should check the URL in the Address box on the Address bar and make sure every character is typed correctly, then try again.

Figure 1-21 ◀
URL Not Found
error message

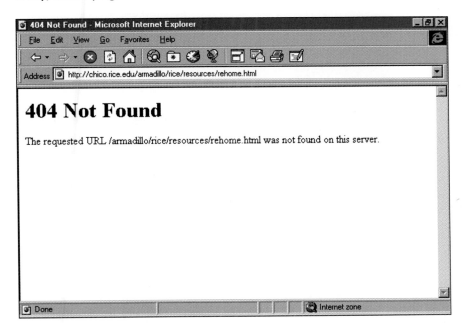

Remembering two important facts about a URL will make it significantly easier to use a URL to access an Internet site:

- Domain names in a URL are case-sensitive. A URL must be typed with the same capitalization shown. The URL http://www.Mysite.com is different from http://WWW.mysite.com. Unless the server can interpret case-sensitive addresses, you will get an error message when a URL doesn't exist with the exact name and capitalization entered. Whether you copy a URL from a magazine article or get it from a friend, make sure you copy the characters and their cases exactly.

- Internet sites continuously undergo name and address changes. A network server might have changed names, the file might be stored in a different folder, or the page you want might no longer be available. Remember, no one person or organization controls the Internet. Organizations and individuals can add files, rename them, and delete them at will. Often when a URL changes, you can find the forwarding address (URL) at the old URL. Other times, a site will simply vanish from a server, with no forwarding information.

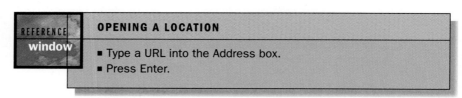

REFERENCE
window

OPENING A LOCATION

- Type a URL into the Address box.
- Press Enter.

Lyle Sanchez, one of the educators, wants to find an interesting site that he can show his students as an "in-class field trip." He asks you to help him. You are going to use a set of Web pages designed by the publisher of this book for these tutorials. The URL for the Web page you need is http://www.course.com/downloads/NewPerspectives/msie4. You can type this URL directly in the Address box on the Address bar.

To open a location:

1. Launch Internet Explorer and make sure Standard and Address toolbars are visible and the buttons display icons without Text Labels.

   TROUBLE? If you need help starting Internet Explorer or setting the options, refer to the appropriate sections earlier in this tutorial.

2. Click the **Address** box to highlight the current entry, which should be the URL for your home page.

   TROUBLE? If the current entry is not highlighted, highlight it manually by dragging the mouse from the far left to the far right of the URL. The entire entry must be highlighted so that the new URL you type replaces the current entry.

3. Type **http://www.course.com/downloads/NewPerspectives/msie4** in the Address box. Make sure you type the URL exactly as shown. Notice the two slashes after the protocol identifier; the protocol identifier is always followed by the two slashes. See Figure 1-22.

Figure 1-22 ◀
Opening a Web
page with
its URL

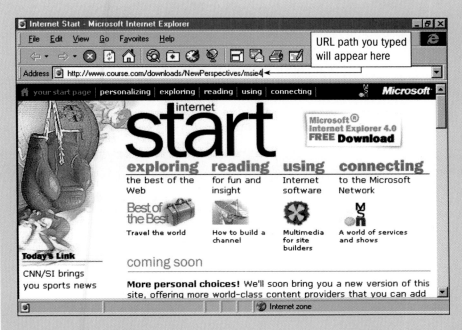

4. Press **Enter**. Internet Explorer will follow the same steps as it did when you clicked hypertext to link to a site and will connect you to the selected Web page. See Figure 1-23.

> **TROUBLE?** If you receive a Not Found error message, the URL might not be typed correctly. Repeat Steps 2 through 4, making sure that the URL in the Address box matches the one shown in Figure 1-22. You can correct a minor error by double-clicking in the Address box, using the arrow keys to move to the error, and then making the correction. If the URL matches Figure 1-22 exactly, or if you see a different error message, press the Enter key to try connecting to the Web page again. If you see the same error message, ask your instructor or technical support person for help.

Figure 1-23 ◀
Opened
Web page

URL of current
Web page

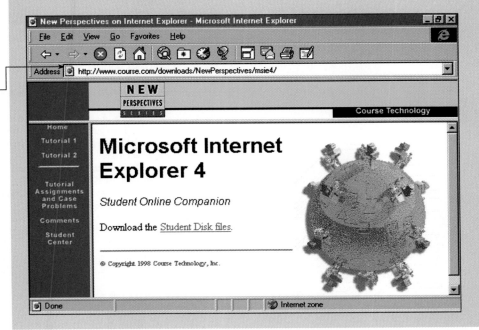

Moving Among Web Pages

In Internet Explorer, you can flip among Web pages you've visited in a session as though they were pages in a magazine that you have held with a finger. Rather than memorizing and retyping URLs of places you have visited, you can use toolbar buttons to move back one page at a time through the pages, move forward again one page at a time, or return to the "front cover" of your home page. Internet Explorer "remembers" which pages you've been to during your current Web session, and it provides navigation buttons on the Standard toolbar so that you can easily move through those pages. See Figure 1-24.

Figure 1-24 ◀
Navigation
buttons in
Internet
Explorer

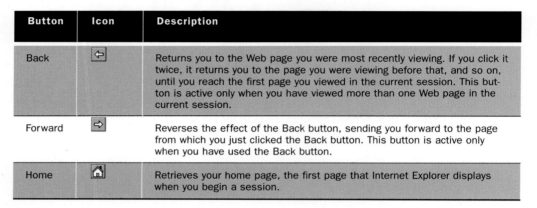

Button	Icon	Description
Back	⇦	Returns you to the Web page you were most recently viewing. If you click it twice, it returns you to the page you were viewing before that, and so on, until you reach the first page you viewed in the current session. This button is active only when you have viewed more than one Web page in the current session.
Forward	⇨	Reverses the effect of the Back button, sending you forward to the page from which you just clicked the Back button. This button is active only when you have used the Back button.
Home	⌂	Retrieves your home page, the first page that Internet Explorer displays when you begin a session.

To visit and then move among visited Web pages:

1. Click the **Tutorial 1** link in the left frame of the Web page to open the Learning to Navigate page. This Web page contains hypertext links to educational resource sites available on the Internet. Lyle wants to look at the Field Trips/Museums link.

2. Click the **Field Trips/Museums** link in the Subject Areas list to see the list of sites available from this Web page. See Figure 1-25.

Figure 1-25 ◀
Field
Trips/Museums
list

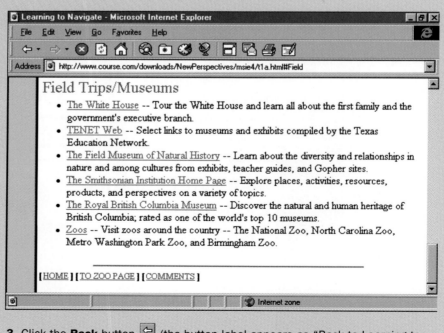

3. Click the **Back** button ⇦ (the button label appears as "Back to Learning to Navigate"; when possible the label identifies the page to which you will return). The Learning to Navigate page reappears on your screen.

TROUBLE? If you click the small arrow to the right of the Back button, a list opens. Click the arrow again to close the list, and repeat Step 3. This time make sure you click ⇦ .

4. Click ⇦ until you return to your home page. Notice that the Back button dims, indicating that you have reached the first page you viewed since you started Internet Explorer; you can move back only as far as the home page.

TROUBLE? If your Back button is already dimmed after you return to the Learning to Navigate page, then you are at your starting point, and your Internet Explorer installation does not have a home page that appears upon startup. Just continue with Step 5.

5. You have moved backward through the earlier pages and now want to return to the Field Trips/Museums list. Click the **Forward** button ⇨ until the Field Trips/Museums list appears. Notice that the Forward button is dimmed again, indicating that you are looking at the last page you visited.

TROUBLE? If your Forward button is not dimmed, you have linked from the Learning to Navigate page to another Web page. Continue clicking the Forward button until it is dimmed; this is your furthest point of travel.

6. Click the **Home** button 🏠 to return to your home page.

TROUBLE? If the Home button is dimmed, your Internet Explorer installation does not designate a home page location, and the initial page content area when you started Internet Explorer was blank. Just continue with the tutorial.

You've seen that it's simple to navigate through Web pages, but sometimes the pages take quite a while to load. Michelle tells the workshop participants that pages load more quickly when they don't contain images.

Loading Images

Images, the graphics and pictures such as drawings or photographs that accompany a Web page, make Internet documents more attractive and informative and can enhance comprehension. For example, if you're studying modern history, you can find up-to-date information on the Internet about the geography and current events of warring countries. Because the countries' borders change so quickly, maps that accompany these articles may be more current than any printed atlas.

The use of graphics, however, significantly increases the time a Web page takes to load. A page that contains only text loads in seconds whereas one containing elaborate images can take minutes. Clearly, a trade-off exists between speed and quality. Deciding which factor to favor depends on the situation. When you have a lot of time or enjoy the richness of images, you might want to automatically load the images for every page. When you want to look at a large number of pages in a short amount of time, you probably want to load just text. With Internet Explorer, you can switch between these two options as frequently as you want.

If you opt to hide images, a graphic image on a Web page is represented with an icon similar to 🖼. Although this option offers speed, the advantage of loading images automatically is that you can see and use all the links that are on the page. Remember that images can also be links to other Web pages. Unless you load the images, you won't be able to see these links.

Michelle asks you to find sites that the teachers might want to use in their classes. You'll view the next pages without graphics so that they will load faster.

REFERENCE window

VIEWING IMAGES ON DEMAND

- Click View, then click Internet Options.
- Click the Advanced tab.
- In the Multimedia section, click the Show pictures check box to deselect it.
- Click the OK button.

To view Web pages without images:

1. Click **View**, then click **Internet Options**.

2. Click the **Advanced** tab.

3. Scroll down to the Multimedia section, then click the **Show pictures** check box to deselect it. See Figure 1-26.

Figure 1-26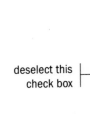
Setting image preferences

deselect this
check box

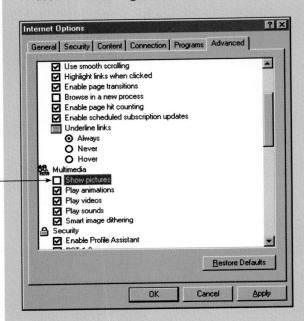

4. Click the **OK** button. The images still appear on the page because you already loaded images for your home page. On the next link you activate, the images will be hidden.

5. Click the **Back** button until you see Field Trips/Museums.

6. Click the **Zoos** link to open the Zoos page, which contains links to several national zoos. Notice that you connect very quickly, and icons replace the images. See Figure 1-27.

Figure 1-27 Zoos page with image icons

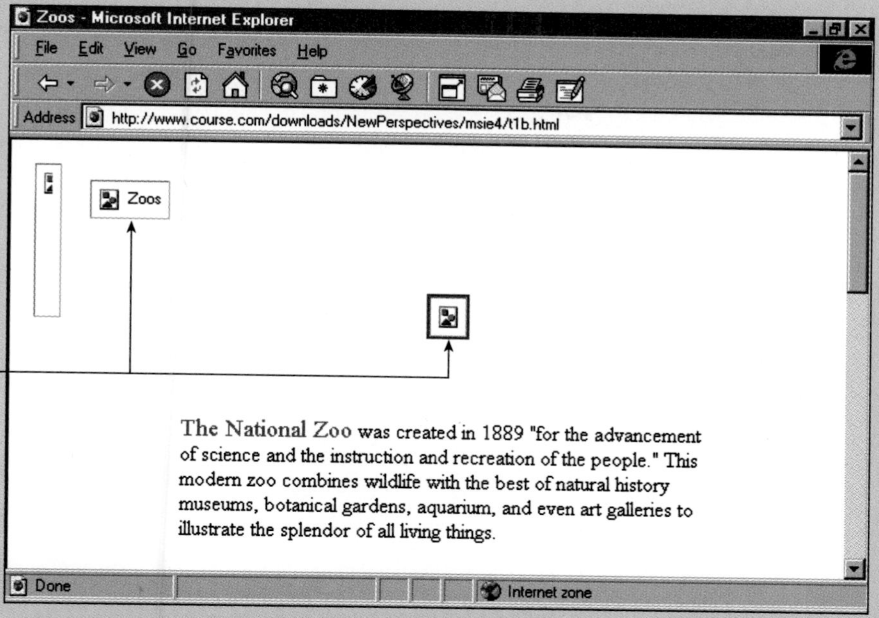

icons replace images

7. Scroll through the **Zoos** page and read the descriptions. Notice there are no hypertext links.

You suspect that the images on this Web page might be links to other pages that the teachers might want to see because none of the text contains links. When you are viewing pages without pictures, you can still examine an individual picture using the picture's **shortcut menu**, a menu that opens when you click an object on the screen with the right mouse button; this is called **right-clicking**. Shortcut menus display commands relevant to the object you right-click. You decide to view the large image with the blue outline.

To view an individual image when images aren't loading automatically:

1. Point at the large image with the blue border and notice that the pointer changes from ↖ to ☝. This indicates that the graphic contains links.
2. Right-click the image with the blue border. See Figure 1-28.

Figure 1-28 Opening an image icon's shortcut menu

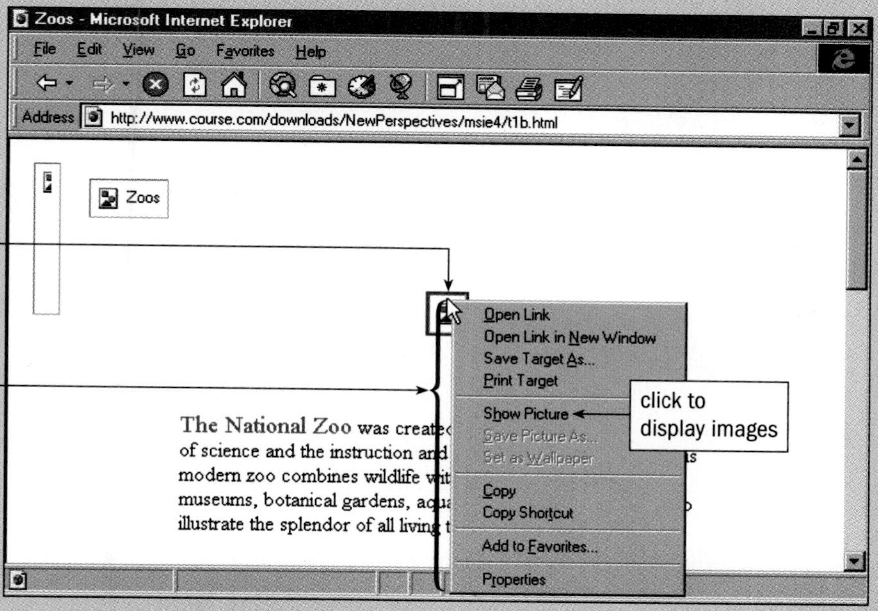

click this icon with right mouse button to open shortcut menu

shortcut menu

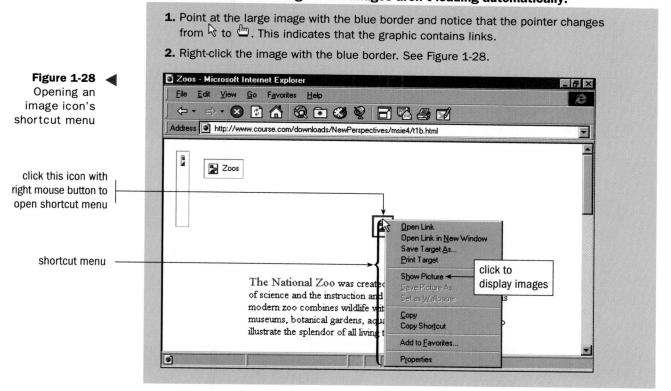

> **TROUBLE?** If your shortcut menu shows some dimmed commands, don't worry. You just clicked the image border instead of the image itself. Continue with Step 3.
>
> **TROUBLE?** To right-click an object, you click it using the right mouse button instead of the left mouse button.
>
> 3. Click **Show Picture** in the shortcut menu that opens. The graphic image appears. Each zoo is represented by a graphic, and each graphic is a link targeting each zoo. When you pass the pointer over each zoo image, the target changes in the Status Bar.

Graphics can contain important information and links, so unless you are in a hurry, it's best to view Web pages with graphics intact. You decide to reset Internet Explorer so that graphics are shown automatically. When you change settings for a page (or when the page changes for some other reason), you can use the Refresh button ⟳ to reload the page.

To load the images:

> 1. Click **View**, then click **Internet Options**.
>
> 2. Click the **Advanced** tab.
>
> 3. Scroll down to the Multimedia section, then click the **Show pictures** check box to select it.
>
> 4. Click the **OK** button.
>
> 5. Click the **Refresh** button ⟳. The page reloads from top to bottom with the images. When it's completely loaded, your page should look like Figure 1-29. The page is much more interesting to view this way and contains other links you couldn't see with the icons.

Figure 1-29 ◀
Zoos page with
images loaded

images replace icons ——

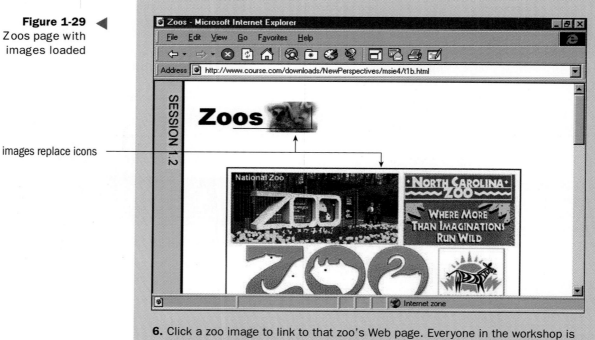

> 6. Click a zoo image to link to that zoo's Web page. Everyone in the workshop is amazed at the clarity of the photographs and the richness of the page. They agree that these types of resources would encourage students to investigate subjects more thoroughly.
>
> 7. Click the Back button ⟵ to return to the Zoos page.

Because your settings now specify showing pictures, any new page you connect to will show pictures. When, however, you are in a hurry and don't need to see pictures, deselecting the Show pictures option can save you time, because a page loads more quickly when the browser doesn't have to display graphic images.

Printing a Web Page

Although reducing paper consumption is an advantage of browsing information online, sometimes you'll find it useful to print a Web page. For example, you might want to refer to the information later when you don't have computer access, or you might want to give a copy of the Web page to someone who doesn't have access to a computer or to the Internet.

Although Web pages can be any size, printers tend to use 8½ × 11 inch sheets of paper. When you print, Internet Explorer automatically reformats the text of the Web page to fit the page dimension. Because lines might break at different places or text size might be altered, the printed Web page might be longer than you expect. You can specify the number of pages you want to print in the Print dialog box.

You decide that the directory of zoos is a good handout for the teachers in the workshop, so you decide to print out a copy. Michelle suggests that you print just the first page for the teachers. If the teachers want other information, they can return to the site and see the material online.

To print a Web page:

1. Click **File**, then click **Print**.

2. If necessary, click the **Pages** option button, type **1** in the from box, press the **Tab** key to move to the to box, and then type **1**. This indicates that you want to print only the page range 1–1 of the document, or just the first page of the document. Your completed dialog box should look similar to Figure 1-30.

Figure 1-30 ◀
Print dialog box

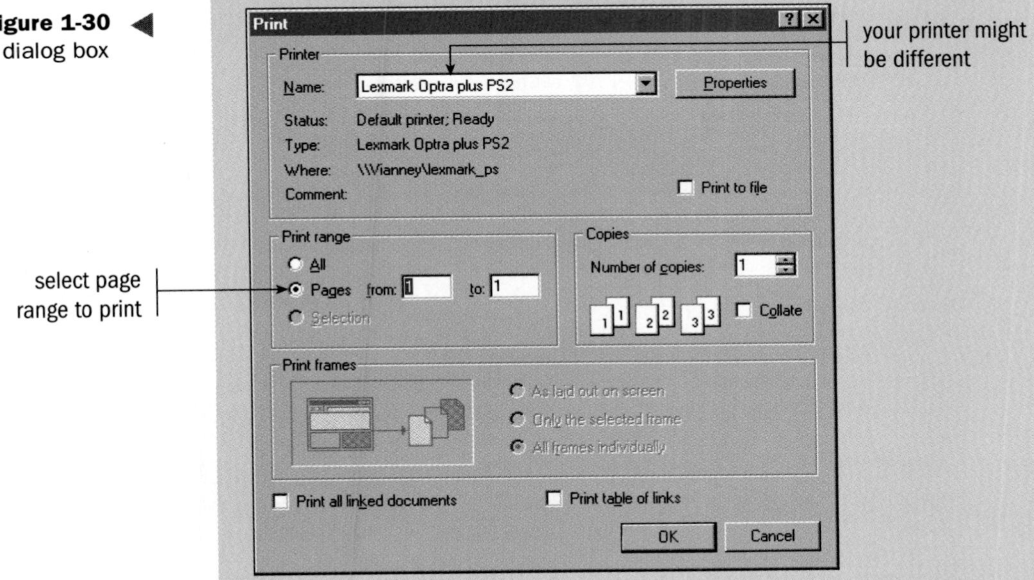

your printer might
be different

select page
range to print

TROUBLE? If your Print dialog box looks somewhat different from Figure 1-30, don't worry. The Print dialog box changes to reflect the options available for the printer you are using. Just continue with Step 3.

3. Click the **OK** button to print the first page of the Web page.

Getting Online Help

Charlotte DuMont, another instructor at the workshop, has been taking notes about how to use Internet Explorer, but she wants to know what to do if she needs help and no one familiar with Internet Explorer is around.

One of the best sources of information and help is always available when you're using any of the Internet Explorer components. Internet Explorer's Help system is an online reference created and maintained by Microsoft for use with its software; you can open the

Help window from the Help menu or by clicking the Help buttons found in certain dialog boxes. The Help system provides a Table of Contents window, an Index, and a Search feature that helps you locate topics by keyword.

Even though the workshop members just saw how to load pages without pictures, Charlotte isn't sure she remembers the precise steps. She asks you to help her find information about this option. You suggest looking up the word "pictures" in the Index.

To get online Help:

1. Click **Help**, then click **Contents and Index**. The Help window opens.
2. Click the **Index** tab. See Figure 1-31.

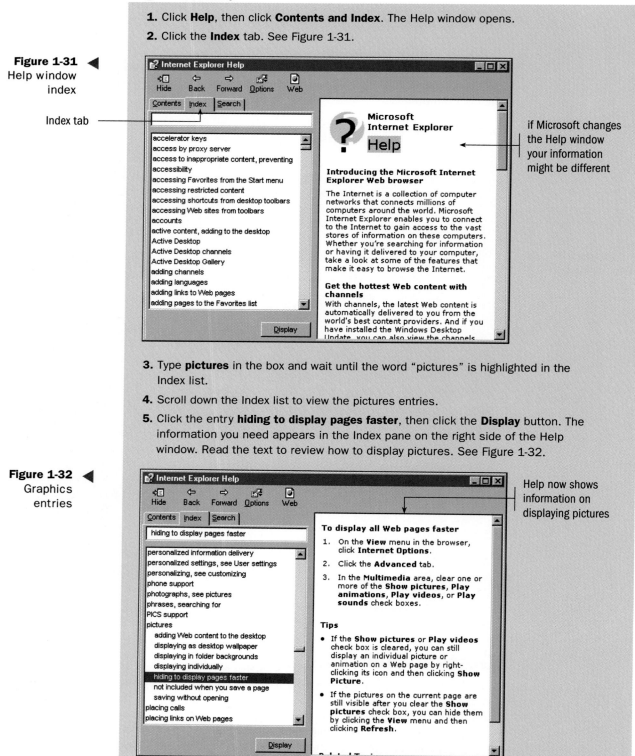

Figure 1-31 ◀
Help window index

Index tab

if Microsoft changes the Help window your information might be different

3. Type **pictures** in the box and wait until the word "pictures" is highlighted in the Index list.
4. Scroll down the Index list to view the pictures entries.
5. Click the entry **hiding to display pages faster**, then click the **Display** button. The information you need appears in the Index pane on the right side of the Help window. Read the text to review how to display pictures. See Figure 1-32.

Figure 1-32 ◀
Graphics entries

Help now shows information on displaying pictures

Internet Explorer

6. Click the **Close** button ☒ to close the Help window.

7. Click **File**, then click **Close** to close Internet Explorer.

Michelle ends the workshop with comments from the educators about incorporating the Internet in their classes. Lyle suggests that the information superhighway might bridge some of the gaps between metropolitan and rural schools as well as between wealthy and disadvantaged districts by providing common, equally accessible, resources to all. As technology costs decrease and states encourage network connections in their public schools, distinctions such as these will begin to fade.

Quick Check

1. Someone has given you the URL of an interesting Web page. How can you view that Web page?

2. In the URL http://www.irs.ustreas.gov/prod/cover.html, what is the protocol? What is the server address? What is the name of the Web page file? In which folder is it located?

3. Is the Web page located at the URL http://www.CTI.COM/HOME.html the same as the Web page located at URL http://www.cti.com/home.html? Why or why not?

4. What is FTP?

5. When you see a URL with ".edu" in it, what do you know about that site's Web server?

6. You can easily flip through Web pages using the _____, _____, and _____ toolbar buttons.

7. Why might you want to load text only and not pictures?

8. True or False: A printed Web page cannot contain any graphics or special formatting.

Tutorial Assignments

Michelle wants to gear her next workshop for college-level educators. She needs to find out how much the Internet is being used for educational purposes in higher education, what types of sites and information are available, and who is involved with this new approach to education.

She asks you to look at trends in the Internet and answer the following questions: How is the Internet affecting higher education? Do you think the overall trends will be positive? What are some of the possible negative side-effects?

Michelle suggested a few Web pages from which you can begin looking for answers. Do the following:

1. If necessary, launch Internet Explorer.

2. Open the Web page at the URL http://www.course.com/downloads/NewPerspectives/msie4.

3. Click the Tutorial Assignments and Case Problems link.

4. Scroll down until you see the Tutorial 1 Tutorial Assignments section.

5. Connect to the World Lecture Hall link in the "Universities Around the World" section.

6. Follow one of the links that interests you and see if you can find any information you can use to answer Michelle's questions. If you try any busy or defunct sites, follow a different link path.

7. Print the first page of the World Lecture Hall page you linked to.

8. Return to the Tutorial Assignments and Case Problems page.

9. Connect to the Distance Education on the WWW link in the Tutorial 1 Tutorial Assignments section.

10. Scroll through the page. Navigate links as necessary to answer these questions: What are four main kinds of services? What is the relevance of the WWW to distance education?

11. Print just the first two pages of this Web page.

12. Submit to your instructor the printout and the answers to Michelle's questions based on the information you found in Step 6 and your answers to Step 10.

Case Problems

1. University Informational Pages   Karla Marletti, director of admissions at Southern University, noticed that an increasing number of universities are placing Web pages on the Internet. She wants her university to remain current in its use of technology and decides that the school should put a Web page on the Web. She is not sure what layout or design would be most appealing for the page or what type of information should be included. She asks you to find a couple of Web pages that you think have attractive and effective designs with interesting and helpful content.

If necessary, start Internet Explorer, then do the following:

1. Open the Web page at the URL "http://www.course.com/downloads/NewPerspectives/msie4."

2. Click the Tutorial Assignments and Case Problems link.

3. Scroll down until you see the Tutorial 1 Case Problems section.

4. Connect to the University Informational Pages link to find a listing of universities with Web pages.

5. Visit three Web pages for universities within the United States and then visit two Web pages for universities outside the United States.

6. Choose Web pages for two universities that you think have an unusual or attractive layout and interesting and relevant content.

7. Print the first page of your two favorite university Web pages. On the hard copy, explain what you liked about that Web page and submit your explanation to your instructor.

2. The Fresno Daily   Helen Wu, a staff journalist for The Fresno Daily, a newspaper serving the community of Fresno, California, just received an assignment to write a feature article on how the Internet is changing the way people spend their leisure time. As part of her article, Helen wants to discuss the current size of the Internet and its rate of growth. She asks you to find statistics on the current number of Internet domains, the current number of Internet hosts, the current number of Web sites, and the percentage that these figures have grown since they were counted last.

If necessary, launch Internet Explorer, then do the following:

1. Open the Web page at the URL "http://www.course.com/downloads/NewPerspectives/msie4."

2. Click the Tutorial Assignments and Case Problems link.

3. Scroll down until you see the Tutorial 1 Case Problems section.

4. Connect to one of the two *Fresno Daily* links to find a listing of relevant Web pages.

5. Navigate through the Web pages to look for the statistics Helen needs.

6. When you find a Web page that contains a relevant statistic, print the information you need.

7. When you have all the information, write a short report about your findings on the back of the printout.

8. Circle the URL of each page you used. *Hint:* When you print a Web page, Internet Explorer inserts a header and footer that include the page name, page number, URL, and date. Check the footer of the printed Web page.

3. The Carpet Shoppe   The Carpet Shoppe imports and sells handwoven rugs from Thailand, Burma, and India. Four times each year, Al Sanchez, the owner, travels to these countries to replenish his inventory of new carpets.

Al has decided that it's time to convert to computerized inventory and accounting systems. Al isn't sure whether to purchase a Macintosh or an IBM-compatible system. He wants a portable computer that he could bring on his buying trips. With a laptop computer, not only will he have the most current figures at his fingertips, but he will also be able to communicate with his employees at home without worrying about the time difference or the cost of international phone calls. He wants a top-of-the-line note-book computer that won't become obsolete quickly. The more RAM, the bigger the disk storage space, and the faster the modem, the better.

He asks you to find information such as the model name, model number, and features about different brands of computers. Most of the bigger computer manufacturers place Web pages on the Internet with their latest computer models and prices, so you can begin looking there.

If necessary, launch Internet Explorer, then do the following:

1. Open the Web page at the URL "http://www.course.com/downloads/NewPerspectives/msie4."

2. Click the Tutorial Assignments and Case Problems link.

3. Scroll down until you see the Tutorial 1 Case Problems section.

4. Find information about a top-of-the line notebook computer from Apple.

5. Print any Web pages that contain relevant information.

6. Find information about a top-of-the line notebook computer from IBM.

7. Print any Web pages that contain relevant information.

8. Write a summary report of the information you found, and make a recommendation regarding which notebook computer you think Al should buy.

4. Marketing 305 Consumer Behavior   The students of Marketing 305 (MK305) have prepared a survey to study consumer behavior in online environments. They plan to compile a report that discusses what consumers think about two malls available on the Internet, how products' prices compare to their local malls, and what percentage of people are willing to shop online.

If necessary, launch Internet Explorer, then do the following:

1. Open the Web page at the URL "http://www.course.com/downloads/NewPerspectives/msie4."

2. Click the Tutorial Assignments and Case Problems link.

3. Scroll down until you see the Tutorial 1 Case Problems section.

4. Navigate through two online shopping malls looking at various products.

5. Print one sample product description from each mall.

6. Compare a similar product available at each mall. See how information about the product is presented as well as its price.

7. Return to the Tutorial Assignments and Case Problems page and locate the MK305 survey link.

8. Connect to the MK305 survey page.

9. Answer the survey questions. When you are done, click the Submit button. Global Marketers Inc. displays a completed survey.

10. Print the completed survey and submit it to your instructor.

Lab Assignments

The Internet World Wide Web

This Lab Assignment is designed to accompany the interactive Course Lab called Internet World Wide Web. To start the Lab, click the Start button on the taskbar, point to Programs, point to Course Labs, point to New Perspectives Applications, then click Internet World Wide Web. If you do not see Course Labs on your Programs menu, see your instructor or technical support person.

The Internet World Wide Web One of the most popular services on the Internet is the World Wide Web. This lab is a Web simulator that teaches you how to use Web browser software to find information. You can use this lab whether or not your school provides you with Internet access.

1. Click the Steps button to learn how to use Web browser software. As you proceed through the steps, answer all of the Quick Check questions that appear. After you complete the steps, you will see a Quick Check Summary Report. Follow the instructions on the screen to print this report.

2. Click the Explore button on the Welcome screen. Use the Web browser to locate a weather map of the Caribbean Virgin Islands. What is its URL?

3. A SCUBA diver named Wadson Lachouffe has been searching for the fabled treasure of Greybeard the pirate. A link from the Adventure Travel Web site leads to a Wadson's Web page called "Hidden Treasure." Click the Explore button. Locate the Hidden Treasure page and answer the following questions:
   a. What was the name of Greybeard's ship?
   b. What was Greybeard's favorite food?
   c. What does Wadson think happened to Greybeard's ship?

4. In the steps, you found a graphic of Jupiter from the photo archives of the Jet Propulsion Laboratory. In the Explore section of the lab, you can also find a graphic of Saturn. Suppose one of your friends wanted a picture of Saturn for an astronomy report. Make a list of the blue, underlined links your friend must click to find the Saturn graphic. Assume that your friend will begin at the Web Trainer home page.

5. Enter the URL "http:\\www.atour.com" to jump to the Adventure Travel Web site. Write a one-page description of this site. In your paper include a description of the information at the site, the number of pages the site contains, and a diagram of the links it contains.

6. Chris Thomson is a student at UVI and has his own Web pages. In Explore, look at the information Chris has included on his pages. Suppose you could create your own Web page. What would you include? Use word processing software to design your own Web pages. Make sure you indicate the graphics and links you would use.

Finding What's Out There

Using the Internet as a Resource at the Peter H. Martin Public Library

CASE

Peter H. Martin Public Library

The Peter H. Martin Library is a well-established public library supported by local and federal government funding as well as local civic groups. Last year, the Board of Directors authorized Anna Ferri, the library's technical assistant, to develop and implement a plan that incorporates Internet access to expand the library's existing resources. The library already had an Internet connection to a host computer within the city and a **local area network** (LAN), a group of computers in one location that are connected so they can share data, files, and software. The library's LAN connects the microcomputers throughout the building to the server, the computer that stores the data and programs accessed by other computers in the LAN, in Anna's office. One of the programs on the LAN is a computerized cataloging system that it shares via the Internet with other regional libraries. Visitors can search for books at any participating library by title, author, or subject.

Anna wants to provide online services that supplement the library's holdings. To fulfill these goals, Anna:

- Created a home page that gives information about the library's services and layout.

- Installed Internet Explorer on the computers throughout the building so all the library's computers have Internet access.

- Added technical support for library users who dial into the system from their home computers.

- Organized training sessions for library personnel and the general public on how to use the Internet as a research and reference tool.

The response from the community so far has been very positive. Because of the library's Internet access, more people are spending time there researching topics for business, school, and personal enjoyment. The library staff spends a lot of time showing people how to surf the Internet and find information. Anna asks you to work at the Information Desk, assisting patrons in answering questions about the Internet.

SESSION

2.1

In this session, you will explore your computer's file associations; listen to an audio clip; use popular navigational guides; browse sites and learn efficient ways to return to sites; and add, use, and delete links to favorite pages in the Favorites folder.

Viewing External Files

Anna informs you that library users often want access to files on the Internet, not just Web pages. She advises you to familiarize yourself with accessing the variety of files available on the Web. Hyperlinks on a Web page can point to many different types of files. Internet Explorer recognizes and can display files such as HTML Web page files and certain types of graphic images. However, when Internet Explorer encounters a file it cannot display on its own, called an **external file**, it searches your computer to see if there is other software available that it could use to display the file. Internet Explorer uses a three-step process to determine what to do when you click a link that targets an external file:

1. First, Internet Explorer checks the file extension of the link's target. A filename usually has two parts, separated by a dot: the name itself and a **file extension**, usually three or four letters long which identifies the file type. A Web page named index.htm, for example, has the extension "htm."

2. Then, Internet Explorer matches the file extension to a list of file extensions and their corresponding programs, called **file associations**. Your computer's operating system maintains a list of file associations.

3. Finally, Internet Explorer checks which program is associated with that file extension, and starts that program if it can find it.

For example, if you click a link targeting a doc file, Internet Explorer might discover that your computer associates doc files with Microsoft Word word-processing software. Internet Explorer then automatically starts Word. Figure 2-1 illustrates this process.

Figure 2-1 ◀
Linking to an
external file

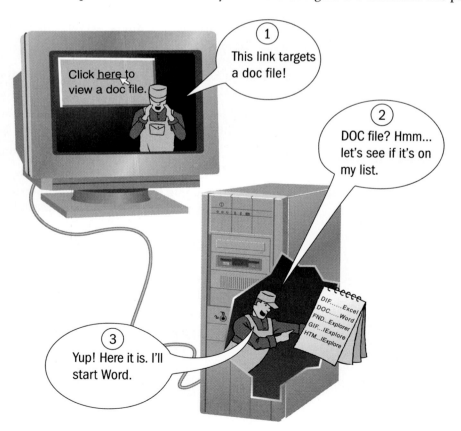

You know that as you help people use the library's Internet connection, patrons will approach you for information about accessing files of many different types on the Web. You decide to explore the file association list on your computer to see which programs are associated with which files. Every computer has a different list, depending on the software it contains. You're especially curious about how sound files with the AU extension are handled.

To check your computer's file associations:

1. From your computer's desktop, start My Computer.

   TROUBLE? How you open My Computer depends on your mouse settings. Try clicking the My Computer icon on the desktop once. If the My Computer window opens, proceed to Step 2. Otherwise, press Enter. The My Computer window should now open.

2. Click **View** on the My Computer menu bar, then click **Folder Options**.

3. Click the **File Types** tab. A list of registered file types appears.

4. Click any file type in the Registered file types list. The File type details area identifies the program that handles that file type.

5. Now you're going to check how AU sound files are handled, because you know that many Web sites feature AU sound files. Scroll down and click **Sound Clip** in the Registered file types list, then notice which program handles it. See Figure 2-2. On the computer shown in the figure, AU files are handled by the command RUNDLL32, which runs a program called ActiveMovie. If no command or program is identified on your screen, you might have trouble playing AU files.

   TROUBLE? If there is more than one Sound Clip option, click each one until you see AU listed as one of the Extensions.

   TROUBLE? If Sound Clip does not appear in the Registered file types list, see if there is an entry under AU. If not, it's possible your computer is not set up to recognize AU sound files. Ask your technical support person or instructor for assistance.

Figure 2-2 ◀
Checking file
associations

Sound Clip file type
is selected; this
computer has two
Sound Clip options

AU extension

details about the
Sound Clip file type

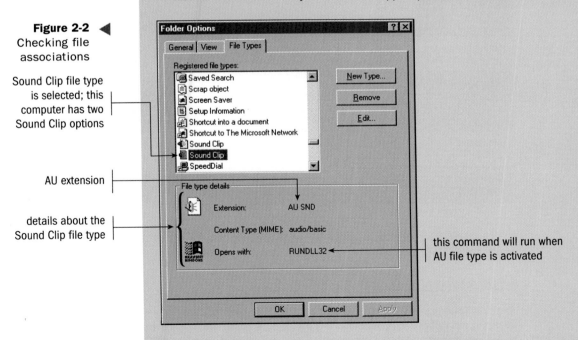

this command will run when
AU file type is activated

6. Click the **Cancel** button to close the Folder Options dialog box without saving any changes you might have inadvertently made.

7. Close the My Computer window.

You now know that when you click a link targeting an AU file, the program indicated in the File type details section will automatically start.

When you click a link for an external file, Internet Explorer might start a program automatically. For example, if your computer has a movie player, it might start automatically when you click a movie clip link. Otherwise Internet Explorer asks what you want to do with the link's target by opening the dialog box shown in Figure 2-3.

Figure 2-3 ◄
Dialog box that appears when you click a link targeting certain file types

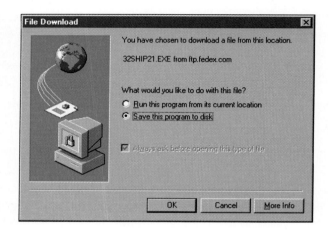

Figure 2-4 describes the options found in the File Download dialog box. You'll learn more about downloading in Session 2.2, but for now you should understand what options to select when you simply want to view, not save, an external file on the Internet.

Figure 2-4 ◄
File Download options

Option	Result
Run this program from its current location	Places the file into a temporary directory and then attempts to match the file extension with the software on your computer. If it can't locate an associated program, a message box warns you that access is denied, and the procedure is aborted.
Save this file (or program) to disk	Allows you to save the file to your hard disk for later viewing, perhaps on a computer with different software.
Always ask before opening	Allows you to specify whether you feel confident that this type of file or program is always safe to open or run directly from the Internet. Taking the precaution to evaluate a file before you open it can help prevent certain files from harming your computer.
More Info	Opens the Internet Explorer Help system to a screen that describes your options and provides security warnings.
Cancel	Cancels the connection and foregoes displaying the file.

Now that you've learned how Internet Explorer handles external files, you're ready to assist any library patron who wants to access such a file.

Listening to an Audio Clip

Two teenagers, Sasha and Janine, stop by the Information Desk and ask you about the library's new Internet connection. You suggest that they begin by looking at the library's home page. Anna created the home page to orient visitors to the library's setup, tell them about the available services, and personally welcome them to the library with a recording by the head librarian. Sound, added to text and images, helps to make a Web page more dynamic and "alive" than a static printed page. Hearing someone greet you to a page is more welcoming than just reading the words. With sounds on a Web page, you can hear the roar of a lion, listen to the beat of a healthy heart, and play the latest song from your favorite band.

Internet
Explorer

Any sound on a Web page is actually a file, called an **audio clip**, which can be stored in different formats. Some formats provide a better quality sound, but create a larger audio clip. The file extension of the audio clip indicates its file type. There is no standard audio file type, but you can expect to see audio files on the Web in the formats shown in Figure 2-5.

Figure 2-5 ◀
Common audio
file types

File type	Description
AU	A basic audio file type that lacks the high-fidelity quality of other audio file types; is nevertheless popular because AU files can be run on practically any computer system, and they are smaller than similar sounds saved in other formats.
AIFF	High-fidelity sound developed by Apple and used primarily on Macintosh computers.
RA	Real Audio; allows you to hear live broadcasts. These files play as they download.
WAV	High-fidelity sound developed by Microsoft and IBM and considered a standard on Windows/PC computers.

Each type of audio file needs to be interpreted by a **playback device**, software that identifies the file and its format and then uses a sound card to play it through your computer's speakers. If your computer has the appropriate software and the file associations are properly set, when you click an audio clip link, a playback device starts automatically and plays the clip. (For some devices, you might need to click the Play button.) Not all software works with every type of audio file. If your computer does not have the correct playback device for an audio clip that you click, Internet Explorer warns you and prompts you to abort the connection. Depending on your version of Windows, a playback device is probably already associated with audio clips. Your computer might have this software already loaded, but you should check your file associations—you may need to load it yourself.

If your computer doesn't have a playback device or doesn't have the necessary hardware (including a sound card and speakers) to play audio clips, you will receive an error message in the next set of steps.

To open the Peter H. Martin Library home page and listen to an audio clip:

1. Launch Internet Explorer and make sure the Standard toolbar displays text labels, the Address and Links toolbars are visible, and the Explorer bars are hidden. Make sure images are set to load automatically.

2. Replace the current entry in the Address box on the Address toolbar with the URL **http://www.course.com/downloads/New Perspectives/msie4**, then press **Enter**.

3. Click the **Tutorial 2** link to open the library's home page.

4. Position your pointer over the audio clip graphic link 🔊 on the Peter H. Martin Library home page. See Figure 2-6.

   TROUBLE? If your Links toolbar shows different buttons, don't worry. The Links toolbar is customizable so users can change it to display different buttons.

Figure 2-6 ◄
Peter H. Martin
Library
home page

click to hear
audio clip

information box
appears when you
point to this link

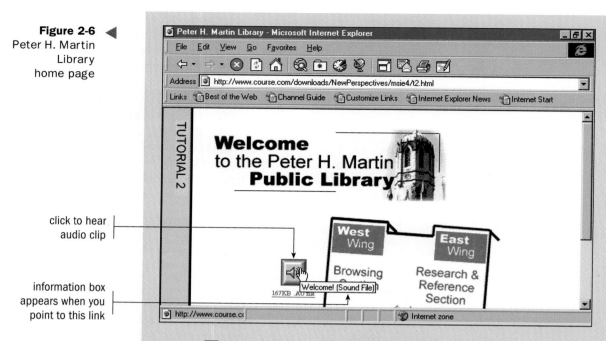

5. Click [image]. The File Download dialog box opens.

6. Click the **Open this file from its current location** option button, because you want to listen to the file without saving it to your disk.

   TROUBLE? If the File Download dialog box doesn't open but instead the sound plays, your computer is set to play that type of file automatically without asking you what you want to do with it. Skip Step 7.

7. Click the **OK** button. You might need to wait a minute or two as your playback device starts and loads the audio clip. If the playback device opens but you don't hear a sound, try clicking the **Play** button [image]. Figure 2-7 shows the Microsoft playback device, which plays the clip automatically. Be patient; it might take a minute.

   TROUBLE? If you don't hear a sound, even after clicking the Play button, your computer might not have audio capabilities or the sound might be turned down (a common tactic in computer labs to reduce noise). Check with your instructor or technical support person.

   TROUBLE? If a message appears warning you that the file can't be accessed, your computer does not recognize this type of audio file and you cannot hear the audio clip. For now, close the dialog box and continue with the tutorial. You might need to acquire a playback device, or you might need to check your computer's file type associations. Use the instructions in the previous section to check the Sound Clip file association.

Figure 2-7 ◄
Playback
device

filename

click to pause
audio clip

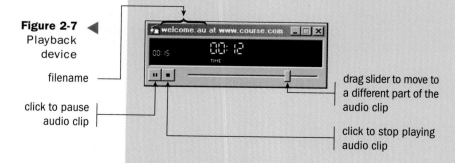

drag slider to move to
a different part of the
audio clip

click to stop playing
audio clip

8. If necessary, close the playback device. You might need to click its button on the taskbar, then click the **Close** button [X].

Now that Sasha and Janine have seen the library's welcome page, you decide to show them how navigational guides work.

Using a Navigational Guide

With so much information available on the WWW, many people spend their time searching for unique, interesting, or newsworthy sites. Some of these sites feature unusual layouts or interesting text, graphics, or sounds. Microsoft Corporation routinely scouts the Internet for interesting or newsworthy sites, then places links to those URLs on pages that you can access from the Links toolbar. Figure 2-8 describes the buttons that appear on the Links toolbar. Your toolbar might show different buttons, depending on your Internet Explorer configuration. If, for example, you installed Internet Explorer 4 as an upgrade to a previous version, you might see buttons such as Microsoft Product News, Today's Links, and Web Gallery. The only button you need in this tutorial is Best of the Web, which should be on the Links toolbar even if your installation is an upgrade.

Figure 2-8 ◀
Buttons on the
Links toolbar

Button	Description
Best of the Web	Connects to a page on Microsoft's Web page that showcases interesting Web pages, divided into topics such as Best of the Best, Business & Finance, Living, Sports, and so on.
Channel Guide	Connects to Microsoft's Web site, from where you can access the Active Channel Guide.
Customize Links	Opens a Web page stored on your computer that offers help on customizing your computer's Links toolbar.
Internet Explorer News	Connects to a page on Microsoft's Web site that contains news about the Internet Explorer software.
Internet Start	Connects to Microsoft's home page, called Internet Start.

Microsoft updates these pages periodically, so they are a good starting point for surfing. You can find similar types of lists on the WWW compiled by other groups or individuals. A list or index of Web pages organized around a general theme or subject is called a **navigational guide**.

Sasha wants to check out the links on the Best of the Web page. This page groups Web pages into topical categories, so to view a Web page on the Best of the Web list, you must first select a category.

One disadvantage to sites on the Best of the Web and other similar lists is that the lists are frequented by many people and the pages can suddenly become extremely popular, overwhelming the URL's server. As a result, you might be unable to link to these pages or even to different pages housed on the same server.

To look at the Best of the Web page:

1. Click the **Best of the Web** button on the Links toolbar to link to a list of Web pages collected by Microsoft Corporation. See Figure 2-9. The page is updated regularly, so yours will look different from the one shown here.

   TROUBLE? If the Links toolbar does not appear on your screen, click View, point to Toolbars, then click Links to display the Links toolbar. Drag the Links toolbar below the Address toolbar, if necessary.

   TROUBLE? If the site is busy, you might not be able to connect. After a reasonable period of time, click the Stop button 🗙 to abort the link, then repeat Step 1.

TROUBLE? If the Best of the Web button does not appear on your Links toolbar, try connecting to Microsoft's Web site with the URL http://www.microsoft.com or http://home.microsoft.com and locating the Best of the Web page from there. If you can't locate the Best of the Web page, ask your instructor or technical resource person how to locate the Best of the Web page.

Figure 2-9
Best of the
Web page

click to open
Microsoft's Best of
the Web list

category list

a select list of
featured sites that
Microsoft considers
"best of the best"

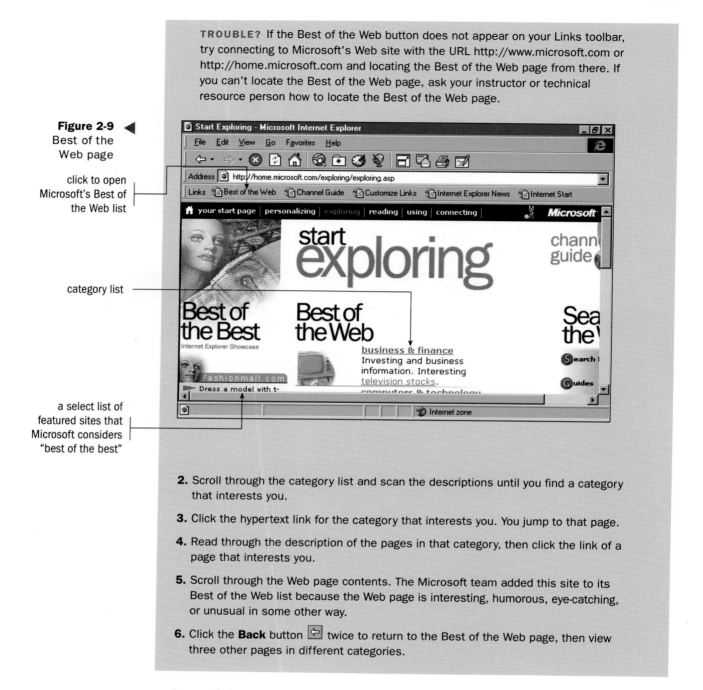

2. Scroll through the category list and scan the descriptions until you find a category that interests you.

3. Click the hypertext link for the category that interests you. You jump to that page.

4. Read through the description of the pages in that category, then click the link of a page that interests you.

5. Scroll through the Web page contents. The Microsoft team added this site to its Best of the Web list because the Web page is interesting, humorous, eye-catching, or unusual in some other way.

6. Click the **Back** button ⇦ twice to return to the Best of the Web page, then view three other pages in different categories.

Some of the pages you visit might include advertisement links. Many Web sites earn revenue by selling advertising links on their page to organizations. These advertisements change regularly.

Returning to Sites

Sasha and Janine have navigated through quite a few sites, and now they are ready to return to the library's home page. You've already seen how to use the Back button to return to a previously visited site. Internet Explorer also makes it easy to return to pages by maintaining a list of the most recent sites you have visited since launching Internet Explorer. This list, available on the File menu, returns you to a page you viewed earlier in the session with a single click. The checkmark indicates your current location. Although you can click the Back button repeatedly to return to a page, the File menu list is usually a quicker way to go where you want if you've navigated multiple Web pages.

You decide to show Sasha and Janine how to return to the library's page using the File menu list. Then you'll show them the navigational guide that Anna created for the Peter H. Martin Library.

To return to the Peter H. Martin Library page:

1. Click **File** to open the File menu. See Figure 2-10. Yours will look different, depending on which sites you linked to using the Best of the Web pages.

Figure 2-10 ◀
List of recently viewed sites on the File menu

visited sites

first site is your home page; yours might be different

click to return to the Peter H. Martin Library home page

current Web page (Best of the Web in the Living category; yours might be different)

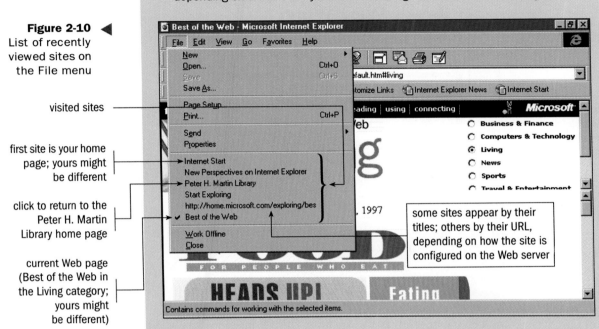

some sites appear by their titles; others by their URL, depending on how the site is configured on the Web server

2. Click the **Peter H. Martin Library** entry on the File menu list.

   TROUBLE? If you can't find the library home page on the File menu, enter http://www.course.com/downloads/NewPerspectives/msie4 in the Address box, then press Enter. Then click the Tutorial 2 link. If the URL fills in automatically for you as you type, the AutoComplete feature is running on your computer. Internet Explorer's AutoComplete feature fills in a URL automatically if it matches it to a URL you've entered before.

3. Click the **Browsing Section** area on the left side of the floor plan, shown in Figure 2-11.

   TROUBLE? If nothing happens, you might not have clicked the correct area. Make sure the pointer changes to 🖑, indicating that you are clicking a link.

Figure 2-11 ◀
Accessing the library's browsing section

click to connect to the browsing section

4. In the Library West Wing page that opens, shown in Figure 2-12, click the **Navigational Guides** link to see a list of popular navigational guides.

Figure 2-12
Connecting to
the library's
navigational
guides

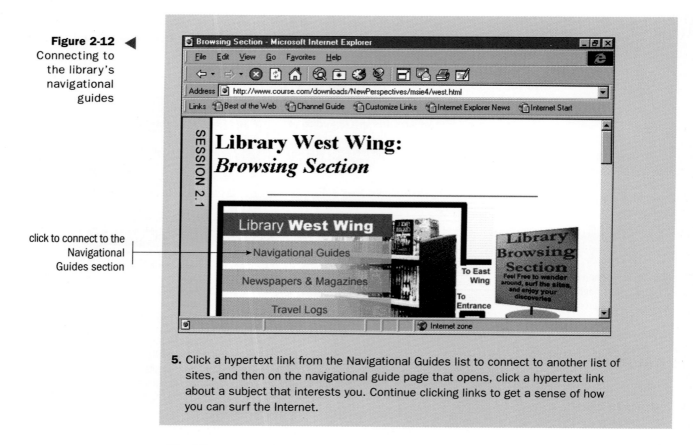

click to connect to the
Navigational
Guides section

5. Click a hypertext link from the Navigational Guides list to connect to another list of sites, and then on the navigational guide page that opens, click a hypertext link about a subject that interests you. Continue clicking links to get a sense of how you can surf the Internet.

The File menu only recalls the most recent sites you have visited in the current session (the number of sites on the menu depends on your browser's settings). If you want to view information on all recently visited links, including those in previous sessions, you can view the History Explorer bar. **Explorer bars** appear on the left side of your screen and contain lists of links that assist you in finding the pages you want. Four Explorer bars are available: Search, Favorites, History, and Channels. The History Explorer bar provides a list of the servers you've visited each day for a period of days specified in your browser's settings.

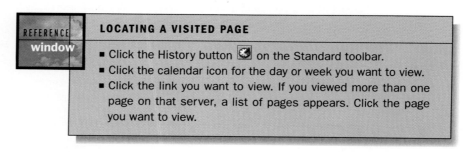

REFERENCE window

LOCATING A VISITED PAGE

■ Click the History button 🌐 on the Standard toolbar.
■ Click the calendar icon for the day or week you want to view.
■ Click the link you want to view. If you viewed more than one page on that server, a list of pages appears. Click the page you want to view.

You want to show Sasha how he can use the History Explorer bar to return to a page.

To use the History Explorer bar to return to a page:

1. Click the **History** button 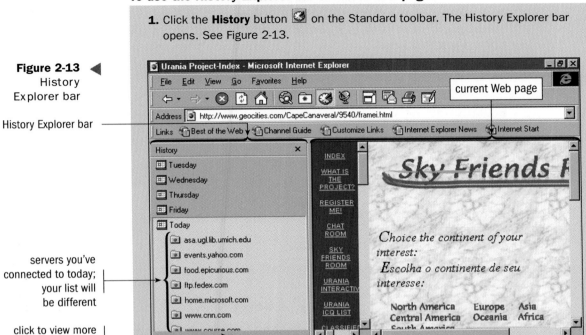 on the Standard toolbar. The History Explorer bar opens. See Figure 2-13.

Figure 2-13 ◀
History
Explorer bar

History Explorer bar

servers you've
connected to today;
your list will
be different

click to view more
links from today

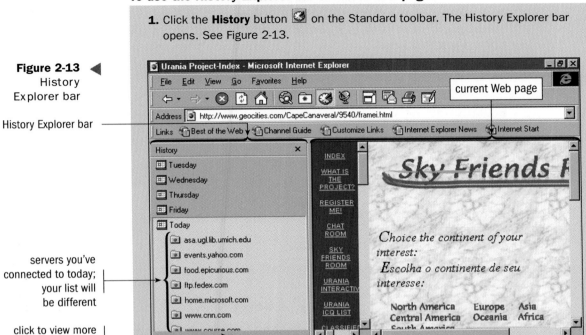

2. Now you'll see how to locate the Peter H. Martin Library site. Click the **www.course.com** link in the Today list (you might need to scroll to see it). A list of sites you've visited on the course server appears. See Figure 2-14.

Figure 2-14 ◀
List of pages
viewed on the
course server

Close button

URL for course server

pages viewed on
course server

click to open Peter H.
Martin Library
home page

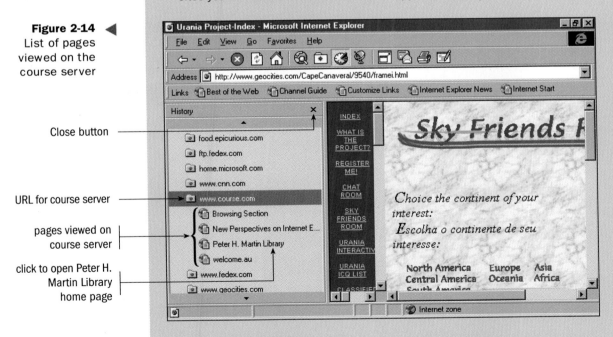

3. Click the **Peter H. Martin Library** link on the History Explorer bar. You return to the Peter H. Martin Library home page.

4. Click the **Close** button ⊠ on the History Explorer bar to close the History Explorer bar.

Sasha asks if the library's navigational guides might be able to help him plan his next vacation. He'd like to learn about travel in Malaysia. You assure him the information is there, and you tell him about another navigational trick. The Back and Forward buttons each contain arrows that you can click to open Back and Forward lists, which will show all the pages going back to a certain point and all the pages going forward to a certain point. Once you've used the Back list to return to a page, that page disappears from the Back list. The Back and Forward buttons are gray, indicating they are unavailable, if you have not yet navigated any pages in the current session.

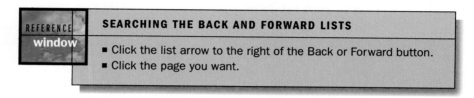

REFERENCE window	**SEARCHING THE BACK AND FORWARD LISTS**
	■ Click the list arrow to the right of the Back or Forward button. ■ Click the page you want.

You'll show Sasha this technique while you explore Malaysian travel pages.

To use the Back and Forward lists:

1. Click the **Browsing Section** link on the Peter H. Martin Library home page to return to that site.

2. Click **Travel Logs**. The Travel Logs section of the Browsing Section page appears.

3. Click the **Virtual Tourist II** link, then scroll down to see a map of the world. See Figure 2-15. The Virtual Tourist II page is a visual presentation of links rather than text. You can click any point on the map to link to a different page and get additional information about that country or region.

   TROUBLE? If the Virtual Tourist II site is busy, try another travel link. It might not be map-oriented, but it may still contain links to travel destinations.

Figure 2-15 ◄
Virtual Tourist II
Web page

click to open
map of Asia

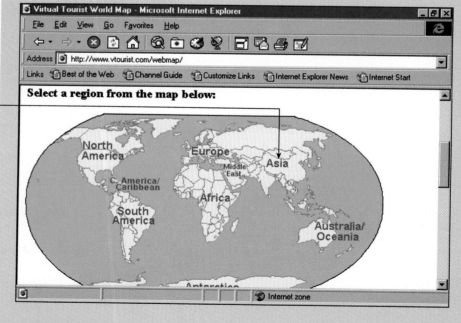

4. Click **Asia** to open a map of Asia.

5. Click **Malaysia** to link to its travel page. Scroll down until you see the Tourism link. See Figure 2-16.

Internet
Explorer

Figure 2-16 ◀
Malaysia page

Tourism link

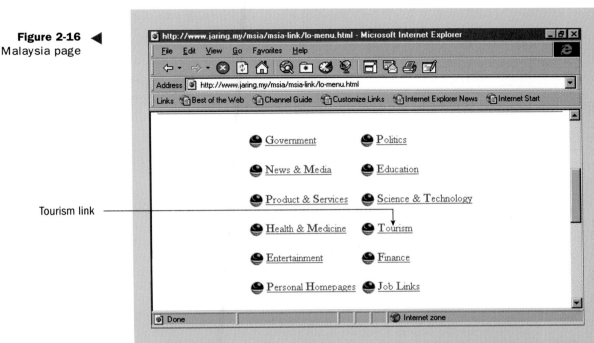

TROUBLE? If the Malaysia site is busy or you are on a travel Web page other than Virtual Tourist II, click another link until you find one that is available. Then substitute the name of the Web pages you have located for the Web pages mentioned in the steps.

6. Click **Tourism** to link to its travel page. Notice the available topics.

7. Now use the Back list to return to the Virtual Tourist World Map. Click the list arrow to the right of the Back button. The Back list appears. See Figure 2-17.

Figure 2-17 ◀
Back list

Back list arrow

Back list

click to return to
Virtual Tourist
World Map

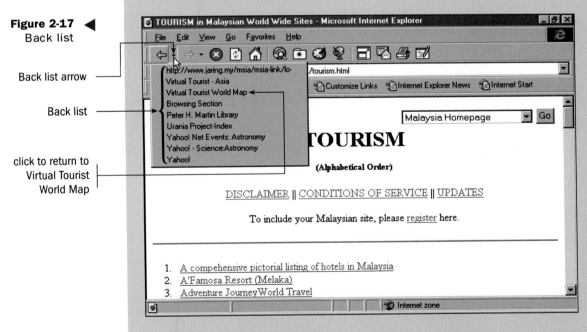

8. Click **Virtual Tourist World Map**. You will return to the Virtual Tourist page. Now try returning to the Tourism page using the Forward list. Click the list arrow next to the Forward button so that the Forward list appears.

9. Click the **TOURISM in Malaysian World Wide Sites** link.

TROUBLE? If this link appears with a URL instead of a title, click the URL.

You've now learned several methods of returning to sites. Under what circumstances should you use the various methods? Consider these guidelines:

- When you want to return to one of the pages you just viewed, use the Back and Forward lists.

- When you want to return to a page you viewed earlier in the session, but not necessarily within the last few links, use the File menu. The File menu, however, lists a small number of pages, usually 5–10.

- When you want to return to a page that you viewed quite some time ago, or in a different session, such as the day or week before, use the History Explorer bar.

- If you want to return to a page whose URL you typed in previously, you can use the Address bar's list arrow. If you want to type a URL that you've typed before, you can also type several characters and then press Ctrl+Enter to use the AutoComplete feature, which attempts to fill in a URL based on a list of previously visited sites. For example, if you entered the Microsoft site at one time and now you want to return to it, you could type "microsoft" and AutoComplete would fill in http://www.microsoft.com for you.

Sasha tells you he's always wanted to visit Malaysia. He'd like to explore this page some more. Janine, however, wants to keep looking at other places. You'll show Sasha how to mark this Web page so he can easily find it later.

Creating a Favorites Collection

While surfing the Net, you might find an interesting or unusual site to which you want to return. Rather than trying to remember the URL of that site, you can add it to your list of favorite pages, stored in the Favorites folder on your hard drive. You can access the pages in your Favorites folder from the Favorites menu or the Favorites button on the Standard toolbar.

Sasha wants to add the Malaysia tourism page to his Favorites folder so he can open it easily.

Adding a Page to the Favorites Folder

Adding a page to the Favorites folder is helpful when you want to return to a specific Web site, try other links from that page, or show someone else a certain site. You can add any Web page to your Favorites folder by using the Add to Favorites option. You might not be able to modify your Favorites folder, because your lab manager might have prevented the Favorites list from being changed. If this is the case, read through the following steps and consult your instructor.

To add the Tourism page to your Favorites folder:

1. Click **Favorites** to open the Favorites menu.

2. Click **Add to Favorites**. The Add Favorite dialog box opens. See Figure 2-18.

Figure 2-18 ◄
Adding a page
to the Favorites
folder

make sure No
option is selected

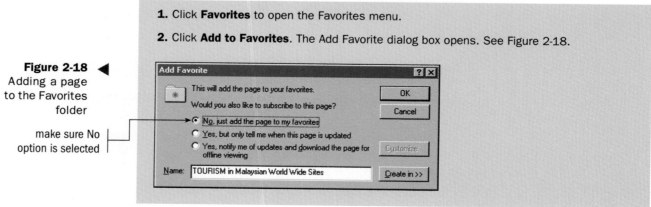

3. Click the **OK** button to add the current Web page, the Malaysia tourism page, to your list of favorites.

4. Click **Favorites** again to open the Favorites menu and display the Favorites list, which now includes TOURISM in Malaysian World Wide Sites, probably at the end of the list. If your list is quite long, you might need to click the down arrow at the bottom of the Favorites menu to view the TOURISM in Malaysian World Wide Sites page. Notice that the page is listed by its title, which is more descriptive than its URL. See Figure 2-19.

> **TROUBLE?** If a different title appears, you were on a different Web page. You can either locate the TOURISM in Malaysian World Wide Sites page and repeat this set of steps, or you can continue using a different page.

Figure 2-19 ◄
Favorites list

your list will differ ——————

page you just added ——————

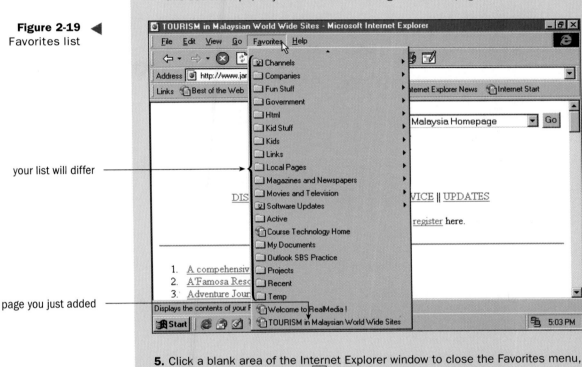

5. Click a blank area of the Internet Explorer window to close the Favorites menu, then click the **Back** button twice to move to a different Web page.

Now that the Web page you added to the Favorites folder is no longer the current page, you can show Sasha how to refer back to it.

Accessing a Page in the Favorites Folder

Because the menu bar is available no matter what Web page you are looking at or how long you have been surfing, you can click any page in the Favorites folder to return directly to that Web page. The pages you have placed in the Favorites folder are available until you delete them from the list.

You'll show Sasha how to get back to the Malaysia tourism Web page.

To access a page in the Favorites folder:

1. Click **Favorites**.

2. Click **TOURISM in Malaysian World Sites**.

> **TROUBLE?** If you added a different page, click that instead. If the page you added doesn't appear on the list, click the down arrow at the bottom of the menu to view additional pages.

Sasha is glad to see that the Favorites folder is so easy to use. He notices, however, that the Peter H. Martin Library Favorites folder includes folders in addition to bookmarks. He asks you to explain.

Managing Favorites Folders

Most browser users organize their favorite pages into folders grouped by category so it is easier to find a certain page. The Peter H. Martin Library Favorites folder, for example, organizes its favorite pages into folders with names such as Art and Literature, Government, Local Pages, and so on.

You can create folders in the Organize Favorites window. This window lists both folders, indicated by , and favorite Web pages, indicated by 📄.

REFERENCE window	**CREATING A FOLDER FOR FAVORITE PAGES**
	▪ Click Favorites, then click Organize Favorites. ▪ Click the Create New Folder button. ▪ Type the folder name, then press Enter.

You decide to show Sasha how to create a Travel folder and then add the Malaysia tourism page to that folder from within the Organize Favorites window. Then you'll show him how to add a page to a folder "on the fly" with the Add to Favorites command.

To create a Travel folder:

1. Click **Favorites**, then click **Organize Favorites** to open the Organize Favorites window.

   TROUBLE? If your Favorites list is too long and you had to scroll down it to see the page you added, you will now need to click the up arrow at the top of the menu. Then click Organize Favorites.

2. Click the **Create New Folder** button 📁.

3. Type **Travel** in the box, then press **Enter**.

4. Locate and click the **TOURISM in Malaysian World Wide Sites** page you added to the Favorites folder earlier (it is probably at the bottom of the list).

5. Click the **Move** button. The Browse for Folder dialog box opens. Locate and click the **Travel** folder. See Figure 2-20.

   TROUBLE? If your list shows file details, you are using Details view instead of List view. You could leave your view in Details view or click the List button 📋 to change the view in the Organize Favorites dialog box.

Figure 2-20 ◀
Adding a page
to a folder

List button displays
files in List view,
without file details

page you added to
Favorites folder; you
might have to scroll
to find this page

Travel folder you just
created; you might
need to scroll to see
it (your folder window
might look different)

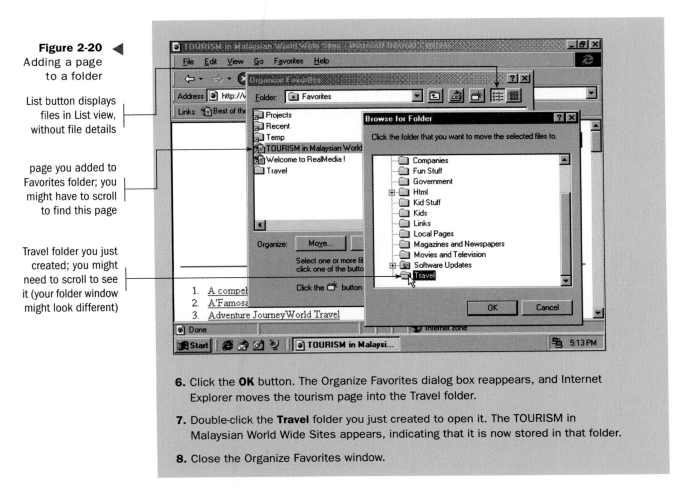

6. Click the **OK** button. The Organize Favorites dialog box reappears, and Internet Explorer moves the tourism page into the Travel folder.

7. Double-click the **Travel** folder you just created to open it. The TOURISM in Malaysian World Wide Sites appears, indicating that it is now stored in that folder.

8. Close the Organize Favorites window.

Once you have added a page to a folder, you access it by opening the Favorites menu and then navigating to the folder you want. The pages in that folder appear in a menu that cascades off to the side of or below the Favorites menu. You can also access favorite pages from the Favorites Explorer bar. You decide to show Sasha this method.

To access a page stored in a folder using the Favorites Explorer bar:

1. Click the **Back** button twice to go to a different page.

2. Click the **Favorites** button ⬚. The Favorites Explorer bar appears on the left side of the Internet Explorer window.

3. Click **Travel**. The page you stored in the Travel folder appears. See Figure 2-21.

TROUBLE? If you don't see the Travel folder, you might need to click the down arrow at the bottom of the Favorites Explorer bar until it scrolls into view.

Figure 2-21 ◄
Favorites
Explorer bar

Favorites Explorer bar ——

new folder ——

page moved
into folder

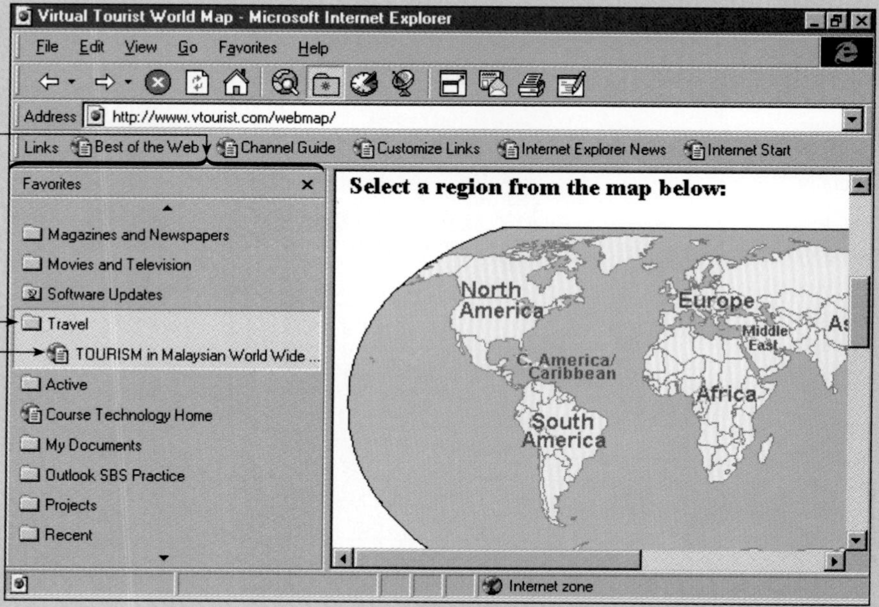

4. Click **TOURISM in Malaysian World Wide Sites**. You return to the Malaysia tourism page.

5. Click the Explorer bar **Close** button [×] to close the Favorites Explorer bar.

You are back to the tourism page. Now you're going to add a page to the Travel folder using the Add to Favorites window instead of the Organize Favorites window. You'll first open a different page on another place Sasha is interested in: Italy.

To add a page to a folder from the Add to Favorites window:

1. Click **File**, then click **Virtual Tourist World Map** to return to that page.

   TROUBLE? If that page title no longer appears on your File menu, use the Navigational Guides on the Peter H. Martin Library Browsing Section page to locate it.

2. Click **Europe**.

3. Click **Italy**. A map of Italy appears. Because Sasha isn't sure which city he wants to visit, you decide to add this page to his Travel folder.

   TROUBLE? If you can't link to this country's page, choose a different country.

4. Click **Favorites**, then click **Add to Favorites**.

5. Click the **Create in** button and locate and click the **Travel** folder. See Figure 2-22.

Internet Explorer

Figure 2-22 ◀
Adding a page
to the Travel
folder

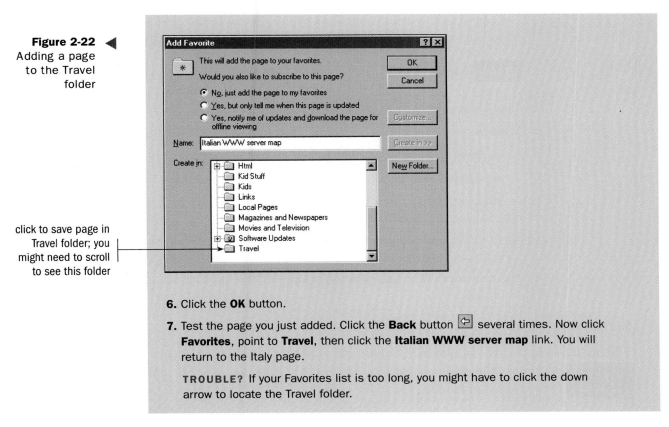

click to save page in
Travel folder; you
might need to scroll
to see this folder

6. Click the **OK** button.

7. Test the page you just added. Click the **Back** button [⬅] several times. Now click **Favorites**, point to **Travel**, then click the **Italian WWW server map** link. You will return to the Italy page.

   TROUBLE? If your Favorites list is too long, you might have to click the down arrow to locate the Travel folder.

Sasha asks how you remove a page from your Favorites folder.

Deleting a Page from the Favorites Folder

Deleting, or erasing, pages from the Favorites folder is almost as easy as adding them. It's always a good idea to delete any Web page that you no longer use or that has become outdated. This will help keep your list of favorite pages manageable and organized. In the Organize Favorites window, you can delete individual pages or entire folders. If you delete a folder, you delete not only the folder but also all the pages it contains.

REFERENCE
window

DELETING PAGES OR FOLDERS FROM THE FAVORITES FOLDER

- Click Favorites, then click Organize Favorites.
- Click the page or folder you want to delete.
- Click the Delete button.

You decide to delete the entire Travel folder.

To delete the Travel folder:

1. Click **Favorites**, then click **Organize Favorites** to open the Organize Favorites window.

2. Click the **Travel** folder.

3. Click the **Delete** button.

4. Click the **Yes** button when asked if you are sure.

5. Close the Organize Favorites window.

6. Close Internet Explorer.

Sasha thanks you for your instruction and leaves for home eager to further explore the travel information available on the Internet.

Quick Check

1. True or False: Internet Explorer uses its own software to interpret every type of file format.

2. What happens when you click a link targeting an external file but no software starts?

3. Name three audio file types and provide a short description of each.

4. To see a list of especially good Web sites, you can go to Microsoft's _____ page.

5. A disadvantage to using a URL link placed on Microsoft's navigational guide pages is a(n) _____ demand for the URL's server.

6. After browsing a number of Internet sites, you can trace your path by viewing the _____ menu.

7. You can store a Web page you might want to visit again in the _____.

SESSION

2.2

In this session, you will conduct search queries, save text and images to a file, and explore how to download files. You will also learn about useful utilities that help you with file transfer.

Searching the Web

Surfing the Web is often a slow-paced, read-for-pleasure type of activity. Another, more focused, use of the Internet involves fact-gathering and research. You might use the Internet to find information about a term-paper topic, to learn about opening a new business, or to report statistics to a government agency. A common thread in all these research goals is that they have a specific topic or theme.

Just as you return from lunch, Yoko Muramoto approaches the Information Desk to get assistance in finding information about opening a take-out restaurant serving Japanese food in the Marquette County, Michigan area. Some questions include: What is the population of the area? What are the current interest rates for bank loans? What government resources exist for small businesses? The answers to these questions and many others can be found on the Internet, but locating the information might be challenging.

The Search Explorer bar makes available many popular **search services**, software that helps you find information on the Web. Search services such as Excite, Infoseek, Lycos, and Yahoo are featured on the Search Explorer bar, which you can access by clicking the Search button 🔍 on the Standard toolbar. These services are organized on the search page so you can select the one you want. As you gain familiarity with the different search services, you'll develop preferences for which service you want to use based on the type of information you're looking for.

Search services help you find information in two ways: you can either search by query, which means you request information on a specific topic, or you can search using a subject guide, which is similar to using a subject catalog in a library. Yoko will first perform query searches and then will use a subject guide to locate information on the Japanese restaurant industry.

Searching by Query

To manage the growing number of files and documents on the Internet, commercial organizations collect information and store it in databases. A **database** is a collection of related information that can be searched by topic. The database software contains a **search engine**, which retrieves information from the database based upon a person's query. A **query** is a written request in question form that tells the search engine to find documents that contain a **keyword** (a specified word or phrase). For example, Yoko might want to search for information that matches the keywords "population statistics." The search engine generates a list of sites on the Internet that contain those words.

How is the database created? Most search services employ a **spider**, indexing software that compiles a large index of existing Web pages on a database that you can search to find references to a specific subject. Sometimes called robot, harvester, or worm, the term *spider* has perhaps become the most popular one for indexing software because it extends the Web analogy.

To understand how the spider creates a database, imagine a library that arranges its books randomly on the shelves and doesn't have a catalog index. The only way to locate information about any topic is to pick up a book and start reading and indexing it, jotting down keywords and references to other books. Follow these references and links until you reach a dead end, then repeat this process for all the other books in the library. The resulting list, in effect, is a database of the keywords and bibliography in each reference—a valuable way to locate all reference materials that relate to a keyword, such as Mozart. Now imagine adding to your list the books in all the libraries in your state, the country, and even the world. The resulting database, although time-consuming and tedious to compile, would yield even more information about a topic. A spider creates this type of database by circulating through millions of Web pages, one at a time, reading and storing keywords and links, until the links dead-end. The spider's helper programs organize the database by connecting some of the linked servers, removing duplicate entries, and categorizing the results.

A spider periodically (daily or weekly) connects to servers throughout the Internet in order to update its database. When you submit a query to search a spider's database, the query results include only references that were available and within the spider's range when it last updated its database. If new Web pages have been added since the last update or the spider couldn't access a Web page during an update, the index doesn't contain current references to them. If a Web page is not indexed in the database, it will not turn up in a search.

The enormous task of indexing the Internet is done by relatively few organizations. Spiders on the servers of these organizations take different, but overlapping, routes as they travel the Internet. Each one independently builds and maintains a database, so each database is built on different keywords. A query performed with, for example, the Infoseek search engine usually provides a different result than asking the same query of, for example, the AltaVista search engine. To obtain a broad range of references that will more likely provide the data you need, use several search services when researching a topic.

Before you use a new search engine, you'll need to determine how you should write a query to get the results you want. When some search engines encounter two words such as population statistics, they assume you mean "population" *or* "statistics" and return pages with either word. Other search engines assume you mean "population" *and* "statistics" and return pages with both words. These types of searches take longer and return fewer pages, but the pages are likely to be more useful.

To help people learn to do research on the Internet, Anna created a small database that you can use to demonstrate searching on the Web. The library's search engine assumes you mean *and*, not *or*, when it encounters two words. Some search engines allow you to specify which kind of search you want to perform; others do not.

To use Anna's search engine, you need to return to the Peter H. Martin Library home page. You can quickly return to a Web page whose URL you have already typed, even in a different Internet Explorer session, by clicking the Address list arrow on the Address bar to view a list of URLs that have been manually entered.

To conduct a query:

1. Launch Internet Explorer. Click the **Address** list arrow, click the **http://www.course.com/downloads/NewPerspectives/msie4** URL, then click the **Tutorial 2** link.

   TROUBLE? If the http://www.course.com/downloads/NewPerspectives/msie4 URL does not appear in the Location list, you'll need to enter it manually. Then click the Tutorial 2 link.

2. Click the **Research & Reference Section** link on the right side of the floor plan to connect to the Research & Reference Section page. See Figure 2-23.

Figure 2-23 ◀
Connecting to the Research & Reference Section

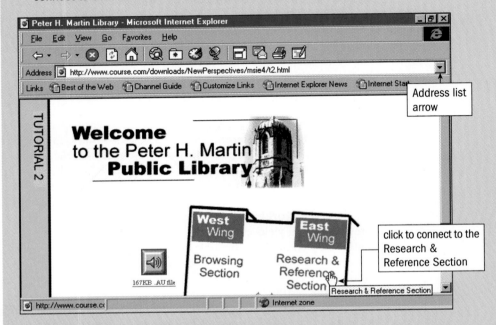

3. Click the **Query Demonstration** link (you might need to scroll down to see it) to open the Query Form used in the library's demonstration.

4. Click the query box and then type **population statistics** to indicate the keywords you want to search for. The list of references returned will include any documents that contain both the words *population* and *statistics*. See Figure 2-24.

Figure 2-24 ◀
Query form

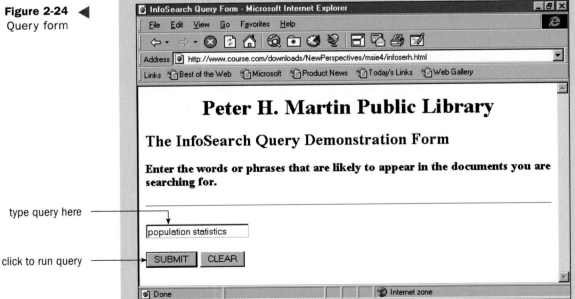

5. Click the **Submit** button to initiate the query search and compile a list of links that connect you to relevant sites. See Figure 2-25.

TROUBLE? If a Security Alert dialog box warns you that sending information over the Internet might not be secure, click the Yes button. You can click the check box if you want to disable this warning in the future. Security is important because whenever you send or receive information over the Internet, you are exposing yourself to a security risk. Internet Explorer allows you to specify what level of security you want to maintain, and depending on your configuration, this message might or might not appear.

Figure 2-25 ◀
Query
results list

relevance measure ⎯⎯⎯⎯⎯

located references ⎯⎯⎯⎯⎯⎯→

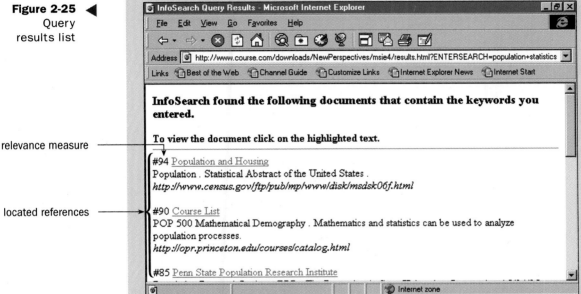

6. Scroll through the Query Results list and see if the data is relevant. The number on the left side of each link indicates, on a scale of 0 (least relevant) to 100 (most relevant) how relevant each link might be, based on criteria set up by the database manager. After scrolling through the links and noting those she might want to return to, Yoko decides to query the Census Bureau directly.

7. Scroll to the bottom of the page, click the **Click here to proceed to the next step** link to try another query, type **Census Bureau by county** in the query box, then click the **Submit** button. The first entry in the list that appears, Data Maps, has a relevance of 95. Yoko decides to explore this link.

8. Click the **Data Maps** link. The United States map appears. Click the Michigan Upper Peninsula, labelled **MI**, as shown in Figure 2-26.

TROUBLE? If the Data Maps site is busy, read through these steps and try them again later.

Figure 2-26 ◀
State data map

source is U.S.
Census Bureau

click to connect
to Michigan
county maps

each state is a
hypertext link

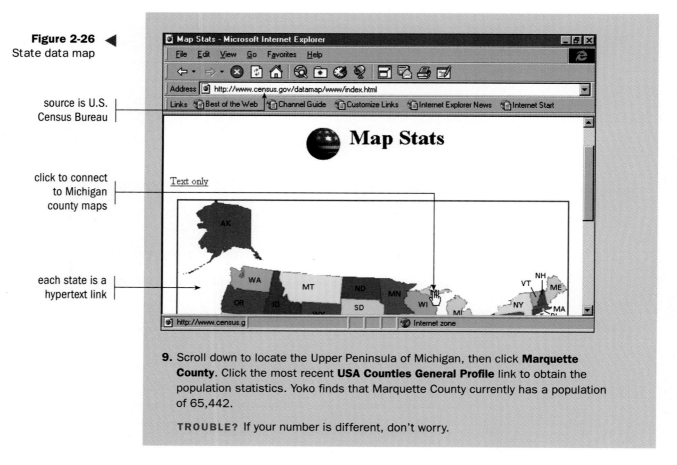

9. Scroll down to locate the Upper Peninsula of Michigan, then click **Marquette County**. Click the most recent **USA Counties General Profile** link to obtain the population statistics. Yoko finds that Marquette County currently has a population of 65,442.

TROUBLE? If your number is different, don't worry.

Yoko has found the population statistics she was looking for, but you add a note of caution. Sometimes a query might be too general, which results in a large list of references that includes unrelated data. Other times, the query might be too specific and returns few or no references. In either case, you'll need to revise the query so that it is more or less inclusive, as necessary. Try adding adjectives or nouns that help focus the search, or try choosing synonyms that are more specific to your needs. Using the root of words can also help. Sometimes queries are case-sensitive, so capitalize any word that might be capitalized in references.

The search engine Yoko has been using so far is the one Anna created for the Peter H. Martin Library. Its database is not a large one. Now that Yoko knows how to search using a query, she wants to try one of the search services available on the Search Explorer bar. She'll start by using Infoseek, which lets you search the Web and many other services on the Internet, including newsgroups.

Yoko decides to use Infoseek to see what information is available on Japanese food.

To search for pages on Japanese food:

1. Click the **Search** button 🔍. The Search Explorer bar appears.

2. Click the **Choose provider** list arrow, then, as shown in Figure 2-27, click **Infoseek**.

Figure 2-27 ◄
Searching
with Infoseek

click to open Search
Explorer bar

click to view list
of search providers

list of search
providers

Search Explorer bar;
a different search
provider might appear

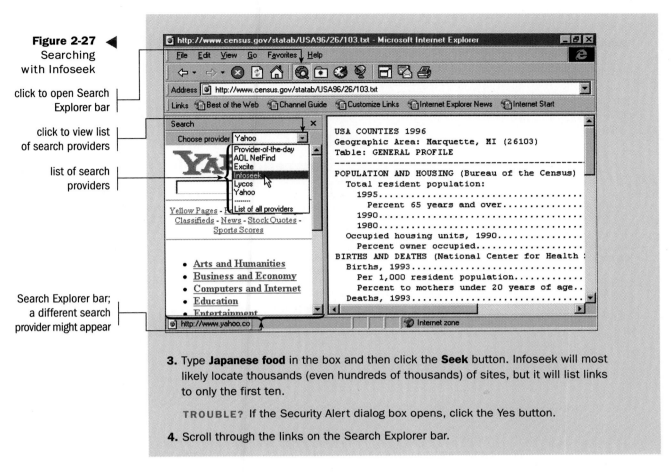

3. Type **Japanese food** in the box and then click the **Seek** button. Infoseek will most likely locate thousands (even hundreds of thousands) of sites, but it will list links to only the first ten.

    TROUBLE? If the Security Alert dialog box opens, click the Yes button.

4. Scroll through the links on the Search Explorer bar.

Yoko is impressed with the breadth of the pages located in the search. She realizes there's a lot more information here than she can ever take in, and she resolves to come back later to see how other Japanese restaurants are maintaining a presence on the Web.

Now Yoko decides to use the Excite search service to find additional census information.

To use the Excite search service:

1. Click the **Choose provider** list arrow on the Search Explorer bar, then click **Excite**.

2. Type **Census Bureau by county** in the box, then click the **Search** button.

3. Scroll through the links to see the first batch, and click the first one. The search results appear in the Internet Explorer window, as shown in Figure 2-28. Your results will be different because the database is constantly updated.

Figure 2-28 ◄
Excite
search tool

if you click link in
results list, page
appears here

type search
query here

click to
perform search

results list

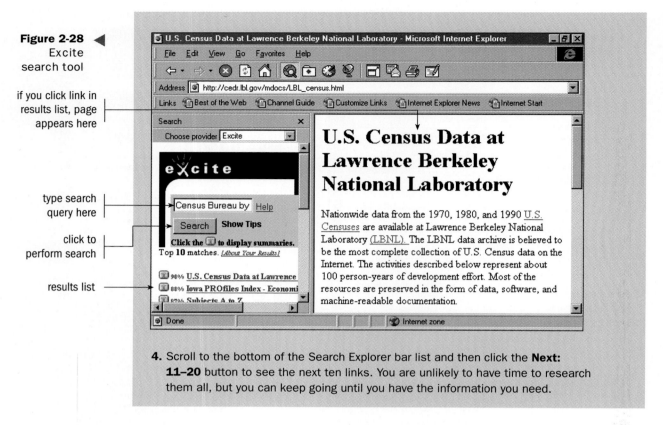

4. Scroll to the bottom of the Search Explorer bar list and then click the **Next: 11–20** button to see the next ten links. You are unlikely to have time to research them all, but you can keep going until you have the information you need.

You have now used two search services, Infoseek and Excite, to locate information by performing queries. Now Yoko wants to try a different kind of search: a subject search.

Searching Through a Subject Guide

Sometimes when you begin studying a topic, you don't know what keywords to use in a content search. Instead, you can search for applicable information by subject. Subject lists are organized first by general and then successively more specific subjects as you search.

Yoko knows that many new businesses fail within a short time, due in part to lack of planning and knowledge of where and how to get resources. Because her restaurant will be a small business, she thinks the government might provide funding or consulting assistance at the federal, state, or local level. She wants to know all her options but isn't sure where to begin looking. A subject search using a navigational guide is a good starting point. Yoko wants to use the Yahoo subject guide to find information on starting a small business.

To search by subject with Yahoo:

1. Click the **Choose provider** list arrow, then click **Yahoo.**

2. Scroll down, if necessary, and click a **Business** link. See Figure 2-29; the list you see might be different depending on which guide you are using.

Figure 2-29 ◀
Subject guide

list of main
categories

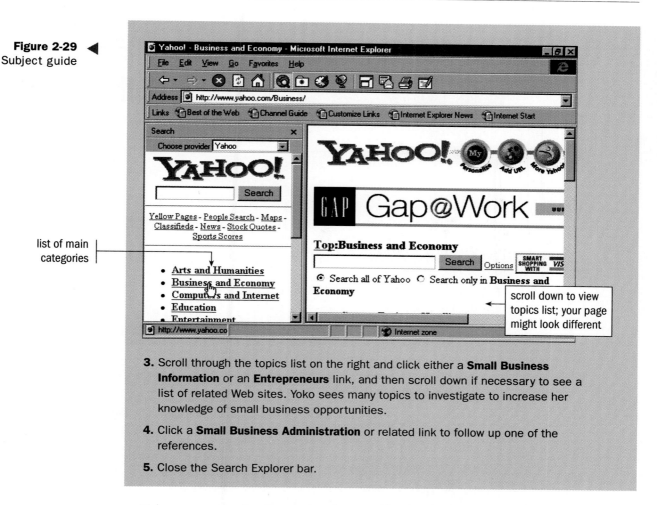

3. Scroll through the topics list on the right and click either a **Small Business Information** or an **Entrepreneurs** link, and then scroll down if necessary to see a list of related Web sites. Yoko sees many topics to investigate to increase her knowledge of small business opportunities.

4. Click a **Small Business Administration** or related link to follow up one of the references.

5. Close the Search Explorer bar.

Yoko comments that because such a wealth of material is available about small businesses, she'll never be able to read it all before the library closes. Printing all these Web pages would require a lot of paper and time. You suggest that she save the pages she wants to look at on a disk. First, though, you pass on an Internet Explorer search tip: you can perform a quick, rough search by typing the word *find* in the Address bar, followed by a search word. When you press Enter, the Internet Explorer AutoSearch feature displays a list of links you might try, courtesy of the Yahoo search service.

Saving Text and Images to a File

Saving Web pages on a disk not only saves you paper and the time it would take to print the pages; it also reduces the amount of time you spend online. This can save you a lot of money if you pay a connection charge for using an online service provider. If the fee is charged per minute of connection time, reading Web pages online can become very costly.

You can save a Web page on disk in text format or HTML format. When Internet Explorer saves a file as text, it saves only the text. Thus when you open a file you've saved as text, the formatting, special fonts, and color do not appear.

Alternatively, you can save a Web page as an HTML file, so if you open the saved file in Internet Explorer it will look similar to the Web page, including the special fonts and colors. However, Internet Explorer does not save the graphics that accompany the file, and although it saves the links, not all links will work locally on your machine, depending on how the links were originally configured.

Moreover, because the file is a coded HTML **source document**, a file embedded with special characters that allow browsers to display the file, some word-processing programs will be unable to interpret the HTML codes. You can, however, open the file in Internet Explorer or in word processors that can interpret HTML files, such as Microsoft Word. If you open the HTML file in Notepad or a similar text editor, you will see the codes.

One final note: If you are viewing a page with frames, you will be unable to save the text, because framed pages use special HTML codes that affect how text appears. The steps, therefore, direct you to find a page that is not framed.

Saving a Web Page as a Text File

Yoko wants to save the Web page that she is reading about the small business association.

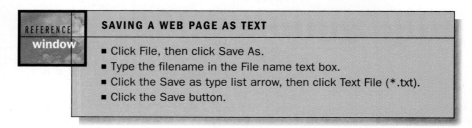

REFERENCE window	**SAVING A WEB PAGE AS TEXT**
	▪ Click File, then click Save As.
	▪ Type the filename in the File name text box.
	▪ Click the Save as type list arrow, then click Text File (*.txt).
	▪ Click the Save button.

To save the current Web page as a text file:

1. Make sure the page you are viewing is not a framed page. If it is, return to your search results and choose a different page. Select a page that has text, not just graphics and links.

2. Insert your Student Disk into drive A or the appropriate drive on your computer.

3. Click **File**, then click **Save As** to open the Save As dialog box.

   TROUBLE? If the Save As command is dimmed, you might not have finished loading the entire Web document. Click the Refresh button 🔄 on the toolbar to reload the Web page.

4. Click the **Save as type** list arrow to see the file type options.

5. Click **Text File (*.txt)** in the Save as type list box so the Web page is saved as readable text rather than as HTML coding.

6. Click the **Save in** list arrow and choose **3½ Floppy (A:)**.

7. Type **business** in the File name box to name the file being created. See Figure 2-30.

Figure 2-30 ◀
Saving a Web
page as
a text file

type filename here —

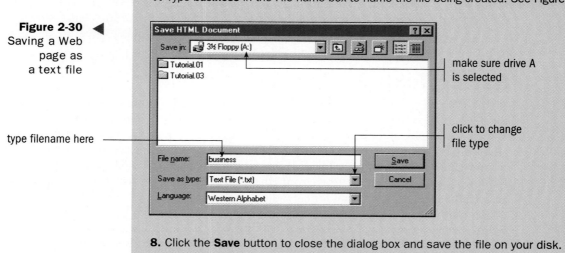

make sure drive A
is selected

click to change
file type

8. Click the **Save** button to close the dialog box and save the file on your disk.

Before Yoko saves any more pages, she should double-check that the page saved properly.

Opening a Text File

Because you saved the document as a text file, you could open and edit it with any word-processing program. You can also open the file from Internet Explorer and edit it using Microsoft FrontPage Express, the Web page editor that accompanies the Internet Explorer suite. When you open a text file using the Internet Explorer Open command, Internet Explorer displays the text in the Internet Explorer window.

REFERENCE window

OPENING A TEXT FILE

- Click File, then click Open.
- Click the Browse button and specify the folder you want to look in.
- Click the Files of type list arrow, then click Text (*.txt) from the Files of type text box.
- Click the file you want to open, click the Open button, then click the OK button.

For now you'll just open Yoko's file from within Internet Explorer to verify that it saved properly.

To open a file:

1. Click **File**, then click **Open**. The Open dialog box opens.

2. Click the **Browse** button, then click the **Look in** list arrow and select the drive containing your Student Disk.

3. Click the **Files of type** list arrow, then click **Text Files** to display the business file you just saved in the file list. Click the **business.txt** file, then click the **Open** button.

4. Click the **OK** button in the Open dialog box. The contents of the text file appears in the Internet Explorer window. Notice that no color, special fonts, links, or graphics are saved. See Figure 2-31.

Figure 2-31 ◄
Viewing a text file in Internet Explorer

content remains though formatting and images are not saved; your content might differ

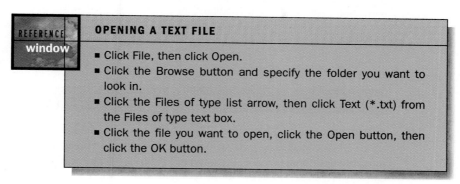

```
Net Earnings has surveyed the key management books that can help
         small business succeed. You can get any of our recommended title:
         for 10% off list price. And they can be shipped directly to you
         within just 2 or 3 days. Just click the title to order now.

Financial Basics of Small Business, by Beverly Manber and James O.
         Gill.
         A compendium of valuable information about the money side of sma
         business. Lots of practical tips with insights into the banking
         finance industry.
         Strategies for Small Business Success, by Jane Applegate.
         The nationally known commentator on small business surveys the d
         and dont's of American entrepreneurial success. Her message is t:
         there are many different ways to achieve your business goals.
```

5. Use the History Explorer bar to return to the library's Research & Reference Section page. Remember that this target is on the www.course.com server, so you need to click that link first in the History Explorer bar.

TROUBLE? If the Notepad window opens, close it.

6. Close the History Explorer bar once you have returned to the Research & Reference Section.

Yoko mentions that she might want to use a graphic from a Web page on her promotional material. You suggest that she save a graphic from the library's Web pages so she can see how to save images.

Saving an Image from a Web Page

You can save images you see on Web pages as separate files. Image files can be saved in a variety of file formats. The two most common image file types are GIF and JPEG. As with audio files, the difference between the types of file is image quality and file size. You'll also need software that can interpret these different image file types if you want to view and use them.

You'll save an image from the library's Web page for Yoko.

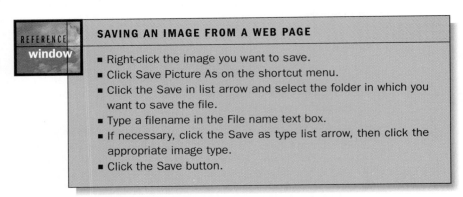

REFERENCE window

SAVING AN IMAGE FROM A WEB PAGE

- Right-click the image you want to save.
- Click Save Picture As on the shortcut menu.
- Click the Save in list arrow and select the folder in which you want to save the file.
- Type a filename in the File name text box.
- If necessary, click the Save as type list arrow, then click the appropriate image type.
- Click the Save button.

To save an image from a Web page:

1. Right-click the Library East Wing image; you might need to scroll to see it. The shortcut menu opens. See Figure 2-32.

Figure 2-32 ◄
Saving an
image on a
Web page

click image with right
mouse button to
open shortcut menu

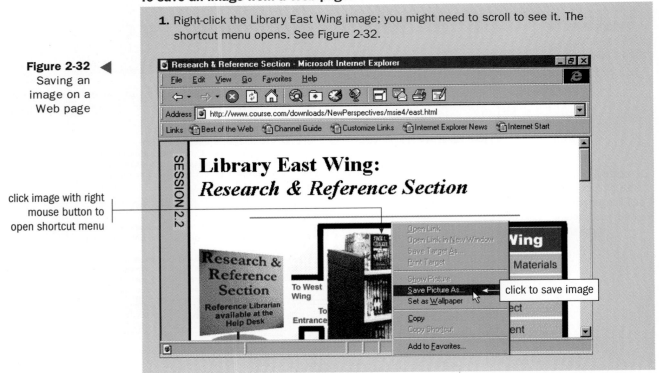

2. Click **Save Picture As** to open the Save As dialog box.

3. Click the **Save in** list arrow and select the drive containing your Student Disk.

4. Type **Image** in the File name box to name the file on your disk.

5. Make sure that GIF File (*.gif) appears in the Save as type text box, then click the **Save** button. The Save As dialog box closes, and the image is saved on your disk. Now you'll open the file in Internet Explorer and view the image to verify that it saved properly.

6. Click **File**, and then click **Open**. The Open dialog box opens.

7. Type **a:\image.gif** in the box, then click the **OK** button. The image appears in the Internet Explorer window.

Yoko plans to save a number of documents and useful images that have information about starting a small business.

Downloading External Files

Yoko noticed there are many external files referenced in the Web pages she has browsed—that is, files that don't appear in the browser window but that instead can be viewed only in a separate program. She asks if there is an easy way to save those files without first opening them.

Many files on the Internet are available for transfer to your hard drive so you can use them later. For example, a financial company might place its fund prospectus on its Web site for potential investors to examine. Software developers often post trial versions of their software on the Web for potential buyers to preview.

You can transfer a file over the Internet from a Web server onto your hard drive with relative ease. File transfer over the Internet is so easy, in fact, that it has revolutionized the way people today share information.

For years, the common way to retrieve files from the Internet was with the File Transfer Protocol (FTP). **FTP** provides a means of logging onto, or connecting to, a computer elsewhere on the Internet, called a **remote computer**, viewing its directories, and transferring files to and from your local computer. You can quickly recognize an FTP site by its URL, which begins with "ftp://" instead of "http://". These sites are often referred to as **anonymous FTP sites** because to access the files on the site you have to log onto the remote computer, entering "anonymous" as your username and your e-mail address as the password. When you use Internet Explorer to connect to an anonymous FTP site, the logon takes place automatically. In recent years, however, as the World Wide Web has become the primary means of accessing data from the Internet, you no longer need to store files in anonymous FTP sites to make them available to users, although it is still quite common to connect to them when you're searching for a file.

The person who owns or runs a Web server can decide whether to establish a public directory, a portion of the server that stores files that people can upload or download. **Upload** means to transfer a copy of a file from your own computer to a public directory. **Download** means to transfer a copy of a file from the public directory to your own computer.

You decide to show Yoko how to download the sound file on the library's home page. You will save it directly on your Student Disk.

To transfer a file:

1. Return to the Peter H. Martin Library page using any of the navigation methods you learned earlier.

2. Right-click the **audio link** 🔊 .

3. Click **Save Target As** and enter a network password if necessary. Click the **Save in** list arrow, then click **3½ Floppy (A:)**. Notice that the filename is welcome.au. Click the **Save** button. A progress bar informs you of the download status, and when the download is complete, the file is saved on your Student Disk.

4. Click the **OK** button to acknowledge the download complete message.

Now that the welcome audio file is on your Student Disk, you can run it by starting any audio utility.

You have successfully downloaded a file from the Web. Yoko asks if there is anything special she should know when downloading files from the Internet. After a moment's thought, you mention that she should learn about file compression, as she is likely to encounter compressed files if she spends much time downloading files over the Internet. She should also check any files she downloads for viruses, and she should ascertain whether or not the files are in the public domain before she does anything with them. You agree to go over those subject areas with her.

Compressed Files

The length of time a file takes to transfer over the Internet depends largely on the speed of the computer modem and on the size of the file. In order to conserve space on a network server and decrease the time a file takes to transfer, many files are compressed. **Compression** compacts data into a smaller size by scanning a file, eliminating duplicate words or phrases, and replacing them with reference codes, which it keeps in a small internal chart that accompanies the compressed file. For example, the words *Internet Explorer* might be replaced by a code such as *#1* every time the words appear in these tutorials, decreasing the space they require by 15 characters. Apply this same coding to every repeated word in a lengthy document, and its results in a much smaller file. Often, several related files are compiled into a single compressed file. The most common compression program on the Internet today creates files called **zip files**, compressed files with the file extension zip. Zip files are created with the popular PKZIP for DOS or WinZip for Windows compression programs.

For example, say the Kitakuni Japanese Restaurant wants to place a collection of Japanese recipes on their Web site. They might save the collection as a Word file named Recipes.doc. Then they might use the WinZip program to compress the Word file. The compressed file, which is much smaller in size, is named Recipes.zip. They place Recipes.zip on their Web server. Figure 2-33 illustrates this process.

Figure 2-33 ◀
Compressing a file and placing it on a Web server

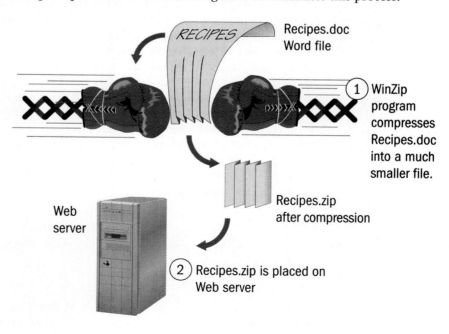

Recipes.doc
Word file

1 WinZip program compresses Recipes.doc into a much smaller file.

Recipes.zip after compression

Web server

2 Recipes.zip is placed on Web server

Once a compressed file is placed on a server, it can be downloaded much more quickly. If you download a compressed file, however, you must use an **uncompression program** that interprets the reference codes and restores the file to its original structure and size. Your compression program might also include an extraction feature that allows you to extract, or uncompress, one file at a time. Some compressed files are self-extracting. A **self-extracting file**, which usually has the exe extension, is able to extract its compressed files without a separate uncompression program.

If you don't have a compression program, you can download one from a Web site that makes software utilities available, following the general steps in the next section on viruses. Ask your instructor for recommendations on a suitable compression and uncompression program and a URL for where you might find it. If you spend much time downloading files on the Internet you will almost certainly encounter compressed files, so learning how to handle them is time well spent.

Viruses

Files stored in public directories are highly subject to viruses. You warn Yoko that she should routinely check any file that she downloads from an unknown source. A **virus** is a destructive program code embedded, or hidden, in an executable file. When you run an infected program, the virus can affect the performance of your computer, display messages or images on your screen, or even damage your data.

In order to protect your computer, you should run an anti-virus program on every file you download and on every disk you get from someone else. An **anti-virus program** looks for suspicious series of commands or codes within an executable file and compares them to a list of known virus codes. If the program finds a match, it removes the virus from your disk. If you haven't opened an infected file, then it doesn't infect your computer. Anti-virus programs are frequently updated because new viruses are constantly appearing.

You can download current anti-virus programs from the Internet and then run them on the files you download. It is unlikely that you would be able to download and install an anti-virus program on a school lab computer, but you might find these steps useful if you have your own computer at home. Skip these steps if you are in a school lab. These steps are necessarily general because they do not recommend one particular product, and the download and installation procedure differs from product to product. Your instructor might be able to recommend a favorite brand of anti-virus software.

To download an anti-virus program:

1. Perform a search for the words *virus protection* or *virus program* until you find a site that supplies anti-virus utilities. Use any search provider you want on the Search Explorer bar.

2. Link to the anti-virus site, and continue to search through the links until you find the virus product you want.

3. Locate a download link. Most vendors have a "try" link and a "buy" link; for now, use the "try" link. If you like the software you can buy it later. You might need to navigate through a few links to actually begin downloading the file. More than likely, you'll need to select the correct version of the program for your operating system. You might also be required to provide your address and other information about how you plan to use the product.

4. Once you have clicked the download link, you will most likely be asked where you want to place the file. Choose a location on your hard disk, such as a special folder you create for the virus software, or in a Program Files folder. Many programs are too big to be easily saved on floppy disks. Wait until the software is downloaded; this could take some time, depending on the speed of your Internet connection.

5. Once the program is installed, locate it on your computer. It is most likely an executable setup file, so to run it, you click or double-click the file, depending on your operating system. Once you run the setup file, an installation program starts automatically and installs the product on your system. Use the product's Help system to learn how to use the product.

Once you have an uncompression program and an anti-virus program, you are ready to download any file off the Web. Yoko, for example, might decide to download the recipes on the Kitakuni Web site. First, she uses an uncompression program to unzip the file and place it in a folder. Then she checks the file for viruses. Only then does she open it. Figure 2-34 illustrates the process.

Figure 2-34 ◄
Downloading,
uncompressing
and checking a
file for viruses

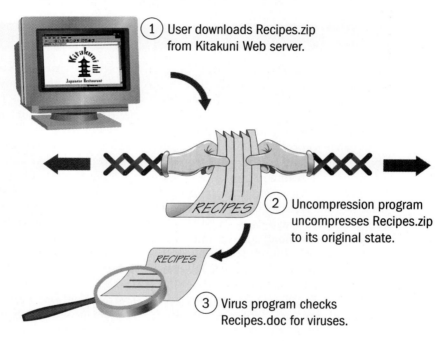

1. User downloads Recipes.zip from Kitakuni Web server.

2. Uncompression program uncompresses Recipes.zip to its original state.

3. Virus program checks Recipes.doc for viruses.

Internet Explorer also allows you to change the security settings on your computer so that you can exclude content that could damage your computer or you can be warned of potentially damaging content, enabling you to check it for viruses before you transfer it to your computer.

Copyrighted Material

As you've seen, saving text and images on your own computer from Internet sites around the world is easy to do, perhaps even easier than photocopying. The quality of the copied material is the same as the original; colors, shading, and graphics do not darken or distort, as they might in a photocopy. This makes it simple to copy an image or text from the Internet and reproduce it for personal, academic, or commercial use. However, similar to those for printed material, restrictions apply to the use of these files.

All printed material, such as books and magazines, and all audio material, such as music CDs or books on tape, are protected from unlimited reproduction by copyright law. A **copyright** is a federal law that allows an author (or the copyright holder) to control how his or her work is used, including how the material is reproduced, sold, distributed, adapted, performed, or displayed. Depending on how much material you want to reproduce from the Internet and your purpose in reproducing it, you might need to obtain permission from the Web page owner (the copyright holder) and, in some cases, pay a fee. Figure 2-35 outlines some guidelines for determining when you need to request permission before reusing

Internet
Explorer

material from the Internet. Remember that people, authors and artists, have made their works available over an electronic medium for increased distribution, not for increased duplication.

Figure 2-35 ◄
Copyright
notices

Copyright Notice	Academic Use	Commercial Use
Copyrighted	Can quote a certain amount without permission. Include proper citation. Request permission to reuse large amounts.	Request permission
No copyright	Assume copyrighted	Assume copyrighted
Source states "Use freely, no restrictions"	Can reuse without permission	Can reuse without permission

If Yoko found a graphic she liked on the Internet, she could use it with its citation if she were writing a research paper on starting a Japanese take-out restaurant. If she wants to use the graphic in a commercial setting for her own profit, Yoko needs to request permission from its creator to use the graphic.

Shareware

A program that you can try before buying is called **shareware**. The people who write these programs enjoy sharing their ideas and creations, hence the name *shareware*. The authors of shareware are not necessarily employees of software companies, but, rather, can be college students, professionals, or hobbyists, who had an idea for a program or an interest in programming. The Internet provides a convenient and inexpensive way to market a program and get feedback on its features.

The authors make their programs available for a free trial; if you decide to keep the program, you must send the author a fee, as outlined in the text file attached to the program. To help ensure that people send in the appropriate fee after a trial period, many authors distribute a demonstration version, which might have disabled features. When you register and purchase the program, you'll receive a full working version and information about updates, or revisions, to the program. Registering and sending payment for any shareware you plan to keep and use will encourage shareware authors to continue to write new versions and create new programs.

Other programs called **freeware** are made available to the public but are free of charge.

Yoko is pleased with all the information she has gathered and what she has learned about researching on the Internet.

Quick Check

1. You submit database queries to a _____ to search the Web for keywords.

2. In a query, which kind of search—an *or* or an *and*—results in more site references? Why?

3. True or False: All sites listed in a query result are relevant to the user's needs.

4. _____ are computer software that periodically index Web page contents and URLs into topics for use in query searches.

5. When you don't know keywords to use for a search, use a _____ guide to search for general topics.

6. Web pages can be saved as _____ files, but these files don't include graphics, formatting, or links.

7 What is the difference between saving a page as text and saving it in HTML format?

8 What are the two most common image file types on the Web?

9 What is an external file?

10 What is the difference between uploading and downloading?

11 True or False: You can insert one GIF image, copied from the Internet, into a college term paper without requesting permission from the Web page owner.

12 True or False: Shareware is free, regardless of how long you use it.

Tutorial Assignments

Yoko Muramoto is continuing with her plans to open a take-out restaurant serving Japanese food, and she regularly checks the Web for new and useful sites that might help her. She is particularly interested in any page that deals with Michigan, small businesses, the restaurant business, or Japanese culture.

Right now Yoko wants additional information about insurance for her business. She learned from other small business owners that the Michigan Insurance Bureau provides information specially geared to small businesses. She thinks they might have a Web page. Yoko also wants to find Web pages for other businesses that deal with Japanese food. She asks you to find the Web page for the Michigan Insurance Bureau and Web pages dealing with Japanese food, recipes, or restaurants.

If necessary, launch Internet Explorer, and then do the following:

1. Open the Web page at the URL http://www.course.com/downloads/NewPerspectives/msie4.

2. Click the Tutorial Assignments and Case Problems link.

3. Scroll down until you see the Tutorial 2 Tutorial Assignments.

4. Click the Search by Content link at the Peter H. Martin Library Research & Reference Section.

5. Click the WebCrawler link.

6. Enter "Michigan Insurance Bureau" in the query box and press Enter.

7. Print the list of sites returned by WebCrawler.

8. Is a link to the Michigan Insurance Bureau shown? If so, click that link and then save a copy of the Michigan Insurance Bureau page as a text file. If not, connect to a link for the state or government of Michigan and look further for the Michigan Insurance Bureau site. If there is not a link to the Michigan Insurance Bureau, save the current page as a text file.

9. Use the File menu to return to the Research & Reference Section page.

10. Choose a different search provider on the Search Explorer bar and type the "Michigan Insurance Bureau" query again. How do the results differ? Print this list and staple it to the first, indicating which search service you used for each query. Submit this to your instructor.

11. Return to the Research & Reference Section page using the Back list, and then click the Search by Subject link.

12. Click the Yahoo link.

13. Proceed through the more detailed levels of entertainment and foods subjects to find a list of Web pages related to Japanese food by clicking appropriate links.

14. Open a Web page related to Japanese food.

15. Add this page to your Favorites folder.

16. Create a folder called Japanese Food and move the page you just saved into that folder.

17. Open three additional Japanese Web pages and add each to your Japanese Food folder.

 18. Save an image from one of the Japanese Web pages you see. Open the image in Internet Explorer, then print the image.

 19. Return to your favorite Japanese Web page so you can add it as a button on your Links toolbar. Click Favorites, click Add to Favorites, click the Create in button, then click Links. Test the button you just added. You might need to click the scroll arrow on the Links toolbar to view the button you added.

 20. Open the Organize Favorites window, open the Links folder, then delete the link you just placed on the Links toolbar. Also delete the Japanese Food folder and its contents.

Case Problems

1. LaFrancois Travel Danielle LaFrancois, owner and chief agent at the LaFrancois Travel Agency, uses the Web to keep tabs on various festivals and activities taking place at tourist sites around the country. She recently learned of some inexpensive airfare to Edinburgh, the capital of Scotland. The tickets will be available at that price for only a short time so she wants to find some current information on Edinburgh and Glasgow, a nearby city, to help encourage people to purchase the tickets. She asks you to use the Web to find the following information for both cities: what activities are upcoming, a list of museums and galleries, and some other places of interest.

If necessary, launch Internet Explorer, then do the following:

1. Open the Web page at the URL "http://www.course.com/downloads/NewPerspectives/msie4" and then click the Tutorial Assignments and Case Problems link.

2. Scroll down until you see the Tutorial 2 Case Problems section.

3. Click the Travel Logs link in the Browsing Section of the Peter H. Martin Library.

4. Open the City.Net link and add that page to your Favorites folder.

 5. Navigate through the maps of Europe to locate information about Edinburgh. Save any information you find on the Edinburgh page as a text file.

6. Return to the Travel Logs in the Browsing Section page using the history list.

 7. Investigate Glasgow using the Virtual Tourist II or City.Net links. *Hint:* Follow the United Kingdom links under Europe.

8. Print the Glasgow document for your instructor. Write a short note on the back stating whether you think Glasgow or Edinburgh offer the better tourist attractions at this time.

9. Locate a link to an external file, such as an audio or video clip, on one of the travel Web pages you encountered. Download the file by right-clicking the file and clicking Save Picture As.

 10. Once you have downloaded the file, check its file type by viewing its extension in My Computer or Windows Explorer.

11. Check which program is associated with this file type by viewing the File Types tab in the Folder Options dialog box (accessible through My Computer's View menu). Start that program if you have it, and then open the file you just downloaded. Write a short report for your instructor that identifies the file, the page from which you downloaded it, its file type, and the program associated with that file type.

12. Open the previously saved Edinburgh text file using a word-processing program (such as Word, WordPad, or Notepad), type your name at the top, print the first page of the file, and submit it to your instructor.

2. Reading the News from Halifax Halifax, a city in Nova Scotia, Canada, northeast of Maine, is situated along the Atlantic Ocean, and fishing is a major industry. In recent years, it has also flourished as a tourist town thanks to the natural beauty of the area. David Wu wants to spend his summer working at one of the fishing resorts in the area. Before he packs his bags, he wants to learn a little more about daily living in Halifax. He asks you to use the Web to get the headlines from a Halifax newspaper, find out about the climate, and determine popular sporting events in Halifax.

If necessary, launch Internet Explorer, then do the following:

1. Open the Web page at the URL "http://www.course.com/downloads/NewPerspectives/msie4" and then click the Tutorial Assignments and Case Problems link.

2. Scroll down until you see the Tutorial 2 Case Problems section, then click the Newspapers and Magazines link in the Browsing Section of the Peter H. Martin Library.

3. Follow either the Yahoo's Guide to Media link or the Newspapers on the Net link to reach a listing of newspapers published on the Internet.

4. Locate one of the Halifax newspapers using one of the search services on the Search Explorer bar. (*Hint:* Search for "Halifax newspaper".)

5. Connect to the newspaper and add it to your Favorites folder.

6. Navigate through the pages to obtain the information about today's weather and a local sporting event that David wants.

7. When you have all the information, print the page containing the headlines of a Halifax newspaper for your instructor.

8. On the back of the page, briefly summarize the facts you gathered. Submit this page to your instructor.

9. Save one of the images on the newspaper as a gif file.

10. Open the gif file in the Internet Explorer window and then print the gif file and submit it to your instructor.

11. Remove the newspaper link you added to your Favorites folder.

3. Job Searching on the Web Keisha Williams, a senior at MidWest University, is actively searching for employment in marketing, her major field of study. She'd like to move to Texas. She asks you to help her use the Web to locate resources for job searches and to find some tips on writing résumés. One popular site to find job listings is the CareerMosaic home page, which contains the J.O.B.S. database, which you can use to search for specific jobs in different parts of the country. Unfortunately, you don't know the address of the site, so you'll have to find the Web page before you can search for job listings. The J.O.B.S. database page contains several fields into which you can enter information specific to the job you're seeking.

If necessary, launch Internet Explorer, then do the following:

1. Open the Search Explorer bar.

2. Select one search service and type "CareerMosaic" or "Career Magazine" in the query box, then submit the query as indicated by the search engine.

3. Scroll through the list of sites returned by the query until you see relevant page referrals.

4. Connect to the CareerMosaic or Career Magazine home page.

5. Using the search criteria given by Keisha, look for available positions. In Keisha's case, you should search for jobs related to marketing and limit the search to jobs in Texas. If you don't find any in Texas, expand your search to nearby states.

6. Connect to a link that describes a job you think is appropriate for Keisha.

7. Print the job description page for your instructor.

8. Use one of the navigational methods you learned in this tutorial to return to the home page of the search engine you used earlier.

9. Search for pages that contain résumé writing tips.

10. Investigate the pages that seem the most helpful. Select the one that looks like the best resource and save it on your disk as a text file. Then print the text file for your instructor.

4. Scavenger Hunt on the World Wide Web Now that you've had some experience using search tools on the WWW, you should be able to locate almost any type of information on the Web. Complete the following "scavenger hunt"; use any tool available at the Peter H. Martin Library. As you find an answer, write it down. Submit the answers to your instructor and indicate the URL of the page you used to find the answer.

If necessary, launch Internet Explorer, then do the following:

1. Open the Web page at the URL "http://www.course.com/downloads/NewPerspectives/msie4" and then click the Tutorial 2 link.

2. In what Shakespearean play does a character say "There's no trust, no faith, no honesty in men; all perjured, all forsworn, all naught, all dissemblers" (specify the act and the scene)? *Hint:* Look for the Shakespeare home page, which contains a tool for searching the contents of all Shakespeare's plays and poems.

3. In the movie "Three Little Words," who played the part of Harry Ruby? *Hint:* Look for The Internet Movie Database page and then use a search tool to find a movie titled "Three Little Words."

4. While you are exploring movie pages, try to locate a video clip from a movie. Many movie pages include previews to upcoming movies. Save the video clip on your Student Disk, and then double-click it in My Computer to play it. What software started?

5. What is the current temperature, humidity, wind, and barometric pressure at Caribou, Maine? *Hint:* Look for a page that deals with weather in the Travel Logs section of the Peter H. Martin Library home page.

6. What are the address, phone number, and e-mail address of your congressional representative in the U.S. House of Representatives? *Hint:* Use the Yahoo index to search for government resources.

7. What is the current estimate of the population of the United States, and of the world? *Hint:* Use the Planet Earth home page in the Browsing Section of the Peter H. Martin Library home page.

8. What is the zip code for Nome, Alaska (abbreviated AK)? *Hint:* Check the Frequently Used References at the Peter H. Martin Library.

9. What is the URL for the Smithsonian Institution's home page?

10. When you have found the answers to these questions, write them in a report and submit the report to your instructor.

Corresponding with Outlook Express

Communicating over the Internet at Carey Outerwear

OBJECTIVES

In this tutorial you will learn to:

▪ Configure the e-mail function

▪ Secure, send, receive, reply to, print, and forward e-mail messages

▪ Organize addresses in an Address Book

▪ Send and receive e-mail attachments

▪ Manage messages in folders

▪ Save messages and attachments for future reference

▪ Delete e-mail messages and Address Book entries

▪ Subscribe to and unsubscribe from a newsgroup

▪ Post a message to a newsgroup

▪ Search a newsgroup for information

LAB

E-Mail

CASE

Carey Outerwear

Carey Outerwear is a corporation specializing in high-quality outerwear for campers, hikers, and climbers. The company has outlet stores in several western states and recently opened outlets in Madison, Wisconsin, and Boston, Massachusetts. The main branch, in Seattle, Washington, is hosting the Spring 2000 sales conference June 12–17, 2000. Employees will spend the first part of the week in sales meetings, but for the weekend following the conference, Carey Outerwear is providing its employees with a variety of opportunities to field-test Carey merchandise on organized outings throughout Washington state. You just started working as a summer intern in the Seattle sales department. Your supervisor, John Kruse, has asked you to help organize a guided climb of Mt. Rainier for the conference.

John recommends that you begin by getting in touch with Katie Herrera, one of the salespeople in the Tacoma outlet. John knows that Katie used to work as a seasonal ranger at Mt. Rainier National Park before she joined the Carey sales force, and she will be a good source of information. John gives you Katie's e-mail address and tells you that with **e-mail**, the electronic transfer of messages between hosts on the Internet, you can correspond with people around the world without having to worry about time zones, expensive long-distance charges, or answering machines.

You've also heard that newsgroups are another great Internet source of information. A **newsgroup** is a discussion group on the Internet that focuses on a single topic. There are newsgroups on just about every conceivable topic, from climbing to surfing to the Beatles to crochet. By subscribing to a newsgroup, you can see what others have to say about the topic and can take part in the conversation. You hope that when you have some free time you can explore newsgroups and see how they work.

SESSION

3.1

In this session, you will use the Outlook Express e-mail function to send and receive e-mail messages and attachments, organize addresses in the Address Book, and save attached files.

Configuring Outlook Express for Electronic Mail

As more people connect to the Internet and have access to e-mail programs, communicating by e-mail is becoming increasingly more common. When you need to send information to someone else, an e-mail message can save time and money because you don't need to wait for expensive postal delivery nor do you need to make expensive long-distance phone calls. You can send e-mail to and receive e-mail from anyone in the world who has an e-mail address, regardless of the operating system or type of computer they are using.

You remind John that you haven't yet been assigned an e-mail account at Carey Outerwear. John replies that the company's systems administrator just finished installing Internet Explorer on the computer you will be using, and he hands you a slip of paper with your user ID, password, and e-mail address. A **user ID** is the account name that identifies you on the network. A **password** is a personal code that verifies you have the right to read incoming mail. An **e-mail address** consists of the user ID, the @ symbol, and a host name (the domain address). For example, John's e-mail address is:

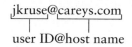

jkruse@careys.com

user ID@host name

Like URLs, every e-mail address is unique. Many people might use the same host, but user IDs distinguish one e-mail address from another.

Before you can use the Internet Explorer e-mail function, you must make sure it is **configured**, or set up, properly. Outlook Express needs the address of your Internet mail servers (one for outgoing mail and one for incoming mail), your name, and your e-mail address before you can use its e-mail function. Your e-mail address is included in every e-mail message you send, both as an identifier and as a return address. Your version of Outlook Express might also be set up to require a password before you can get your mail messages. Your technical support person might have configured these properties for you.

If you have any problems with your e-mail service, write down the information you find about your computer's mail properties and ask your instructor for help.

The Outlook Express window is customizable. You need to be able to view the **Folder List**, which displays the Outlook Express folders in a hierarchy similar to Windows Explorer. Messages, as you'll see momentarily, are organized in folders, and the Folder List helps you organize these folders. The Outlook Express window also features other components that you don't need right now. You'll begin by ensuring that your windows matches the windows shown in the figures.

To configure the properties for e-mail messages:

1. Click the **Start** button ⊞Start, point to **Programs**, point to **Internet Explorer**, then click **Outlook Express**. The Outlook Express window opens. See Figure 3-1.

   TROUBLE? If you are using the full version of Microsoft Outlook, start it as you normally would. Ask your instructor or technical support person for help if you have trouble finding it.

   TROUBLE? If your window looks different, click View, then click Layout. In the Basic area, make sure the Outlook Bar and Folder Bar check boxes are not selected and the Folder List check box is selected. In the Toolbar area, make sure the Top option button is selected and the Show text on toolbar buttons check box is selected. Click the OK button.

TROUBLE? If you see the Inbox instead of the Outlook Express view, click Outlook Express, which appears on top of the Folder List, shown in Figure 3-1.

Figure 3-1 ◄
Outlook
Express
window

toolbar

make sure Outlook
Express is selected

Folder List; you might
see additional folders

drag this border
left or right to
change the width of
the Folder List

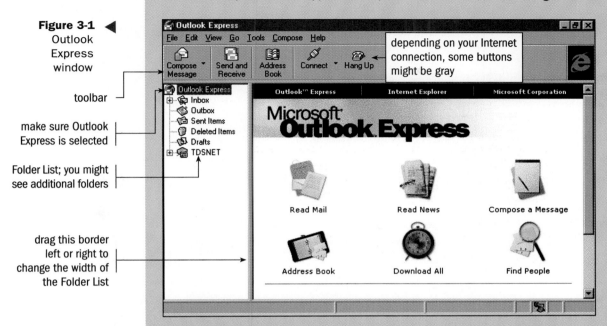

depending on your Internet
connection, some buttons
might be gray

2. Click **Tools**, then click **Accounts** to open the Internet Accounts dialog box.

3. Click the **Mail** tab. See Figure 3-2.

Figure 3-2 ◄
Mail accounts

account name; yours
will be different

click to set up new
account

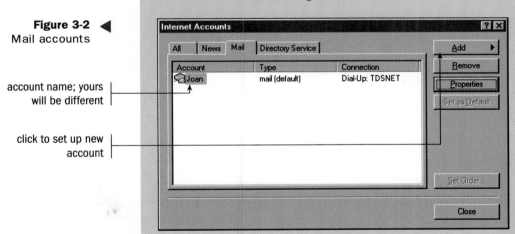

4. Click the account with your name.

TROUBLE? If no account appears with your name, no account has been set up for you. If you know your computer's Internet or modem settings, you can set up an account yourself by clicking the Add button and then clicking Mail. The Internet Connection Wizard starts. This wizard walks you through the steps of setting up a mail account. If you don't know the answers to all the questions the wizard asks, you will need to get further assistance from your technical support person or Internet Service Provider. You are unlikely to be able to set up an account in a school lab.

5. Click the **Properties** button. Your name and e-mail address should appear in the account Properties dialog box; Outlook Express uses this information when you send and receive e-mail. See Figure 3-3.

TROUBLE? If the name and e-mail address boxes are blank, ask your instructor or technical support person what to enter in them.

Figure 3-3 ◀
Configuring
e-mail
preferences

your user information
will be different

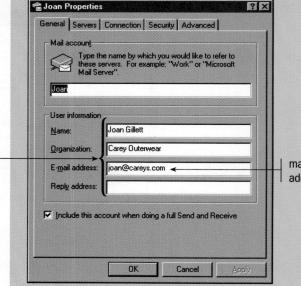

make sure your e-mail
address appears here

6. Click the **Servers** tab to check your mail server information. Your account name (user ID) and password should appear, along with your outgoing and incoming mail server addresses. See Figure 3-4.

TROUBLE? If any of these four boxes is blank, ask your instructor or technical support person what to enter in them.

Figure 3-4 ◀
Checking mail
server
information

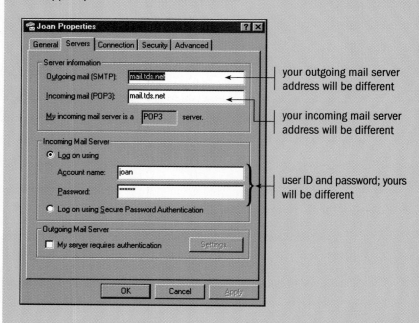

your outgoing mail server
address will be different

your incoming mail server
address will be different

user ID and password; yours
will be different

7. Click the **OK** button to close the account Properties dialog box and then close the Internet Accounts dialog box.

Now that you have ensured that Outlook Express can handle your e-mail, you're ready to send e-mail messages. Outlook Express organizes all the messages it handles, outgoing and incoming, into folders, or compartments that allow you to sort your messages: As you'll learn later, you can also create subfolders within the folders that allow you to file and store your messages in groups. Figure 3-5 describes the Outlook Express folders that you can use to store mail.

Figure 3-5 ◀
Outlook Express
folders

Folder	Description
Inbox	Stores all incoming messages and messages that you've read but haven't discarded or filed. Includes two subfolders: Personal Mail, where you can file personal messages, and Return Receipts, where Outlook Express stores a receipt indicating that a message you sent has been received (this occurs only if you set up Outlook Express to use this feature).
Outbox	Stores messages that you've finished composing and plan to send as soon as you connect to the Internet.
Sent Items	Stores a copy of every message you've sent.
Deleted Items	Stores the messages you've discarded. They remain in this folder until you delete them, at which point they are permanently gone.
Drafts	Stores messages that you have begun but are still drafting.

Securing E-mail

When you send confidential information in an e-mail message or an attachment, you need to be concerned about who might be able to access your message. Outlook Express offers several security features that allow you more control over your e-mail. You can obtain a **digital ID**, a secret code that is attached to the e-mail you send. This ID proves your identity to others and allows you to send and receive **encrypted**, or coded, messages to ensure their privacy. E-mail that uses digital signatures and encryption is marked with special icons in Outlook Express: tells you the message is digitally signed, and tells you the message is encrypted.

Incoming e-mail can also be a concern. E-mail from certain sources can contain **active content,** or code that automatically installs and runs on your computer, such as scripts or ActiveX controls (don't worry if you haven't heard these terms; all you really need to know is that they have the potential to damage your system). You can control how much access these codes have to your computer by assigning a given source to a security zone, and you can then assign a certain level of security to that zone. For example, you might place Web sites that you trust in a restricted zone and then assign a low level of security to that zone. For all other sites, you can assign a medium or high level of security so that active content from those sites cannot run at all or cannot run unless you allow so.

All security settings are controlled on the Security tab of the Options dialog box, available on the Tools menu. You won't work with security settings in this tutorial, but you should be aware that they're there, in case you need to configure security for your e-mail sometime in the future.

Sending E-mail

An e-mail message uses the same format as a standard memo: it typically includes From, Date, To, and Subject lines, followed by the content of the message. The To line indicates who will receive the message. Outlook Express automatically supplies your name or e-mail address in the From line and the date you send the message in the Date line. The Subject line, although optional, alerts the recipient of the message's topic. Finally, the message content area contains the text of your message. You can also include additional information, such as a Cc line, which indicates who will receive a copy of the message or a Bcc line, which indicates a "blind" copy that no other recipients will see.

When you prepare an e-mail message, you should remember some commonsense guidelines:

- Think before you type; read before you send. Your name and your institution's name are attached to everything you send.

- Type in both uppercase and lowercase letters. Using all uppercase letters in e-mail messages is considered shouting, and messages in all lowercase letters are difficult to read and decipher.

- Edit your message. Keep your messages concise so the reader can understand your meaning quickly and clearly.

- Send appropriate amounts of useful information. Like junk mail, e-mail messages can pile up quickly. If you must send a longer message, attach it as a file.

- Find out if personal e-mail messages are allowed on a work account. E-mail is not free (businesses pay to subscribe to a server), nor is what you write and send from the workplace confidential (your employer, for example, can access your e-mail).

Outlook Express also allows you to create messages on electronic stationery. There are several **stationery templates**—HTML files with predesigned backgrounds and text, including a party invitation, a birthday greeting, and a holiday letter. You can create your own stationery template by designing and saving an HTML file and using it while composing messages. To use stationery in an e-mail message, click the Compose Message list arrow and choose the stationery template you want. Your recipient must be able to read HTML e-mail. You won't use stationery in this tutorial, but you might find it fun to experiment with on your own.

REFERENCE window	**SENDING AN E-MAIL MESSAGE**
	■ Click the Compose Message button.
	■ Enter the e-mail address of the recipient in the To box.
	■ Press Tab until you reach the Subject box, then type the subject of the message.
	■ Press Tab, then type the content of the message in the message content area.
	■ Click the Send button.

You decide to send a message to Katie in which you introduce yourself and ask for her help. Her e-mail address is kherrera@course.com. You also decide to send a copy of the message to yourself so you can make sure your mail servers are interpreting your requests correctly.

E-Mail

To send an e-mail message:

1. Click the **Compose Message** button . The New Message window opens, which allows you to compose a new message.

   TROUBLE? If you receive an error message, check your mail server settings using the procedure you learned in the previous section. Record your settings and ask your instructor or technical support person for help.

2. Type **kherrera@course.com**, then press **Tab**.

3. Type your own e-mail address, then press **Tab** twice.

4. Type **Spring 2000 Mt. Rainier guided climb** in the Subject box, then press **Tab**. Make sure you type this subject exactly as shown.

5. Type the following message in the content area:

I am a summer intern at Carey Outerwear in Seattle and I am helping organize the Mt. Rainier guided climb for the Spring 2000 sales conference. John Kruse suggested I contact you for information on guide services. Thanks in advance.

[your name]

6. Click the **Send** button.

TROUBLE? If a message dialog box opens, indicating that Outlook Express was unable to connect to the server, you might need to check the configuration of your outgoing mail server. Use the procedure you learned in the previous section to do so, and ask your technical support person for help if necessary.

The time it takes to send an e-mail message depends on the size of the message, the speed of your Internet connection, and the quantity of Internet traffic at that time. When you send an e-mail, your local server examines the host name. Messages addressed to people at the same host site as the person sending the e-mail are processed and distributed without connecting to the Internet. Messages addressed to people at other host sites are sent out over the Internet. Because the Internet is so vast, your local mail server is not connected to every other host, so e-mail is rarely sent along a direct path to the recipient. Instead, the message is handed from one host to another until the e-mail reaches its destination. Figure 3-6 shows how the Internet routes an e-mail message from a student at the University of Alaska to a student at the University of the Virgin Islands.

Figure 3-6 ◀
Internet
e-mail routes

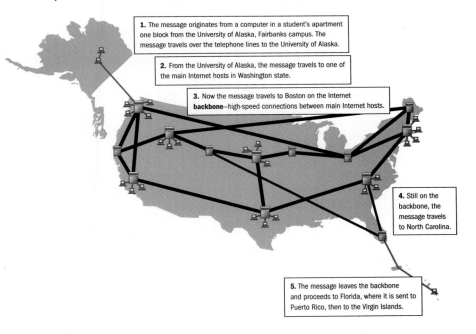

1. The message originates from a computer in a student's apartment one block from the University of Alaska, Fairbanks campus. The message travels over the telephone lines to the University of Alaska.

2. From the University of Alaska, the message travels to one of the main Internet hosts in Washington state.

3. Now the message travels to Boston on the Internet **backbone**—high-speed connections between main Internet hosts.

4. Still on the backbone, the message travels to North Carolina.

5. The message leaves the backbone and proceeds to Florida, where it is sent to Puerto Rico, then to the Virgin Islands.

The message you just sent to kherrera@course.com was actually sent to a server maintained by the publisher of this book. That server is set up to send an e-mail message back to you instantly. In real life, of course, you don't usually get replies to your messages that quickly.

Receiving E-mail

Recall that e-mail messages people send you are handled by an incoming mail server. That server is similar to a post office in that it collects all mail associated with a given region (host) and holds it for pickup and delivery by a mail carrier (e-mail program). Acting as your mail carrier, Outlook Express contacts the incoming mail server, requests any mail addressed to your user ID, and delivers it to your computer folder.

Rather than being limited to a fixed delivery schedule, you can check your e-mail at any time. When you ask Outlook Express to check for incoming mail, the incoming mail server returns only e-mail messages that have arrived since you last checked. Some people check for new e-mail messages sporadically during the day, while others check at regular intervals, such as every hour or every morning and evening. You can also have Outlook Express check for messages at a specified interval using the General tab of the Options dialog box, available on the Tools menu, but you won't do that now.

E-mail messages can be stored on the incoming mail server or in your own computer's memory. When e-mail is left on the server, you can access it from any computer with an e-mail program, whether at school, home, or work. Once you move the e-mail to a specific computer, however, you can access it only from that computer. Storing many e-mail messages on a computer can consume a lot of disk space. To conserve space, some network administrators don't allow people to store e-mail messages on the server after they have been read.

You decide to see whether or not Katie got your message and responded.

To check for incoming mail:

1. Click the **Send and Receive** button 🖼. If a dialog box opens requesting your password, enter your password and then click the **OK** button.

   TROUBLE? If you don't know your password, ask your instructor or technical support person for help.

2. Close the Outlook Express dialog box once it informs you that the requested tasks were completed successfully.

3. Click the **Inbox** button on the Folder List. The Inbox button indicates the number of new messages you've received, if any. See Figure 3-7. Your Inbox folder might contain additional e-mail messages from other people as well.

Figure 3-7 ◀
Receiving
messages

new messages are
stored in the
Inbox folder

you might receive a
different number
of messages

unread messages
appear in boldface;
you might have
additional messages

contents of
selected message

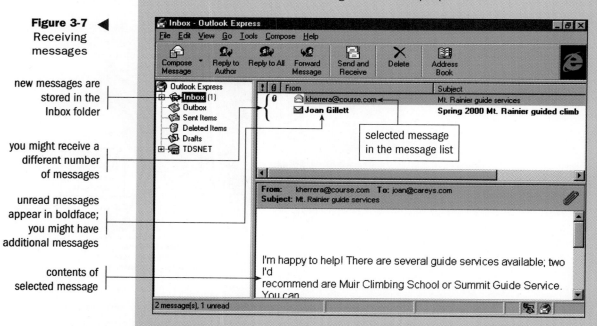

TROUBLE? If a message dialog box opens, indicating a problem with the incoming mail server, it's possible that your computer is set to remove messages from the server after they have been read. Click the OK button, then continue with the tutorial, but recognize that you might not be able to perform all the steps.

TROUBLE? If you have received no messages, it's possible that your mail server has not received or sent the messages yet. Occasionally, some mail servers cause mail to be delayed. Come back later to see if your mail has arrived, or consult your technical support person.

You should have received at least two new messages since you last checked your e-mail messages, including a copy of the message you sent to Katie (Sender should be yourself) and the reply from Katie (actually sent from the publisher of this book).

Viewing a Message

Incoming messages are automatically saved to the Inbox folder. The folder window is divided into two preview panes, or parts. The top pane, the message list, lists the messages in that folder, including the sender, the subject (truncated if it's too long), and the date received. Your window might list additional columns. You can change the width of the columns in the message list by dragging the vertical separation line between columns in the pane borders in the appropriate direction. Bolded messages have not yet been read. The message list displays a variety of icons that help you determine the status of the message: for example, ✉ tells you the message has been read; ✉ tells you the message has not been read; 📄 tells you the message is in progress in the Draft folder.

When you select an e-mail message from the message list, the contents of that message appear in the message content pane below it, and it no longer appears in boldface, indicating that you've displayed it. You can hide the lower pane if you want to view only the message list, or you can resize the two panes by dragging the pane border in the appropriate direction. For example, to enlarge the message pane so you can see more of a message at once, drag the top border of the pane toward the top of the window until the pane is the size you want.

You decide to start by reading the copy of the message you sent to Katie.

To read an e-mail message:

1. If necessary, click the message you sent yourself, which has the subject "Spring 2000 Mt. Rainier guided climb," in the message list. The contents of that message appear in the lower pane.

2. Now try adjusting the column widths. Point at the vertical line between one of the column borders, shown in Figure 3-8, until your pointer turns to ↔. Now drag the pointer slightly to the right to see more of the column, or to the left to see less.

   TROUBLE? If your window shows additional columns, don't worry. You can determine what information to display by clicking View, clicking Columns, then adding or removing between the Available columns list and the Displayed columns list.

Figure 3-8 ◀
Changing
column width

drag this border to the
right to enlarge From
column or to the left
to shrink it

message list

message contents

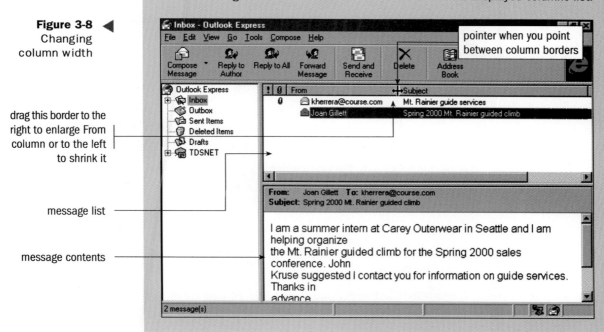

By successfully viewing the copy of the message you sent to yourself, you've verified that Outlook Express is configured properly on your computer.

Replying to a Message

Often, you'll want to respond to an e-mail message. Although you could create and send a new message, it's easier to use the Reply feature, which automatically inserts the e-mail address of the sender and the subject into the proper lines in the message window. The reply feature also "quotes" the sender's text to remind the sender of the message to which you are responding. When you reply to an e-mail message, you can respond to the original sender of the message, or to anyone else who received the message.

You're first going to view the message Katie sent you, this time in its own window, and then you're going to reply to it. To open a message in its own window, double-click the message in the message list. This allows you to display more of the message at once.

To open a message in its own window and then reply to it:

1. Double-click the message from Katie in the message list. The message opens in its own window. Maximize this window if necessary, then read the message. Scroll to read it all, if necessary. See Figure 3-9.

Figure 3-9 ◄
Viewing a
message in its
own window

click to reply to
Katie's message

Message window
displays subject and
sender information

contents of
Katie's reply

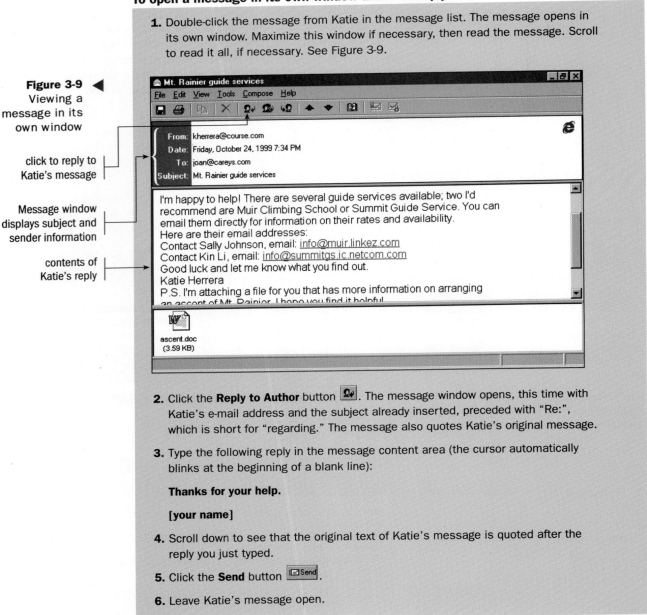

2. Click the **Reply to Author** button [Q]. The message window opens, this time with Katie's e-mail address and the subject already inserted, preceded with "Re:", which is short for "regarding." The message also quotes Katie's original message.

3. Type the following reply in the message content area (the cursor automatically blinks at the beginning of a blank line):

   Thanks for your help.

   [your name]

4. Scroll down to see that the original text of Katie's message is quoted after the reply you just typed.

5. Click the **Send** button [Send].

6. Leave Katie's message open.

Deciding whether or not to quote the sender's original message when you reply to a message depends on several factors. If the recipient might need to be reminded of the message content, it's appropriate to quote. However, long messages take longer to download, so whenever possible you should delete quoted material from your messages.

Printing a Message

You print an e-mail message using the File menu's Print command. You decide to print Katie's e-mail message.

To print Katie's e-mail message:

1. With Katie's message open, click **File**.

2. Click **Print**.

3. Check the print settings in the Print dialog box, then click the **OK** button.

When you retrieve your message from the printer, you might notice that some of the lines are uneven because the font your printer used caused the message word wrapping to change. If you need a high-quality printout of a message, you can save the message as a text file, open it in a word processor, and edit it there so that it looks professional.

Organizing Addresses in an Address Book

Every message sent across the Internet requires an e-mail address, but like the wrong zip code on a letter, any misspelled words or incorrect punctuation in an e-mail address will result in an undeliverable message. Because memorizing many e-mail addresses is a cumbersome task, prone to errors, Outlook Express provides the **Address Book** feature in which you can record both individual e-mail addresses and groups of e-mail addresses. For each address, Outlook Express stores personal, home, business, and other contact information. Including a nickname can be helpful because it substitutes for the e-mail address and is easier for you to type. Only the first name and e-mail address are actually required; all other information is optional.

Once you have Address Book contacts prepared, when you want to send an e-mail message to someone, you just type that person's nickname or click their name from the Address Book list, and Outlook Express will fill in the rest of the address information.

REFERENCE
window

ADDING AN ENTRY TO THE ADDRESS BOOK

- Click Tools, then click Address Book.
- Click the New Contact button.
- Enter a name and an e-mail address in the appropriate boxes, as well as any other information you want to include.
- Click the OK button.

Katie gave you e-mail addresses for two guide services in her message. You also want to add her address to the Address Book. The Reference Window describes how to add an entry from scratch, but if the address you want to add is in a message, there is a simpler way to add it to the Address Book.

To add an address to the Address Book:

1. Make sure Katie's message is open in its own maximized window. Right-click Katie's e-mail address, **kherrera@course.com**, in the From line of the message window, then point to **Add to Address Book**. See Figure 3-10.

Figure 3-10 ◀
Adding an
address to
Address Book

right-click
Katie's address

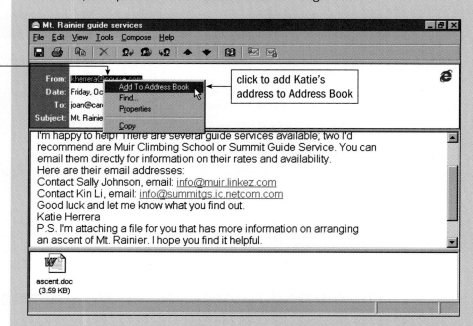

2. Type **Katie** in the First box, press **Tab** twice, then type **Herrera** in the Last Name box. See Figure 3-11.

Figure 3-11 ◀
Entering
Address Book
properties

Katie's e-mail address
automatically
appears

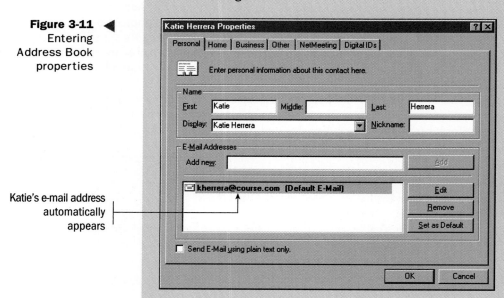

3. Type **katie** in the Nickname box so you can simply type "katie" next time you want to e-mail Katie.

4. Click the **OK** button.

5. Now view the Address Book list to see that Katie's address is included. Click **Tools**, then click **Address Book**. Katie's address appears, along with any other addresses already stored in the Address Book.

The next time you want to e-mail Katie, you can simply use her address from the Address Book, without having to retype it.

Grouping Address Book Entries

When you want to send an e-mail message to a group of people, you could manually select each name or type multiple nicknames every time, but this can be time-consuming and it's easy to miss someone. Instead, you can create a **group**, a specified list of Address Book entries, within the main Address Book. You can copy each entry in the main Address Book into as many groups as you need. When you want to e-mail everyone in the group, you enter the group name in the To box, and the message will be sent to every e-mail address in the group. When you change an individual address card, Outlook Express automatically updates the address in the group.

You decide to create a group called Guides that will contain the e-mail addresses of the two guide services Katie recommended. A group can be created only from addresses that already exist in the Address Book, so you'll first need to add the guide e-mail addresses to the Address Book.

To add names and then create a group:

1. Click the **New Contact** button ![New Contact].

2. Type **Sally** in the First Name box, press **Tab** twice, type **Johnson** in the Last Name box, press **Tab** twice, type **muir** in the Nickname box, and then press **Tab** to the Add new box in the E-Mail Addresses area.

3. Type **info@muir.linkez.com**, then click the **OK** button.

4. Click ![New Contact] again and enter the following information:
   First Name: **Kin**
   Last Name: **Li**
   Nickname: **summit**
   E-mail Address: **info@summitgs.ic.netcom.com**

5. Click the **OK** button. Now you're ready to create the group.

6. In the Address Book window, click the **New Group** button ![icon]. The Properties dialog box opens. Type **guides** in the Group Name box.

7. Click the **Select Members** button. The Select Group Members dialog box opens. Scroll through the entries until you locate Sally Johnson's entry. Click Sally Johnson's entry and click the **Select** button. Repeat for the Kin Li entry. See Figure 3-12.

Figure 3-12 ◀
Creating
a group

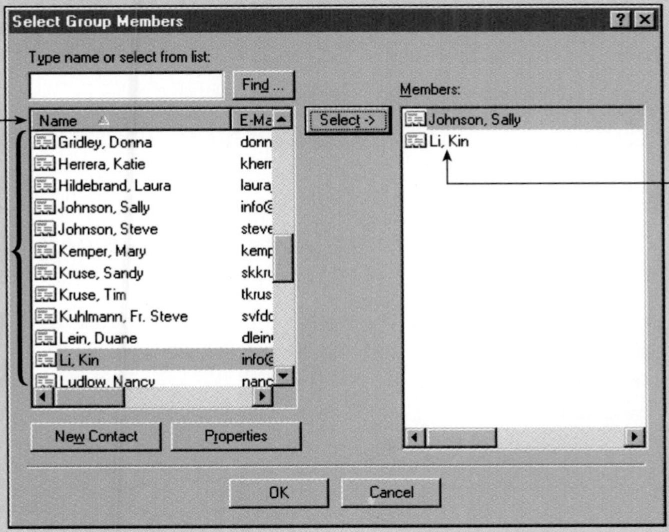

click to alphabetize

list of names in
your Address Book
will be different
and might be
alphabetized by first
name rather than
last name

group members

8. Click the **OK** button. The e-mail addresses are added to the group.

9. Click **OK** in the guides Properties dialog box.

10. Close the Address Book window.

Now that you've finished entering names in the Address Book, you are ready to e-mail the guide services to find out information about availability and rates.

Sending a Message to Multiple Recipients Using the Address Book

Using the Address Book is even easier than creating it. Whenever you want to send an e-mail message to a person or a group of people, you can select any combination or number of personal entries and/or list entries from the Address Book.

You want to send a message to the guides group, and you want to copy it to Katie.

To use the Address Book to address an e-mail message:

1. Close Katie's message.

2. Click the **Inbox** button on the taskbar, then click the **Compose Message** button ▣.

3. Click the address book card icon ▣ next to the To label. The Select Recipients dialog box opens.

4. Scroll to and then click **guides** in the list that appears. Click the **To:** button.

5. Click Katie's entry, then click the **Cc:** box. See Figure 3-13.

Figure 3-13 ◀
Selecting recipients from the Address Book

list of names in the Address Book; yours will be different

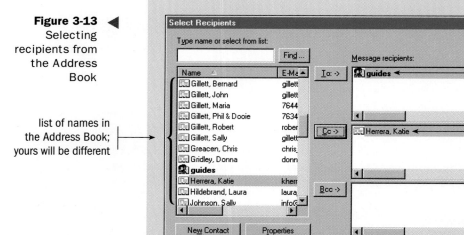

message will go to all members of guides group

Katie will receive a copy

6. Click the **OK** button.

7. Click the Subject box, then type **Information request for Mt. Rainier ascent** in the Subject box. Press **Tab**.

8. Type the following in the message content area: **Please e-mail me information about your guide rates and availability for the weekend of June 18, 2000. Thanks.**
   [your name]

9. Click the Send button ▣Send.

You've sent your request for information, and suddenly you remember that Katie had attached a file to her e-mail message. You decide to look at the file now.

Receiving and Saving Attached Files

When you receive an e-mail message with an attached file, a paper clip icon appears next to the message header in the message list. In the message window, an icon for the attached file appears, which you can click to view the name or names of the attached files.

> **REFERENCE window**
>
> ### VIEWING AN ATTACHED FILE
>
> - Right-click the icon for the file, located at the bottom of the message.
> - Click Open.

You decide to view Katie's attachment and then save it to your disk.

To view an attached file:

1. Open Katie's message in its own maximized window.

2. Right-click the attachment icon in Katie's message. The shortcut menu opens, giving you the opportunity to open, print, or save the attachment. See Figure 3-14.

   TROUBLE? If your ascent.doc icon looks different, you have a different word processor associated with doc files.

Figure 3-14 ◀
File attachment

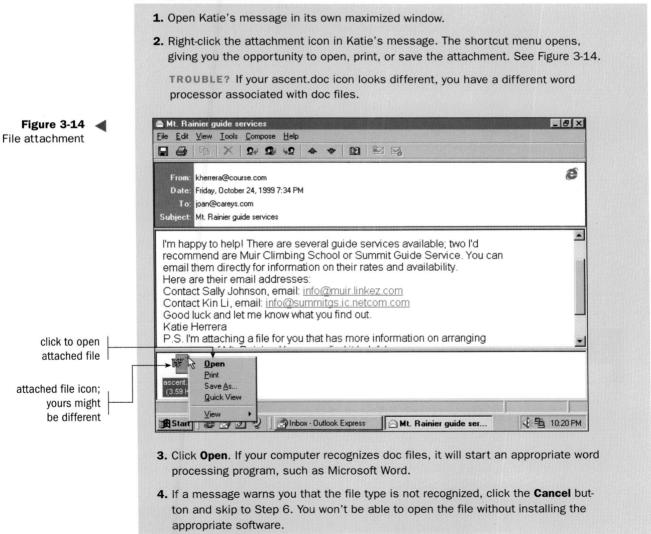

click to open attached file

attached file icon; yours might be different

3. Click **Open**. If your computer recognizes doc files, it will start an appropriate word processing program, such as Microsoft Word.

4. If a message warns you that the file type is not recognized, click the **Cancel** button and skip to Step 6. You won't be able to open the file without installing the appropriate software.

5. Read the document, then click the **Close** button ☒ to close the word processor that opened. Now save the document to your Student Disk. Place your Student Disk in the appropriate drive.

6. Right-click the **ascent.doc** link in Katie's message, then click **Save As**.

7. Type **a:\katie** in the File name box, then click the **Save** button. You can now open the file at any time from your Student Disk.

8. Close Katie's message, click **File**, and then click **Exit** to exit Outlook Express.

The ability to send and receive files with e-mail messages greatly simplifies the process of sharing information over the Internet.

Quick Check

1. Identify the user ID portion and the host name portion of the following e-mail address: pcsmith@icom.net.

2. How can you check the configuration of your e-mail address and name?

3. You just e-mailed a friend with some information but you want to check what you wrote because you're having second thoughts about what you said. Where can you find a copy of the message you sent?

4. Why shouldn't you type your messages in all uppercase letters?

5. A high-speed connection between main Internet hosts is called a _____.

6. Name two advantages the Reply feature has over the Compose Message feature when you are responding to an e-mail.

7. What's the quickest way to add the address of a person from whom you have received a message to your Address Book?

8. True or false: If you change someone's e-mail address in the Address Book, you must also update that address in any groups to which it belongs.

9. How do you know when you've received an e-mail message with an attached file?

SESSION 3.2

In this session you will learn how to organize your messages in folders, to attach a file to a message, to save a message to a file, to forward a message, and to delete unwanted e-mail and Address Book entries.

Managing Messages

You've already seen that Outlook Express uses folders to organize messages passing through your computer. You can further organize your mail by creating subfolders. For example, a student might create a subfolder to file all correspondence with her Latin professor, or an architect might create one folder for each project.

Creating a Folder

Outlook Express displays folders and subfolders in a hierarchy that you can view via the Folder List. When you create a new folder, you need to decide where it will be located in this hierarchy. The top level of the e-mail hierarchy is Outlook Express, and the default folders are on the next level of the hierarchy. Within the Inbox, recall, are two subfolders. You can also create subfolders of subfolders.

Figure 3-15 shows the folders a student has created within the Inbox folder: Homework and Student Government. Within the Homework folder are three subfolders: Calculus, History, and Physics. Within the Student Government folder are two subfolders: Budget and Homecoming.

Figure 3-15 ◀
Message
folder structure

folders student
created in
Inbox folder

subfolders

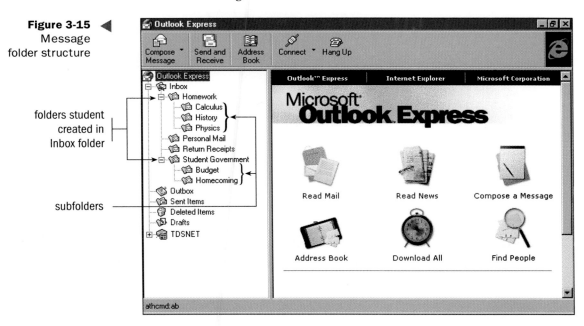

You can show all the folders in the hierarchy or only those at the levels you choose. The plus ⊞ and minus ⊟ boxes indicate whether the folders in that level are visible ⊟ or hidden ⊞.

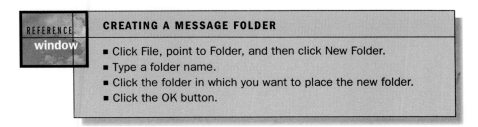

REFERENCE window

CREATING A MESSAGE FOLDER

- Click File, point to Folder, and then click New Folder.
- Type a folder name.
- Click the folder in which you want to place the new folder.
- Click the OK button.

You are going to create a folder called Rainier into which you will file the correspondence you have regarding the Spring 2000 ascent of Mt. Rainier. You'll create that folder within the Inbox folder.

To create a folder within the Inbox folder:

1. Launch Outlook Express, then click **Inbox** in the Folder List.

2. Click **File**, point to **Folder**, then click **New Folder**.

3. Type **Rainier** in the Folder name box.

4. Click **Inbox**. See Figure 3-16.

Figure 3-16 ◀
Creating
a new folder

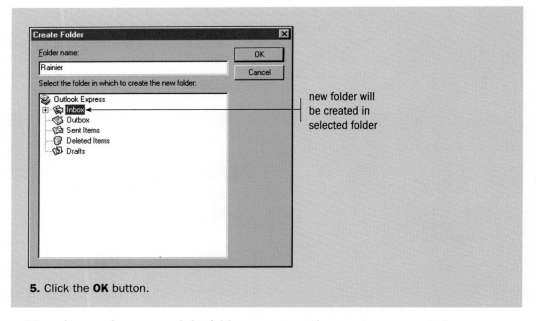

new folder will
be created in
selected folder

5. Click the **OK** button.

Now that you have created the folder, you are ready to save messages in it.

Filing Messages

When a message comes into the Inbox, you can file it immediately or file it later.

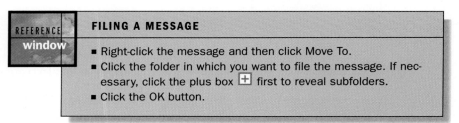

REFERENCE
window

FILING A MESSAGE

- Right-click the message and then click Move To.
- Click the folder in which you want to file the message. If necessary, click the plus box ⊞ first to reveal subfolders.
- Click the OK button.

Once you have created a system of folders, you can view the messages in a particular folder by selecting the folder from the Folder List. You decide to file the message Katie sent you into the Rainier folder. Then you'll examine the contents of the Rainier folder.

To file a message:

1. Right-click Katie's message in the Inbox (this message has the subject "Mt. Rainier guide services" and the sender is kherrera@course.com).

2. Click **Move To**.

3. Click the **plus box** ⊞ next to Inbox, then click **Rainier**. See Figure 3-17.

Figure 3-17 ◀
Filing
a message

make sure minus
box is visible
or Inbox subfolders
will be hidden

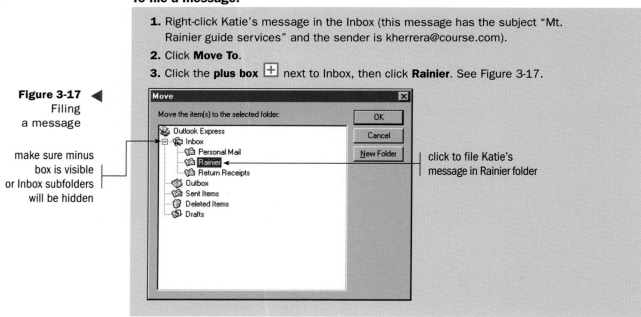

click to file Katie's
message in Rainier folder

4. Click the **OK** button.

5. Now open the Rainier folder to verify that it contains the message you just filed.

6. If necessary, click the **plus box** ⊞ next to Inbox in the Folder List.

7. Click **Rainier**. The message window changes to show the contents of the Rainier folder.

8. Open the Inbox again by clicking **Inbox** in the Folder List.

Some users also file relevant messages they've sent into the folders they've created. For example, you might open the Sent folder and file the message you wrote to the guide services in the Rainier folder.

Receiving Undelivered Messages

Sometimes you send an e-mail message to an Internet address that is no longer active, such as when a person changes his or her e-mail service to another server or switches to a different Internet Service Provider. When your outgoing mail server cannot locate an e-mail address that matches the recipient's address, you will receive an undeliverable mail message. This is similar to the postal service returning a letter because the street address is incorrect.

Because the guide service messages in this tutorial are actually fictional, you should receive one or more returned mail messages from the mail delivery subsystem of your outgoing mail server, telling you that the host was not found. Examine one of these messages now.

To read a returned mail notification:

1. If necessary, check for new e-mail.

2. Double-click a message with "Returned mail" or something similar in the Subject column.

3. Read the message. It should inform you that the e-mail addresses of the two guide services had unknown hosts.

4. Close the returned mail message to return to the Inbox.

If e-mail messages you send are returned undelivered, you should verify the e-mail addresses that you used. Make sure that everything is typed correctly and the person is still using that e-mail address.

Attaching a File to a Message

When two people work in the same office or use the same local area network (LAN), it is relatively easy to share files because they share a common server and can open each other's files. When people not sharing the same network work in different states or even different countries, however, they must use other means. Attaching a file to an e-mail message is an easy and effective way to send files, so long as both people use the same or compatible e-mail programs. The recipient receives the attached file just as quickly as any other electronic message.

REFERENCE
window

ATTACHING A FILE TO AN E-MAIL MESSAGE

- Click the Compose Message button and fill out the New Message window with the recipient and subject information and any message you want to include.
- Click the Insert File button.
- Locate and select the file, then click the Attach button.
- Click the Send button.

When you attach a file, an icon appears at the bottom of the message. As you've worked on the Mt. Rainier ascent, you managed to locate a graphic image file of a person climbing Mt. Rainier that could be used as an image in the Spring 2000 packet. John Kruse asks you to e-mail it to Connie Samini, the contact person for the promotional materials. Connie's e-mail address is samini@joncag.iip.com. The file, Rainier.bmp, is located on your Student Disk. You decide to mail it to yourself, too, so you can test how to retrieve it.

To attach a file to an e-mail message:

1. Click the **Compose Message** button 📝.

2. Type **samini@joncag.iip.com** in the To line and press **Tab**.

3. Enter your own e-mail address in the Cc line, then press **Tab** twice.

4. Type **Spring 2000 graphic file** in the Subject line, then press **Tab**.

5. Type **Here's a graphic file for the Spring 2000 promotions** in the message content area.

6. Click the **Insert File** button 📎. The Insert Attachment dialog box opens.

7. Type **a:\Tutorial.03\Rainier.bmp** in the File name box, then click the **Attach** button. An icon for that file appears at the bottom of the message. See Figure 3-18.

Figure 3-18 ◄
Attaching a file
to a message

click to attach
a file, Web page,
or address card

icon for attached file

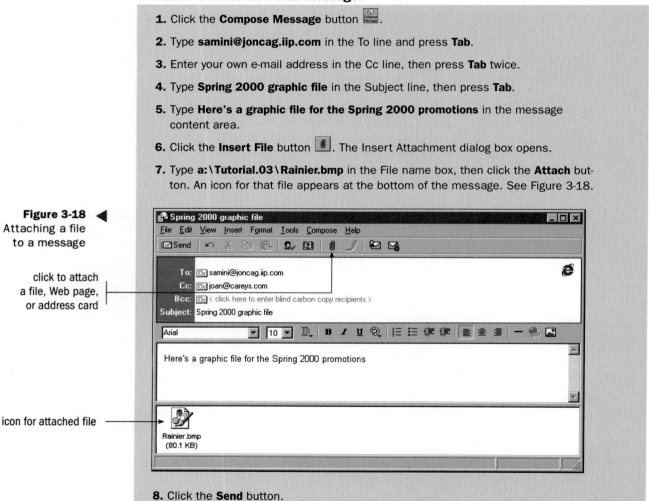

8. Click the **Send** button.

Because there is an attached file, the message is bigger than usual and takes a little longer to send. The message will arrive in Connie's incoming mail, as well as in yours. You decide to check your messages to verify that the file arrived.

To receive the graphics file you just sent:

1. Click the **Send and Receive** button 📧. Because the message you sent to yourself has an attached file, it will take a little longer than usual to get messages.

   TROUBLE? If there are no messages for you, wait a few minutes and then try again.

2. Double-click the **Spring 2000 graphic file** message you just sent to yourself (your name should appear in the From column), and then maximize the window. The picture attachment might appear in the message itself, as well as the icon at the bottom of the message.

3. Right-click the **Rainier.bmp** attachment icon, then click **Open**. If necessary, click the **Open it** option button, then click the **OK** button. If bmp files are associated with Paint, Paint opens to display the Rainier image. See Figure 3-19.

TROUBLE? If the graphic doesn't open in Paint or you receive a warning message that the file type is unknown, your computer might not associate bmp files with a program. Click the Cancel button and skip Step 4. If a different program starts, continue with Step 4.

Figure 3-19
Opening an
attached file
in Paint

attached picture
might appear
in e-mail message

attachment icon

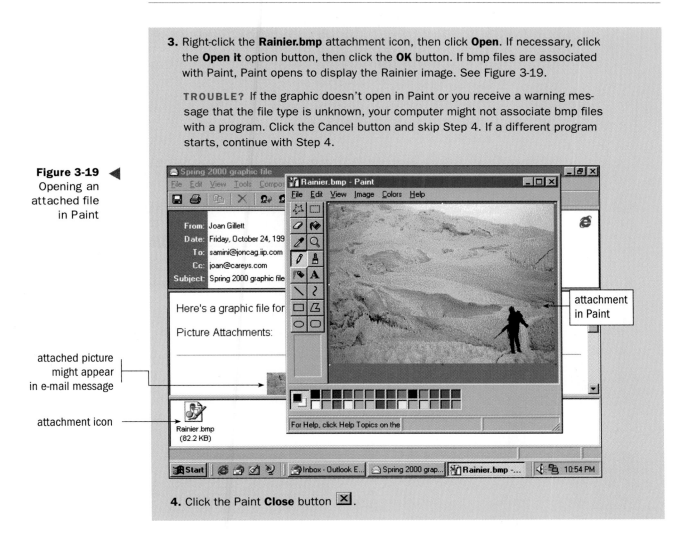

4. Click the Paint **Close** button.

Whether or not Connie can open the attached file will depend on the mail software and graphic software she has on her computer. E-mailing files works only when the mail software is compatible. You might want to check with the recipient before mailing a file to make sure the mail software can handle the message. You can also encode the message in a different format using the Send tab in the Options dialog box (available on the Tools menu). **Encoding** saves the file attachment using coded characters that make it possible for the recipient's mail software to accept the message. The recipient can then use decoding software to interpret the message and restore the file to its original state. Ask your instructor for more information.

Saving a Message to a File

Messages exist in the Outlook Express folders in a format that makes them inaccessible to word processing and other software. You can, however, save a message as a file so that you can store it on a disk or open it in a different program. You can also use the Copy command to copy selected parts of the message, and you can then paste the message text into a different program.

You decide to save the message Katie sent you as a text file.

To save an e-mail message to a disk:

1. Open the Rainier folder, then click Katie's message.

2. Click **File**, then click **Save As**.

3. Type **a:\katie's message** in the File name box.

4. Click the **Save as type** list arrow, then click **Text Files (*.txt)**.

5. Click the **Save** button.

6. Now start a text editor to open the file and view it. Click the **Start** button on the Windows taskbar, point to **Programs**, point to **Accessories**, and then click **WordPad**.

7. Click the **Open** button, type **a:\katie's message.txt**, and then click the **Open** button. The message appears as a text file. See Figure 3-20.

Figure 3-20 ◀
Viewing a saved message in WordPad

Katie's message ────────▶

attached file is mentioned but not included in text file ────────

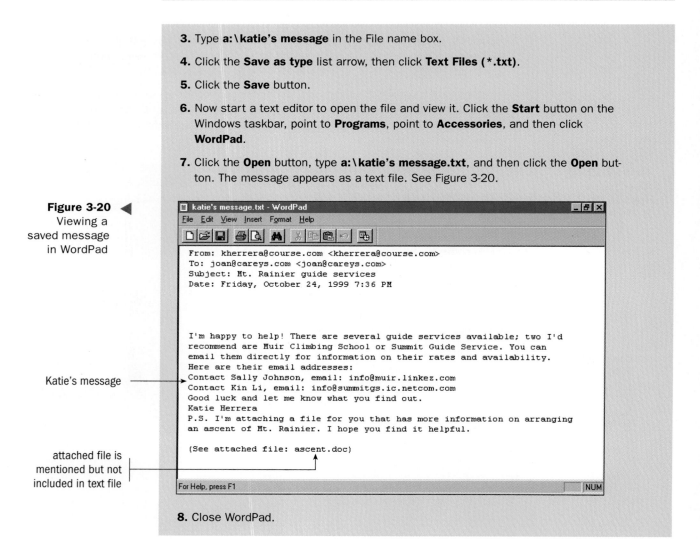

```
katie's message.txt - WordPad
File  Edit  View  Insert  Format  Help

From: kherrera@course.com <kherrera@course.com>
To: joan@careys.com <joan@careys.com>
Subject: Mt. Rainier guide services
Date: Friday, October 24, 1999 7:36 PM



I'm happy to help! There are several guide services available; two I'd
recommend are Muir Climbing School or Summit Guide Service. You can
email them directly for information on their rates and availability.
Here are their email addresses:
Contact Sally Johnson, email: info@muir.linkez.com
Contact Kin Li, email: info@summitgs.ic.netcom.com
Good luck and let me know what you find out.
Katie Herrera
P.S. I'm attaching a file for you that has more information on arranging
an ascent of Mt. Rainier. I hope you find it helpful.

(See attached file: ascent.doc)

For Help, press F1                                                    NUM
```

8. Close WordPad.

Katie's message is now stored as a text file on your Student Disk.

Forwarding a Message

John Kruse has decided to transfer you to a different department. Another intern, Chris Lopez, will take over the Rainier project. You realize that Chris could profit from the information you've gathered from Katie, so you decide to forward Katie's message to Chris.

Forwarding is similar to replying to an e-mail message, except that when you forward an e-mail message, you send a copy of the entire message to another person. When you click the Forward Message button, Outlook Express fills in the Subject box with Fw: [subject] and, if applicable, includes any attached files. When forwarding a message, you can add new comments to the original text of the message in the outgoing message content area.

John tells you that Chris's e-mail address is clopez@careys.com.

To forward mail:

1. If necessary, open the Rainier folder.

2. Click the message from Katie.

3. Click the **Forward Message** button .

4. Type **clopez@careys.com** in the To box.

5. Leave the subject as it appears (Fw: means the message is a forwarded message).

6. Click the message content area, then type: **Here's the information you need for the Rainier project. Good luck.**

7. Click the **Send** button Send .

Chris now has the necessary information to handle the Rainier project, and you are almost ready to move to the new department.

Deleting Outlook Express Information

It's easy for your folders and Address Book to get cluttered with information you no longer need. You should periodically clear out unwanted messages and remove obsolete entries from your Address Book. Because you're moving to a new department, you no longer need any of the Rainier messages or address information.

Deleting a Message

After you have read a message and replied to or forwarded it as necessary, you can delete it. Any message you delete from the Inbox is transferred automatically to the Deleted Items folder. You can recover it from there if you need to, but once you delete the messages in the Deleted Items folder you cannot recover them (unless, however, you are using an IMAP server, in which case you can use the View menu to view deleted messages and you can undelete messages from there).

To delete unwanted e-mail:

1. Open the Inbox.

2. Right-click the returned mail message, then click **Delete**. Repeat this step for any other e-mail in the Inbox that was generated during this tutorial. If you want to delete several messages, press and hold down the **Ctrl** key while you click multiple messages. Then right-click the selection and click **Delete**.

3. Click Sent Items in the Folder List to open the Sent Items folder.

4. Delete any messages in the Sent Items folder that you generated during this tutorial.

You also want to delete the entire Rainier folder and all its contents. You can delete folders from the Folder List.

To delete a folder and its contents:

1. In the Folder List, make sure you can view the Inbox subfolders.

2. Right-click the **Rainier** folder.

3. Click **Delete**.

4. Click the **Yes** button if you are asked to confirm that you want to delete all the messages in the folder.

Deleted messages remain in the Deleted Items folder, providing an opportunity to retrieve them, until you empty the Deleted Items folder. To completely remove e-mail messages and free up storage space available in your computer's memory, you must empty the Deleted Items folder.

To empty the Deleted Items folder:

1. In the Folder List, right-click the **Deleted Items** folder.

2. Click **Empty Folder**. Click the **Yes** button to confirm.

By deleting unwanted messages regularly you save space on your hard drive.

Deleting Address Book Entries

Just as you want to keep your folders clean and up-to-date, you'll want to make sure that the Address Book contains only relevant entries. Periodically, you should remove outdated or no-longer-needed entries from your Address Book. You no longer need addresses you entered in this tutorial, so delete them all from the Address Book.

To delete entries from the Address Book:

1. Click **Tools**, then click **Address Book** to open the Address Book window.

2. Right-click **Guides**, then click **Delete**.

3. Press and hold down the **Ctrl** key, then click **Katie Herrera**, **Sally Johnson**, and **Kin Li**.

4. Press the **Delete** key, then click the **Yes** button to confirm.

5. Click the **Close** button ⊠ to close the Address Book window, then exit Outlook Express.

You've cleaned out all unwanted information from Outlook Express, and you're ready to move to the new department.

Quick Check

1 How can you view the subfolders of a folder in the Folder List?

2 What happens to e-mail messages that have incorrect or obsolete e-mail addresses?

3 If you want to open an e-mail message in your word processor, what should you do first?

4 True or False: Deleting an Inbox message permanently removes the e-mail message from your hard disk.

5 What key should you press to select more than one message?

SESSION

3.3

In this session you will subscribe to a newsgroup, follow the threads in a newsgroup, sort and search newsgroup posts, and unsubscribe from a newsgroup.

Newsgroups

So far in this tutorial you've seen how you can use e-mail to communicate with others and gather information on a topic. Now you'll look at a means of bringing people with a common interest together—**discussion groups**, most commonly called **newsgroups**. There are thousands of newsgroups on the Internet. Interested users subscribe to a newsgroup and then exchange messages with other subscribers on that topic using regular e-mail. The act of sending an e-mail message to a newsgroup is called **posting**; a message sent to a newsgroup is often called a **post**. Newsgroups can be open to everyone or to a private group. A private newsgroup might be created, for example, for scholars who want to limit membership to their peers.

When a newsgroup member posts a message to a newsgroup, the message is sent to a special server called a **news server**, which stores and manages the messages that are posted to various newsgroups. In order to retrieve messages posted to a newsgroup, you need special software called a **newsreader**. Outlook Express can function as a newsreader. When you subscribe to and then open a newsgroup, Outlook Express retrieves the most recent message headers (the text in the Subject line) from the news server. When you see a message you want to read, Outlook Express can download it for you. Figure 3-21 illustrates how messages posted to a newsgroup are disseminated.

Figure 3-21 ◀
Posting to a
newsgroup

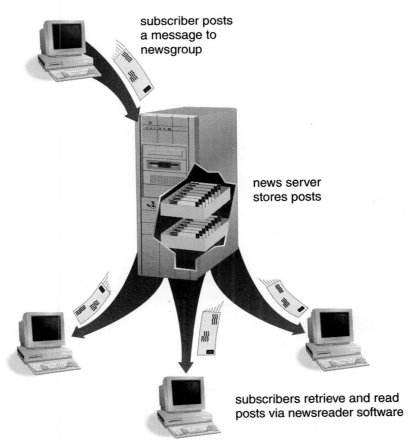

subscriber posts
a message to
newsgroup

news server
stores posts

subscribers retrieve and read
posts via newsreader software

Newsgroup Names

Newsgroup names are defined based on a hierarchy of categories. Figure 3-22 shows a small part of this hierarchy.

Figure 3-22 ◀
Examples of
newsgroup
categories in
the newsgroup
hierarchy

highest level in
newsgroup hierarchy

subcategories of
rec newsgroup

subcategories of
rec.sport newsgroup

subcategories of
rec.sport.football
newsgroup

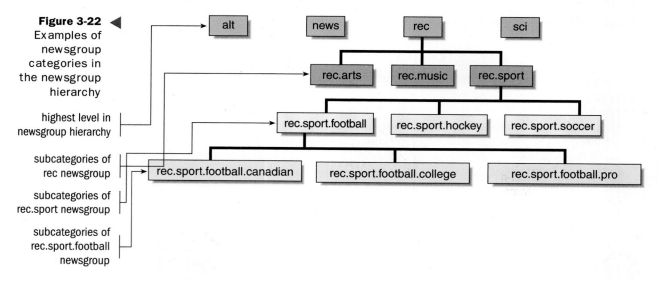

The highest level is the general category to which a topic belongs. Each category has a name (usually an abbreviation). For example, all recreational activities begin with the name "rec." Within the recreational topic category are newsgroups that deal with arts, music, sports, and so on. With the sport category you might find categories such as football, hockey, soccer, and so on. Within the football category you might find categories such as Canadian football, college football, and professional football. The newsgroup for college football has a name consisting of all the codes of the hierarchy, separated by periods: "rec.sport.football.college."

Outlook Express identifies newsgroups by these somewhat cryptic names. Study Figure 3-23 to become familiar with newsgroup names.

Figure 3-23 ◀
Examples of
newsgroup
names

Category	Description	Example
alt	Alternative newsgroups of many different types	**alt.guitar.bass** for discussions about bass guitars
harvard	Newsgroups about Harvard University	**harvard.course.math121** for discussions about the Math 121 course at Harvard
humanities	Newsgroups about topics in the humanities department, such as art and literature	**humanities.lit.authors.shakespeare** for discussions about the works of William Shakespeare
k12	Newsgroups about education K–12	**k12.lang.japanese** for discussions about Japanese language programs in K–12 schools
rec	Newsgroups about recreational activities	**rec.autos.sport.indy** for discussions about car racing at the Indy 500
uk	Newsgroups about the United Kingdom	**uk.politics.electoral** for discussions about electoral politics in the United Kingdom

Threads

When you subscribe to a newsgroup, you have access to all the messages posted by all the subscribers within a time frame established by the news server. Keeping your e-mail organized might seem an easy task when compared to organizing newsgroup messages, given that there can be thousands of people posting on thousands of conversations in a given newsgroup. Newsreader software such as Outlook Express allows you to organize the list of message headers so that subscribers can follow the many conversations without losing the flow.

Outlook Express by default sorts message headers into threads. A **thread** is a batch of messages that follow a single "line of conversation": One person posts a message, several people reply to it, more reply to the replies, and so on until the topic is dropped. Multiple threads can develop simultaneously, just as in a busy room there can be many conversations. Figure 3-24 illustrates how threads are developed in a newsgroup.

Figure 3-24 ◀
Threads you might find in rec.arts. calligraphy

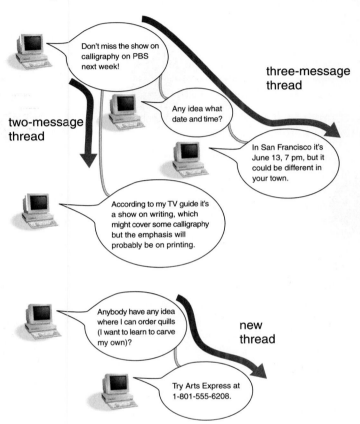

Most threads generate just a few posts, but some (especially controversial topics) can go on for days.

Setting Up a Newsgroup Account

To subscribe to a newsgroup you must first set up a newsgroup account with a news server. Outlook Express must download a copy of the list of all newsgroups supported by your news server to your computer, which could be time-consuming. Once the initial list is downloaded, however, Outlook Express will simply load the list stored on your computer whenever you attempt to subscribe to a newsgroup. If any new newsgroups are created after the initial download, you can view them with the Reset List feature. You won't do that in this tutorial, though, because the list of newsgroups on your news server is unlikely to change over the course of this tutorial.

A few days have passed since you joined the new department at Carey Outerwear, and you decide to spend your lunch hour exploring newsgroups. You don't have any particular goal in mind; you just want to get a feel for what's out there.

It's possible that someone has already set up a newsgroup account on your computer, in which case you don't need to perform this next set of steps unless you want to set up an account for an additional news server. Because different news servers maintain different lists of newsgroups, some people have several news server accounts.

To set up a newsgroup account:

1. Launch Outlook Express.

2. First, check if any newsgroup accounts are currently set up on your computer. Open the Folder List and look at the bottom of the list. If there are any newsgroup icons 📰, then a newsgroup account is already set up on your computer and you can skip Steps 3–6. If there are no newsgroup icons or you want to set up an account with an additional news server, continue with Steps 3–6.

3. Click **Tools**, then click **Accounts**.

4. Click the **News** tab.

5. Click the **Add** button, then click **News**. The Internet Connection Wizard starts. Follow the steps, supplying information where necessary. When you have finished, click the **Finish** button.

   TROUBLE? If you aren't sure of your news server domain name, check with your technical support person or contact your Internet Service Provider.

6. Click the **Close** button. You are prompted to download the list of newsgroups on the server. Click the **Yes** button. You must wait for the newsreader to download the names of all existing newsgroups on your news server; a message box informs you how many have been downloaded. This could take a considerable amount of time, depending on the speed of your Internet connection and the number of newsgroups your news server supports. Be prepared to wait 10 minutes or more. When all newsgroups have been downloaded, the Newsgroups window opens, displaying your news server's list of newsgroups.

   TROUBLE? If 15 minutes have elapsed, your Internet connection might be slow. Ask your technical support person whether you should continue to wait or whether there might be a problem with the connection. If you can determine that you are still receiving data (perhaps your computer indicates data transfer with a blinking icon in the Windows taskbar), continue to wait.

Once you have set up an account with a news server, you are ready to subscribe to any of the newsgroups supported by that server. You decide to view the list of available newsgroups supported by your news server. The list you see depends on what newsgroups your server supports. If you just added a news server account in the previous set of steps, that server's newsgroup list should already be displayed, and you can skip the next set of steps.

To view the list of newsgroups your server supports:

1. In the Folder List, click the news server whose newsgroup list you want to view. News servers are listed at the bottom of the Folder List.

2. If you are not currently subscribed to any newsgroups, a message box asks if you would like to view a list of newsgroups now. Click the **Yes** button. If this message box doesn't appear, click the **News groups** button. The Newsgroups window opens. See Figure 3-25.

Figure 3-25 ◄
List of
discussion
groups

list of newsgroups;
yours will be different,
depending on the
newsgroups
supported by your
news server

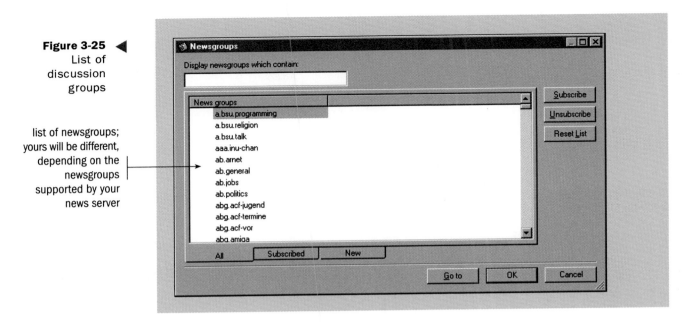

The list of newsgroups appears in alphabetical order. If new newsgroups have been added since the last time you downloaded the list of newsgroups on the server, the ❋ icon precedes that newsgroup name.

Subscribing to a Newsgroup

To subscribe to a newsgroup you can either search for a particular one, as you'll see later, or you can navigate the list of newsgroups until you find the one you want. You decide to look at the newsgroups contained in the alt category, and when you find one that's interesting, you'll subscribe to it.

To subscribe to a newsgroup:

1. Scroll down to the newsgroups that begin with **alt**.

2. Scroll down the list of newsgroups in the alt category. The alt category contains many subcategories, such as alt.animals, alt.autos, and alt.books.

3. Scroll through the alt categories and click a newsgroup that interests you.

   TROUBLE? If you can't find one that interests you, click one whose name is recognizable. This tutorial doesn't recommend a specific newsgroup in order to avoid overloading any one newsgroup with a large batch of new members posting to it.

4. Click the **Subscribe** button. A newspaper icon appears next to the newsgroup. You can subscribe to another newsgroup by clicking the newsgroup and again clicking the Subscribe button, but you won't do that now.

5. Click the **OK** button. The alt group you chose now appears in the message window. See Figure 3-26. Your group should be different.

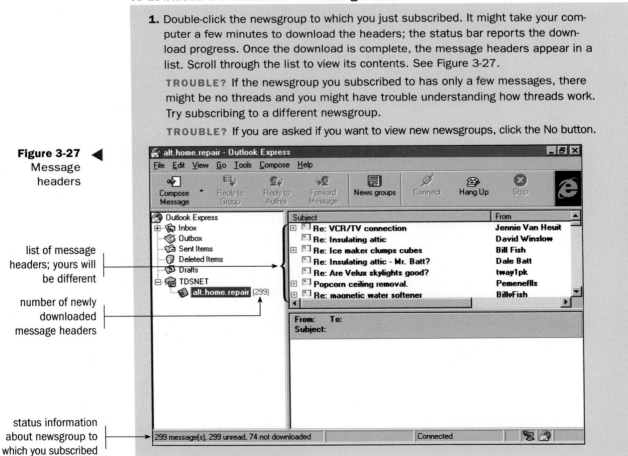

Figure 3-26 ◀
Subscribing to
a newsgroup

newsgroup you
choose will be
different

news server; yours will
probably be different

number of total and
unread messages;
might appear as 0
until you open
newsgroup

Now you are ready to open the newsgroup to which you just subscribed. Outlook Express downloads message headers (not the messages themselves, to save space) 300 at a time, although you can use the menu commands to download just new message headers, new messages, or all messages.

To download the first batch of message headers:

1. Double-click the newsgroup to which you just subscribed. It might take your computer a few minutes to download the headers; the status bar reports the download progress. Once the download is complete, the message headers appear in a list. Scroll through the list to view its contents. See Figure 3-27.

TROUBLE? If the newsgroup you subscribed to has only a few messages, there might be no threads and you might have trouble understanding how threads work. Try subscribing to a different newsgroup.

TROUBLE? If you are asked if you want to view new newsgroups, click the No button.

Figure 3-27 ◀
Message
headers

list of message
headers; yours will
be different

number of newly
downloaded
message headers

status information
about newsgroup to
which you subscribed

Now that you have subscribed, you can view the message headers you have retrieved and select the messages you want to read.

Reading Newsgroup Messages

You read a newsgroup message the same way you read an ordinary e-mail message: You either click it, and the text appears in the lower pane, or you double-click it and the message opens in its own window. Once the first message is open, you proceed through the list of messages using the Next button.

Sorting Newsgroup Posts

The order in which the message headers appear when you click Next depends on how they are sorted in the newsgroup list. By default, Outlook Express sorts message headers by the date sent and groups them by thread, but it can be helpful to sort in a different order. For example, a newsgroup on a popular TV series might have regular posts from the series producer. If you want to read only the posts by the producer, you could sort by sender to locate all posts from that sender.

For now, you should make sure the sort order is by date sent, and that the messages are grouped by thread, so when you read your messages you are able to follow a thread of conversation. You can use the View menu to sort, or you can click the column heading buttons to sort by those columns.

To check the sort order:

1. Click **View**, then point to **Sort By**.

2. Click **Sent** to ensure the messages are sorted by date.

3. Make sure the **Group Messages by Thread** option is preceded by a checkmark. See Figure 3-28.

Figure 3-28 ◄
Sorting messages by date sent, grouped by thread

make sure messages are sorted by date sent

make sure messages are grouped by thread

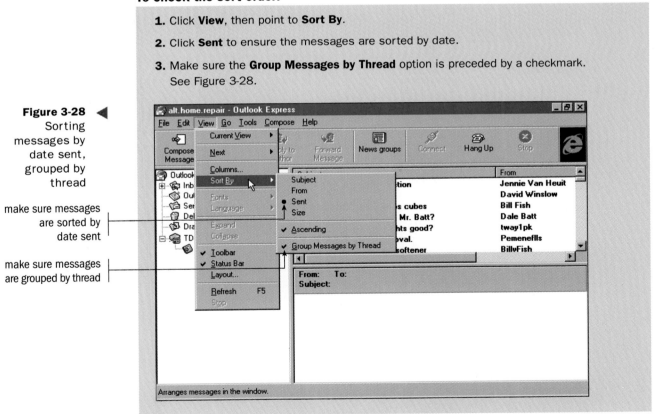

Note that you can also sort your regular e-mail (not just your newsgroup messages) by thread. When you replied to an e-mail earlier in this tutorial, you were actually taking part in a conversation—and Outlook Express tracks replies on a given subject just as it tracks newsgroup threads.

Following a Thread

Outlook Express provides several visual clues to help you keep track of threads of a newsgroup's conversation. For example:

- Any message preceded by a plus box ⊞ or minus box ⊟ indicates the presence of a thread. ⊞ indicates the responses to the initial message are hidden, and ⊟ indicates that they are visible.

- Messages without ⊞ or ⊟ aren't part of a thread in the headers you have downloaded.

- Boldfaced messages have not yet been read; messages without boldface have.

Outlook Express also uses a set of icons that help you track messages. Figure 3-29 introduces some of the icons you'll see when you examine your newsgroup list; study them so you know how to interpret them.

Figure 3-29 ◄
Message icons

Icon	Description
	Message has not been opened.
	Message has been marked read.
	Message has been marked read and is stored in a message file on your computer.
	Message has not been marked read, and header and body are stored in a message file on your computer.
	Message is no longer available on the news server.

Now you're ready to read your newsgroup's messages. Because your list of messages will be different from the list shown in the figures, you'll have to adapt the steps to the newsgroup you selected.

To read the messages in a thread:

1. Scroll to locate a thread, preceded by ⊞.

2. Click ⊞ next to the first message in a thread to view the thread. Click any other ⊞ to view all messages in that thread. See Figure 3-30, which shows a thread beginning with a message that asks about the benefits of finishing basements to make living space. Messages indented one level are replies to the first message in the thread. Messages indented two levels are replies to the message in the message indented one level, and so on.

Figure 3-30 ◀
Viewing a
thread

first message in
thread; because it is
preceded with "Re"
you know it is not the
original message; it
is just the first in the
group of headers you
downloaded

these messages,
replies to the first
message, generated
additional replies

five replies to
first message

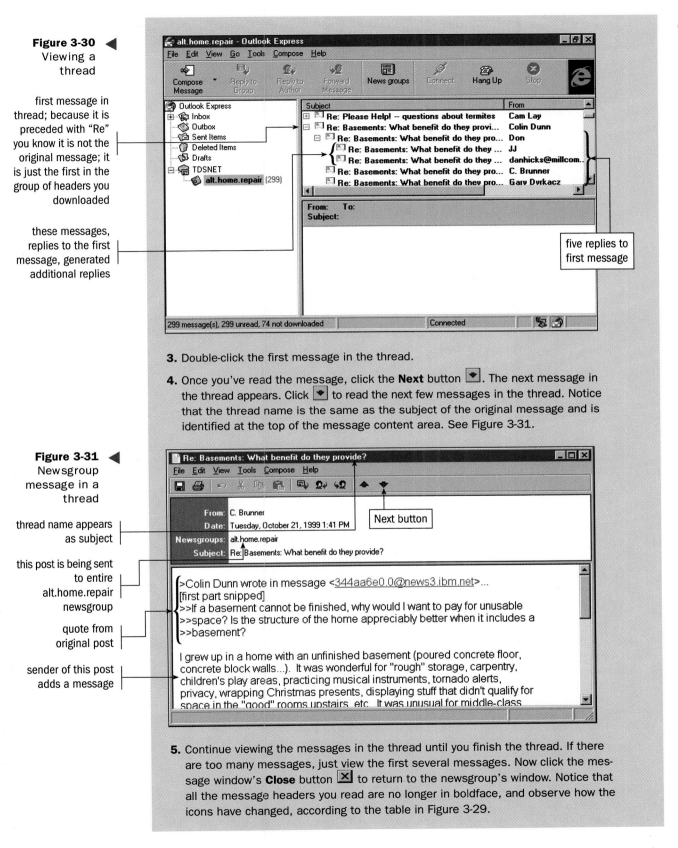

3. Double-click the first message in the thread.

4. Once you've read the message, click the **Next** button [▼]. The next message in
   the thread appears. Click [▼] to read the next few messages in the thread. Notice
   that the thread name is the same as the subject of the original message and is
   identified at the top of the message content area. See Figure 3-31.

Figure 3-31 ◀
Newsgroup
message in a
thread

thread name appears
as subject

this post is being sent
to entire
alt.home.repair
newsgroup

quote from
original post

sender of this post
adds a message

Next button

5. Continue viewing the messages in the thread until you finish the thread. If there
   are too many messages, just view the first several messages. Now click the message window's **Close** button [X] to return to the newsgroup's window. Notice that
   all the message headers you read are no longer in boldface, and observe how the
   icons have changed, according to the table in Figure 3-29.

As you read through the thread, you probably noticed that new posts often quote the
previous posts to which they are replying. When you respond to a post, quote as sparingly
as possible to keep your message short. Some newsreaders do not let you post a message
unless there is more new material than quotes.

Downloading Additional Messages

If you like what you see in a newsgroup, you will probably want to download additional messages. Or you might read messages from a thread but you don't have the first message that initiated the conversation. Try downloading more of the messages in your newsgroup.

To download additional messages:

1. Make sure the newsgroup is open.

2. Click **Tools**, then click **Get Next 300 Headers**.

Outlook Express places the message headers into the list according to the current sort order. Thus, if you added headers belonging to a thread, those headers would be placed in the correct position in the thread.

Posting a Message

Once you have read through some of the posts in a newsgroup, you might be ready to post a message of your own. You can post a follow-up message to a post you are currently reading, or you can post a message on a completely new topic. When you post a response, you can choose to:

- Send a private e-mail message to the sender.
- Post a response to the entire newsgroup.

In a newsgroup, you should usually reply to the group and not the sender, unless there's a good reason for wanting the reply to be private. The idea of a newsgroup is that it is an open forum. Moreover, people don't want their personal e-mail account cluttered up with e-mail from the newsgroup.

You should perform these next steps only if you have a valuable post to send to the newsgroup you chose. If you don't have anything valuable to say, then read through these steps without performing them.

To post a reply to an existing message:

1. Open the message.

2. Click the **Reply to Group** button 🔲. The message window opens with the group's address automatically inserted. See Figure 3-32.

Figure 3-32 ◀
Replying to a newsgroup message

newsgroup address appears as recipient

enter message contents here

original message is quoted; delete as much as you can to keep message short

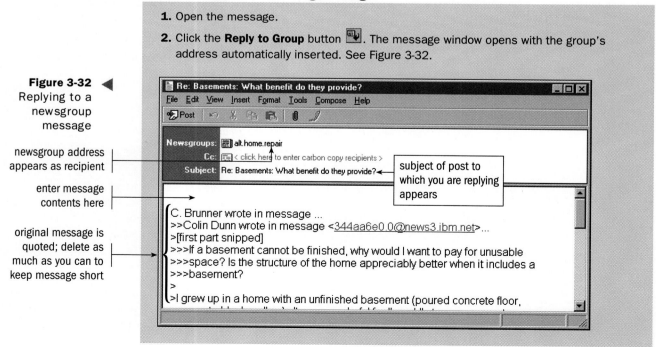

3. Leave the Subject box as is to indicate that your post is a reply and is therefore part of a thread.

4. Enter the message contents as you would with regular e-mail.

5. Click the **Post** button [Post] when you are finished.

   TROUBLE? If you don't think you have a valuable contribution to add to this newsgroup, click the message window Close button [X], then click No to discard changes.

6. Click the **OK** button when warned that it might take a while to post your message.

Your message is added to the list of newsgroup messages as a reply within a thread.

You can also raise a new issue in a newsgroup that might start a new thread, depending on whether other newsgroup members reply. Again, make sure you post a new message only if you have something to say.

To post a new message:

1. Open the newsgroup, then click the **Compose Message** button [Compose Message]. The newsgroup address is again filled in for you.

2. Enter a subject and the message contents.

3. Click the **Post** button [Post].

   TROUBLE? If you have nothing important to post, cancel this message.

4. Click the **OK** button when warned that it might take a while to post your message.

5. Close all open messages.

If you have asked a question or if your message is provocative enough to generate discussion, when you next download messages you might find responses to your message. Depending on how active the newsgroup is, you might need to wait a few days to get an answer, or an answer might appear within the hour.

Searching a Newsgroup

Outlook Express offers search features that make it easy for you to find the newsgroup you want and the information you want. For example, within the Newsgroups window you can search your news server's list of newsgroups for a particular newsgroup. You hope to drive down to California after your internship is over so you decide to look for newsgroups on surfing.

To search for a newsgroup on surfing:

1. Click the **News groups** button [88].

2. Type **surfing** in the Display newsgroups which contain box. After a moment a list of all newsgroups with "surfing" in their names appears. See Figure 3-33. You could click one of these newsgroups and then click the Subscribe button to subscribe to that group, but you won't do that now.

Figure 3-33 ◄
Searching for a
newsgroup

surfing newsgroups;
your list might
be different

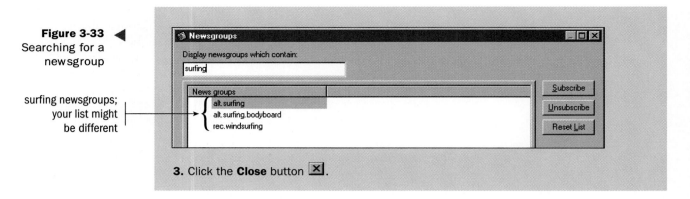

3. Click the **Close** button ⊠.

Within a newsgroup, you can search for posts on particular topics. For example, perhaps you subscribed to a newsgroup of people who like backcountry camping. You are planning a trip to Rocky Mountain National Park and wonder whether there's been any discussion lately about that topic.

To search a newsgroup for messages on a topic:

1. If necessary, open the newsgroup.

2. Click **Edit**, then click **Find Message**.

3. Click the Subject box and type **Rocky Mountain**. (Substitute your own search words for the newsgroup you have open.) See Figure 3-34.

Figure 3-34 ◄
Searching a
newsgroup for
a post on a
topic

choose either sender
or subject

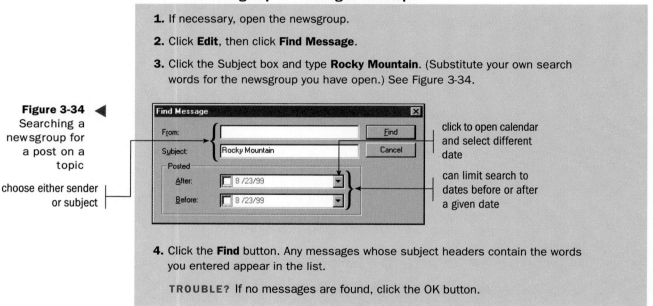

4. Click the **Find** button. Any messages whose subject headers contain the words you entered appear in the list.

TROUBLE? If no messages are found, click the OK button.

The ability to search a newsgroup makes it easier to find information, but you should be aware that because newsgroup contents change so quickly, an unsuccessful search you perform one day might be successful the next.

Unsubscribing

When you have lost interest in a newsgroup, you will probably want to unsubscribe from it so it doesn't clutter up your newsgroup list.

To unsubscribe to a newsgroup:

1. Right-click the newsgroup you joined in this tutorial.

2. Click **Unsubscribe from this newsgroup**.

3. Click the **Yes** button when asked if you are sure you want to unsubscribe from the newsgroup. Click **No** if asked if you want to view additional newsgroups.

4. Click **File**, then click **Exit** to exit Outlook Express.

Newsgroups can be an excellent source of information. Some newsgroups exist just to support people going through hard times, such as coping with a serious illness. Others exist to exchange information and advice on challenges such as home repair. Still others provide an open forum to discuss a hot topic, such as current election issues. The "conversation" in some newsgroups can get rather intense, because people are less inhibited in an anonymous e-mail message than they tend to be face-to-face. Insulting e-mail in newsgroups is so common that it even has a name: **flaming**. If you avoid taking and giving offense, however, your newsgroup experience will probably be positive.

Quick Check

1 True or false: Messages posted to a newsgroup are automatically forwarded to all subscribers.

2 A server that stores the messages posted to a newsgroup is called a _____.

3 When you subscribe to and open a newsgroup, does your newsreader download the text of the messages? Explain your answer.

4 A friend who knows nothing about newsgroups sees rec.arts.painting.oil on your computer screen and asks you to explain what it means. Draw a diagram to accompany your explanation.

5 What is a thread?

6 What might you do to read only the posts by a certain sender?

7 If a message header has no plus box ⊞ or minus box ⊟ next to it in the list of posts, what does that tell you?

8 What is flaming, and why is it more prevalent in newsgroups than in public?

Tutorial Assignments

Your internship is over at Carey Outerwear and you're back at school, after an exciting weekend trip where you actually climbed Mt. Rainier. You want to implement some of the things you learned while in Seattle, especially about e-mail and newsgroups. You plan to e-mail the graphic image of Mt. Rainier to your instructor to show off what you climbed, and then you want to add your instructor's address plus the addresses of some of your friends to your Address Book. You also want to create folders to store your course-related e-mail. Finally, you want to explore more newsgroups to see if you can't find one that you'd like to join and participate in.

1. Make sure Outlook Express is properly configured to send and receive e-mail.
2. Create a new e-mail message to your instructor (your instructor will provide you with the e-mail address to use) and Cc: it to yourself. Enter "From your student [name]" as the subject (insert your name between the brackets). In the message content area, write your instructor a message about what you hope to gain from taking this course.
3. Enter your instructor's name as a new contact in your Address Book.
4. Add the e-mail addresses of three friends to your Address Book. Create a group called "friends" and add the names of your three friends.
5. Create a short message to the friends list you just created and Cc: the message to your instructor. Enter "Class assignment" as the subject and explain briefly in your message that you are testing your e-mail system.
6. In the "Class assignment" message from the previous step, attach the Rainier.bmp file in the Tutorial.03 folder on your Student Disk.
7. Send the Class assignment message. Once you have sent it, open the Sent Items folder and then open the message you just sent.
8. Print the message you sent in Step 7.
9. Create a folder in the Inbox named "Courses." Within the Courses folder, create a folder for each course you are taking.

10. Create another folder in the Inbox named "Work" for storing e-mail related to work. On the back of the printout you created in Step 8, draw a picture of your folder hierarchy.
11. Subscribe to one of the newsgroups in the rec category.
12. Download the first batch of message headers in the newsgroup you just subscribed to.
13. Open any of the messages and print it. On the back of the printout, write the full address of the newsgroup you subscribed to.
14. Search for all newsgroups on the topic "basketball." On the back of the printout you created, write the addresses of a basketball newsgroup in the alt category and in the rec category, plus three additional addresses of any other basketball newsgroups in other categories.

Case Problems

1. E-mailing Freelancers at Custom Cartoons Custom Cartoons provides its clients with cartoon drawings for their promotions and advertisements. Often, when their own cartooning staff is busy with projects, Custom Cartoons contracts projects out to freelance cartoonists. Janey Killips has been assigned to manage a project for a jugglers guild that is hosting a conference in San Antonio next summer. Janey e-mails you and asks if you would be interested in handling the job. You will correspond with Janey via e-mail to get the job done.

If necessary, launch Outlook Express, and then do the following:

1. Create a new message to janey@customcartoons.netez.com.
2. Enter "Jugglers Guild" in the Subject line and use your own words in the message content area.
3. In the message content area, confirm your availability and willingness to do the job.
4. Copy the message to your instructor. Use the Address Book entry you created in the Tutorial Assignments.
5. Add another Cc: line and copy the message to yourself.

6. Add formatting to the message. First, you need to make sure formatting is allowed. Click Format, then click Rich Text (HTML) so that the Formatting toolbar appears. In the message content area, boldface at least one word and italicize at least one word. To boldface a word, you select it and then click the Bold button **B**. To italicize it, you select it and then click the Italic button **I**.

7. Now color one word red. Select the word, press and hold down the Font Color button, and then drag the mouse up and down the color grid that opens and click the color red.
8. Attach the file juggler.bmp, located in the Cases folder of the Tutorial.03 folder on your Student Disk, to the message. Explain in the message content area that this file is a draft of a juggler cartoon.
9. Send the message.

10. Now check your mail. The copied message should appear. Open the message. Print the message, and submit the printout to your instructor.

2. Joining a Newsgroup at Camp Yahara George Hendriks, the maintenance person at Camp Yahara, a summer camp for children with special needs, has hired you to help with some summer maintenance jobs. Many of the outdoor facilities such as the tennis courts, the lake dock, and the obstacle course, need work. Everyone at Camp Yahara has a computer with an Internet connection, and you ask George if he would mind if you spent a little time checking the Internet for advice on some of the repair projects. George replies that a second opinion never hurts, so you decide to subscribe to the newsgroup alt.home.repair, which you know addresses many indoor and outdoor repair and maintenance problems.

If necessary, launch Outlook Express, then do the following:

1. Search for a group named alt.home.repair. If nothing appears, your news server doesn't support this newsgroup. Ask your instructor which newsgroup you should select.
2. Subscribe to the alt.home.repair newsgroup.

3. Open the newsgroup and download the first batch of message headers. If there are none, subscribe to a different newsgroup and repeat this step.

4. Scroll through the message headers until you locate a thread that looks like it might apply to any outdoor or indoor repair job underway at Camp Yahara.

5. Open the first message in the thread and read it. Click the Next button to read through all messages in the thread.

6. Click the Forward Message button to forward the newsgroup message to your instructor; use the Address Book to enter your instructor's e-mail address in the To line.

7. Enter "Camp Yahara" in the Subject line.

8. In the message content area, inform your instructor that you found this message in the alt.home.repair newsgroup.

9. Unsubscribe from the newsgroup.

3. Corresponding with College Students You are interested in what's going on at other colleges and decide to subscribe to one of the many college newsgroups on the Internet. Once you have found a college newsgroup that interests you, you'll post a message to that newsgroup.

If necessary, launch Outlook Express, then do the following:

1. Search for all groups with the word "college."

2. Scroll through the list that appears until you find one that interests you. There are many such newsgroups, ranging from alt.art.college to alt.college.fraternities to soc.college.financial-aid, and so on.

3. Subscribe to the newsgroup that interests you.

4. Download the first batch of message headers.

5. Read through the messages until you find one to which you'd like to respond. Make sure you have something worthwhile to say; the newsgroup won't appreciate it if you write a worthless post. Use the "flavor" of the messages you've read as your guide to tone and length.

6. Reply to one of the messages by posting a message to the entire newsgroup. Copy the message you post to your instructor. Send the message.

7. Wait at least a day. Open the newsgroup again, and if necessary, click Tools and then click Get Next 300 Headers. Locate your message and print it. Submit the printout to your instructor.

8. If there are any responses to your post, reply to that post and add another contribution to the newsgroup. Again, make sure you have something worthwhile to say.

4. Downloading an Uncompression Utility Many of the files that people attach to e-mail messages are zipped to save space. You want to locate a simple uncompression utility so that when you receive an attached file in an e-mail message that is zipped, you'll be able to unzip it. You'll first search for a file named pkz204g.exe, which is a version of pkzip, a popular uncompression utility. Once you've found the file, you'll create a folder on a blank, formatted disk that will store the file. Then you'll download the file into that folder on your blank disk. The pkz204g.exe file is a self-extracting file, which uncompresses or restores its compressed files without a separate uncompression utility. You'll restore the pkz204g.exe file, and then the uncompression program will be available to run on any zip file you receive, either as an attached file, or as a file you download from a Web site.

If necessary, launch Internet Explorer, then do the following:

1. Create a folder on a blank, formatted disk named pkzip. Do not use your Student Disk. To do this, minimize the Outlook Express window. Open My Computer, click 3½ Floppy (A:), click File, point to New, click Folder, type pkzip, press Enter, and then close My Computer.

2. Maximize the Internet Explorer window.

3. Click the Search button, then perform a search for the file pkz204g.exe.

4. Read through the links and click the one that looks most promising. A site with the word "utilities" or "archive" will probably have a copy of this file. Once you locate a promising site, click the PKZ204G.EXE link. If you have trouble, ask your instructor for a workable site.

5. Save the file to the pkzip folder you created on drive A.

6. If you have a virus checker, run it on this file. If you don't, realize that you are putting yourself at risk by running a program that has not been checked. If you are in doubt, ask your instructor.

7. Click the Start button on the Windows taskbar, then click Run.

8. Type a:\pkzip\pkz204g.exe in the Open box, then click the OK button. A DOS window opens, because the program is a DOS utility and shows the steps for uncompressing the file. If you receive a message saying your disk is full, you'll need to copy the file you downloaded over to a blank disk. Once the program is uncompressed, you are ready to run it. It uncompresses into several files; one is pkunzip.exe, the uncompression utility.

9. To run the pkunzip program, you click the Start button, click Run, type:
a:\pkzip\pkunzip.exe path
where path is the path to the file you want to unzip. For example, if you had a file named flowers.zip on drive C and you wanted to unzip it into a folder named c:\flowers, you would type:
a:\pkzip\pkunzip.exe c:\flowers.zip c:\flowers
The first "phrase" in this command indicates the uncompression program you are running; the second indicates the file you are uncompressing; and the third indicates where you want to put the uncompressed files.

Lab Assignments

E-Mail

These Lab Assignments are designed to accompany the interactive Course Lab called E-mail. To start the Lab using Windows 95, click the Start button on the Windows 95 taskbar, point to Programs, point to Course Labs, point to New Perspectives Applications, and click E-Mail.

E-mail that originates on a local area network with a mail gateway can travel all over the world. That's why it is so important to learn how to use it. In this Lab you will use an e-mail simulator, so even if your school's computers don't provide you with e-mail service, you will learn the basics of reading, sending, and replying to electronic mail.

1. Click the Steps button to learn how to work with E-mail. As you proceed through the Steps, answer all of the Quick Check questions that appear. After you complete the Steps, you will see a Quick Check summary report. Follow the instructions on the screen to print this report.

2. Click the Explore button. Write a message to re@films.org. The subject of the message is "Picks and Pans." In the body of your message, describe a movie you have recently seen. Include the name of the movie, briefly summarize the plot, and give it a thumbs up or a thumbs down. Print the message before you send it.

3. Look in your In Basket for a message from jb@music.org. Read the message, then compose a reply indicating that you will attend. Carbon copy mciccone@music.org. Print your reply, including the text of JB's original message before you send it.

4. Look in your In Basket for a message from leo@sports.org. Reply to the message by adding your rating to the text of the original message as follows:

Equipment:	Your rating:
Rollerblades	2
Skis	3
Bicycle	1
Scuba gear	4
Snowmobile	5

Print your reply before you send it.

5. Go into the lab with a partner. You should each log into the E-Mail Lab on different computers. Look at the Addresses list to find the user ID for your partner. You should each send a short e-mail message to your partner. Then, you should check your mail message from your partner. Read the message and compose a reply. Print your reply before you send it. *Note: Unlike a full-featured mail system, the e-mail simulator does not save mail in mailboxes after you log off.*

Answers to Quick Check Questions

SESSION 1.1

1 False

2 The Web page that appears when you start Internet Explorer or the page that a person, organization, or business has created to give information about itself.

3 URL

4 in a different color

5 abort

6 The domain in the URL is not registered with the Domain Name Server (DNS).

SESSION 1.2

1 Type it in the Address box, then press Enter.

2 protocol: http; server address: www.irs.ustreas.gov; filename: cover.html; folder: prod

3 No. URLs are case sensitive.

4 File Transfer Protocol, used to transfer files

5 It is an educational institution.

6 Back, Forward, and Home

7 Page loads faster without images.

8 False

SESSION 2.1

1 False

2 The File Download dialog box opens and gives you the opportunity to save the file to disk.

3 AU (basic audio file), AIFF (high-fidelity sound used on Macintosh computers), RA (Read Audio for live broadcasts), and WAVE (high-fidelity sound used on Windows/PC computers) are four examples

4 Best of the Web

5 high

6 File

7 Favorites folder

SESSION 2.2

1 search engine

2 or, because either word can be present

3 False

4 spiders

5 navigational

6 text

7 When you save a page as a text file, only the text is saved: not the formatting

8 GIF and JPG

9 a file that doesn't appear in the browser window but must be viewed in a separate program

10 Upload means to transfer a copy of a file from your computer to a public directory; download means to transfer a copy of a file from a public directory to your computer.

11 True

12 False

SESSION 3.1

1 user ID: pcsmith; host name: icom.net

2 Click Tools, click Accounts, click the Mail tab, click the account with your name, and then click the Properties button.

3 Sent Items folder

4 The recipient might interpret the uppercase letters as shouting.

5 backbone

6 recipient's e-mail address is automatically inserted; contents of message to which you are replying is quoted

7 Right-click person's e-mail address, then click Add to Address Book.

8 False

9 A paper clip icon appears.

SESSION 3.2

1 Click the plus box ⊞ next to the folder.

2 They are returned undeliverable.

3 Save it as a text file.

4 False. It will be stored in the Trash folder.

5 Ctrl or Shift

SESSION 3.3

1 False

2 News server

3 No. It downloads only the message headers; to download the message text you must double-click a message.

4 The newsgroup is in the rec category, which stands for recreational. It is in the painting subcategory of the arts subcategory, and its subject is oil; probably oil painting.

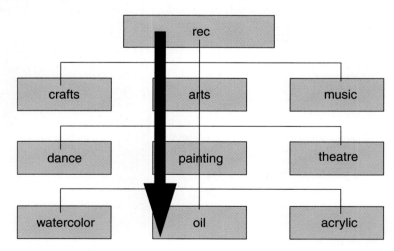

5 a batch of messages that follow a single "line of conversation"

6 sort by sender

7 It is not part of a thread in the message header list you downloaded.

8 insulting e-mail; because e-mail senders are anonymous

Microsoft
Internet
Explorer 4

LEVEL II

TUTORIALS

Read This **Before You Begin**

STUDENT DISKS

To complete the Level II tutorials and end-of-tutorial assignments in this book, you need a Student Disk. Your instructor will either provide you with a Student Disk or ask you to make your own.

If you are supposed to make your own Student Disk, you will need one blank, formatted high-density disk. You will need to copy a set of folders from a file server or standalone computer onto your disk. Your instructor will tell you which computer, drive letter, and folders contain the files you need. The following table shows you which folders go on your disk, so that you will have enough disk space to complete all the tutorials, Tutorial Assignments, and Case Problems:

Student Disk	Write this on the disk label	Put these folders on the disk
1	Student Disk 1: Tutorials 4 and 5	Tutorial.04
		Tutorial.05

When you begin each tutorial, be sure you are using the correct Student Disk. See the inside front or inside back cover of this book for more information on Student Disk files, or ask your instructor or technical support person for assistance.

USING YOUR OWN COMPUTER

If you are going to work through this book using your own computer, you need:

- **Computer System** Microsoft Internet Explorer 4 for Windows must be installed on your computer. This book assumes a full installation of Microsoft Internet Explorer 4.

- **Student Disk** Ask your instructor or lab manager for details on how to get the Student Disk. You will not be able to complete the tutorials or end-of-tutorial assignments in this book using your own computer until you have a Student Disk. The Student Files may also be obtained electronically over the Internet. See the inside front or inside back cover of this book for more details.

To complete the Level II tutorials and end-of-tutorial assignments in this book, your students must use a set of files on one Student Disk. These files are included in the Instructor's Resource Kit, and they may also be obtained electronically over the Internet. See the inside front or inside back cover of this book for more details. Follow the instructions in the Readme or Help file to copy the files to your server or standalone computer. You can view the Readme file using WordPad.

Once the files are copied, you can make Student Disks for the students yourself, or you can tell students where to find the files so they can make their own Student Disks. Make sure the files get correctly copied onto the Student Disks by following the instructions in the Student Disk section above, which will ensure that students have enough disk space to complete all the tutorials and end-of-tutorial assignments.

Tutorial 5 includes steps on how to publish a Web page. You might want to check with your institution's computer labs to ensure your students will have the ability to perform these steps, or else warn your students that they might not be able to complete this section.

COURSE TECHNOLOGY STUDENT FILES AND LAB SOFTWARE

You are granted a license to copy the Student Files software to any computer or computer network used by students who have purchased this book.

Developing Web Pages with FrontPage Express

Creating a Home Page at Avalon Books

OBJECTIVES

In this tutorial you will:

- Create a Web page from scratch using FrontPage Express

- Format large sections of text using paragraph tags

- Create and format numbered and bulleted lists

- Format individual characters or words using character tags

- Insert and format lines and graphic images

- Create a Web page background

Avalon Books

CASE

You work at Avalon Books, a large bookstore in the city of Lakeside. The store offers its customers more than books; it also includes reading rooms, play areas for the kids, and a small cafe. The bookstore sponsors special events such as author signings, poetry readings, and live music. The manager of Avalon Books, Mark Stewart, prepares paper flyers featuring the month's events, and the Avalon Books salespeople insert these flyers into the books customers purchase. However, Mark would like to publicize these events to a wider audience. He especially wants to reach those who have never visited the store or who haven't purchased a book recently and so are unaware of upcoming events. He has asked you to create a Web page to advertise Avalon Books on the World Wide Web. He plans to advertise his Web site in all his promotions.

The FrontPage Express component of Internet Explorer provides three methods to create a Web page. The Personal Home Page Wizard method walks you through a series of steps to create a home page. A second method requires using a **template**, a page created by someone else that you retrieve and use as a model for your own page. Although using a template relieves you from having to spend time on page design, you might find that your page ends up looking too similar to the page it was based on. You can use both the Personal Home Page Wizard and the templates to "jump start" your page by creating the page and then using FrontPage Express to modify it. A third method of creating a new page is starting from scratch with a blank page in FrontPage Express. You enter and format your own text and create your own design using the FrontPage Express tools.

After spending some time thinking about the project Mark has asked you to take on, you decide to use this third method to create the Avalon Books page.

In this session, you will use FrontPage Express to create a Web page from scratch. You will learn how to work offline, to save your document, and to enter and then format text in your page.

Creating a New Page with FrontPage Express

The FrontPage Express component of Internet Explorer gives you the ability to create and edit intranet and Web documents. An **intranet document** is just like a Web page, except that it is available only to an internal network, not to all users on the Web. Thus, a company can make internal company documents available to employees so that they can access them just as they would a regular Web page, but people outside the intranet cannot. See Figure 4-1.

Figure 4-1 ◀
Storing a Web page on the Internet or an intranet

a Web page you store on the Internet server is available to anyone on the Web

intranets exist to exchange internal company documents; A Web page stored on intranet available only to those with intranet access

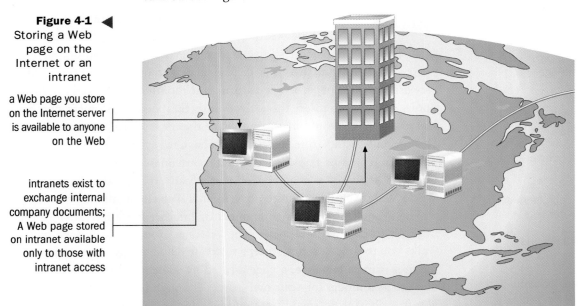

When you create a Web page, you need to decide if your audience will be only your local intranet, if you are on one, or the entire Internet community. Your content should always be dictated by your audience. Once you've created your page, Internet Explorer can help you publish it.

With FrontPage Express you can:

- Create Web documents from scratch, using composition aids.
- Edit and format your documents in a WYSIWYG (what you see is what you get) environment, so that you will see an immediate preview of how the final document will appear.
- Use familiar word processing features such as text formatting and table creation.
- Quickly and easily insert graphic objects and hypertext links into your document.
- Publish your document to a server.

Elements of a Web Page

Creating a Web page involves planning both the content and the appearance of the page. You can plan the content by asking questions like: What information do I want to convey? What links do I want to include?

Once you have settled on your content, you should plan your design. You can include colors, interesting fonts, a stylized background, graphics, and other design elements such as lines and tables. Keep in mind, however, that a browser takes much longer to retrieve a Web page that contains a lot of graphics. If your page takes too long to retrieve, your target audience might lose patience and skip your page.

Mark shows you a flyer he uses to advertise the bookstore's current events, shown in Figure 4-2. He suggests you use this flyer as a basis for the Web page contents.

Figure 4-2 ◀
Mark's flyer

Avalon Books

341 Gorham Avenue, Lakeside, IL (608) 555-4891

Avalon Books is Lakeside's premier bookstore. Come and curl up next to our cozy fire with a good book and a cup of one of our classic coffees. Meet with an author at one of our discussion sessions, or stop by for live music every Friday and Saturday night. Bring the kids any afternoon for storytime and snacks.

Come to Avalon Books for...

- The largest selection of books in the Midwest
- Comfortable reading rooms
- Coffee, wines, and delicious desserts as you read
- A computer lab for kids with the best educational software titles

This week's events

Monday, 10/7

Isaac Anderson discusses humor and science fiction and will sign copies of his new book, *The Time Traveler's Bar and Grill*

Wednesday, 10/9

The Avalon Reading Club will discuss Maureen Dawson's book, *Deconstructing Beethoven*

Friday, 10/11

Soft Jazz by Burns, Sutton, and Davis

The page that Mark sketched contains the following elements:

- A main heading and several subheadings at different levels

- A description of the contents and purpose of the page

- A bulleted list

- Horizontal line that improves the page's appearance

- A graphic image

- Text in different fonts and sizes

- Indented text

You decide to create this page from scratch, by first entering and formatting the text and then by creating a page design.

Going Offline

You can use many Internet Explorer features without actually being connected to the Internet—a plus if you are paying for your Internet connection. When you work without an Internet connection, you are working **offline**. When you start an Internet Explorer component, your computer might attempt to connect to the Internet. If you will be using only FrontPage Express without requiring any Internet resources, you could click the Cancel or Stop button on your Internet connection dialog box to halt the connection.

Starting FrontPage Express

How you start FrontPage Express depends on your circumstances. If you plan to use the Personal Home Page Wizard or to start from a blank page, you need to first start FrontPage Express from the Start menu. Alternatively, you can retrieve any page on the Web in the Internet Explorer browser and open it in FrontPage Express so that it functions as a template. Keep in mind that most Web pages contain copyrighted material that you cannot use without permission.

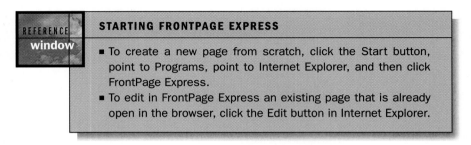

REFERENCE window

STARTING FRONTPAGE EXPRESS

- To create a new page from scratch, click the Start button, point to Programs, point to Internet Explorer, and then click FrontPage Express.
- To edit in FrontPage Express an existing page that is already open in the browser, click the Edit button in Internet Explorer.

To create a new document in FrontPage Express:

1. Click the **Start** button <u>Start</u>, point to **Programs**, then point to **Internet Explorer**.

2. Click **FrontPage Express**. If your computer attempts to connect to the Internet, you can cancel the connection. The FrontPage Express window opens to a blank page.

3. Click the **Maximize** button □ to maximize the FrontPage Express window. Figure 4-3 shows the maximized FrontPage Express window.

   TROUBLE? If you see the Forms toolbar in addition to the Standard and Format toolbar, don't worry. You'll learn how to hide it in a moment.

Figure 4-3 ◀
FrontPage
Express
window

Format toolbar ——

Standard toolbar ——

Format Marks
enabled

document window
displays the page as
you create it

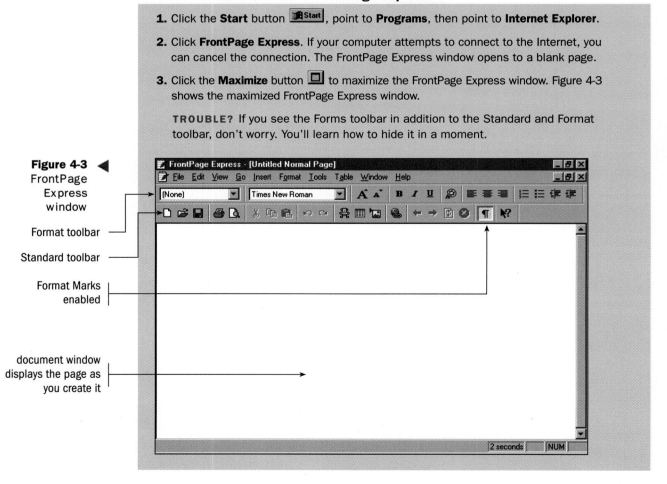

FrontPage Express includes three toolbars: Format, Standard, and Forms. The Format toolbar includes tools that help you format your page; the Standard toolbar includes tools that help you compose your page; and the Forms toolbar includes tools that help you create a form on your page. Because the Avalon Books page won't use forms, you don't need to view the Forms toolbar.

To hide the Forms toolbar:

1. Click **View**.

2. Make sure both the **Standard Toolbar** and **Format Toolbar** options are preceded by a checkmark.

3. If the Forms Toolbar option is preceded by a checkmark, click **Forms Toolbar** to hide the Forms toolbar.

4. Click **View** once more and make sure the **Status Bar** and **Format Marks** options are both preceded by a checkmark.

Your screen should now match the screen in Figure 4-3.

Saving a Web Page

Before you actually begin entering text into your new document, you decide to save it. FrontPage Express lets you save the page directly to the Web or as a file on your disk. You aren't ready to publish the page on the Web, so you will save it as a file on your Student Disk. When you save your page, FrontPage Express gives you the opportunity to give a title to your page. Browsers viewing your page will display this title in the browser title bar.

You decide to enter Avalon Books as the page title and to save the page with the name "Avalon".

To save your Web page and assign it a title:

1. Place your Student Disk in the drive, click **File**, and then click **Save As**.

2. Type **Avalon Books** in the Page Title box. See. Figure 4-4.

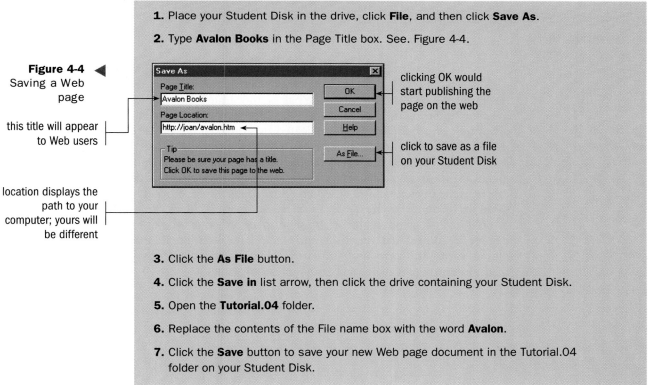

Figure 4-4 ◀
Saving a Web page

this title will appear to Web users

location displays the path to your computer; yours will be different

clicking OK would start publishing the page on the web

click to save as a file on your Student Disk

3. Click the **As File** button.

4. Click the **Save in** list arrow, then click the drive containing your Student Disk.

5. Open the **Tutorial.04** folder.

6. Replace the contents of the File name box with the word **Avalon**.

7. Click the **Save** button to save your new Web page document in the Tutorial.04 folder on your Student Disk.

Notice that the FrontPage Express title bar now displays the path A:\Tutorial.04\Avalon.htm. In the browser, however, the filename will not appear. Instead, the title you entered will appear.

Markup Tags

FrontPage Express works much like a word processor. There are, however, some important differences between a document created with a software program such as Microsoft Word and one created by FrontPage Express for use on the Web. When you create a document using FrontPage Express, you are actually creating a file that consists of HTML codes. **HTML**, which stands for Hypertext Markup Language, is the language in which a Web page is written. HTML uses special codes to describe how the page should appear on the screen. Figure 4-5 shows a Web page as it appears on your computer screen, and behind it, the underlying HTML code. It is this code that is actually transferred over the Web when someone accesses your page.

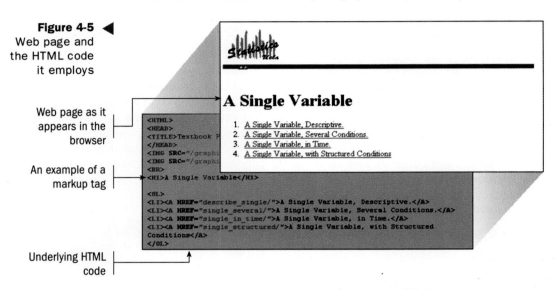

Figure 4-5 ◀
Web page and
the HTML code
it employs

Web page as it
appears in the
browser

An example of a
markup tag

Underlying HTML
code

When the HTML code is transferred over the Web, the browser accessing the page interprets the code to determine the page's appearance and then displays the page according to its interpretation of the code. The appearance of each element in the page, such as a heading or a bulleted list, is indicated by a **markup tag**—a label within angle brackets that identifies the element to a browser. A tag with the label <H1>, for example, stands for "Heading 1" and indicates that the text that follows is a top-level heading in the document. Markup tags are necessarily very general so that many different kinds of browsers can read the document and determine how to display it. Not all browsers display text the same way. Some browsers, called **text-based browsers**, often can't display formatting such as bold or italics and might be able to display only one type of font. These browsers will display Heading 1 text very differently from a browser like Internet Explorer that can display a variety of fonts and formatting. Figure 4-6 shows how two different browsers might interpret text formatted with a Heading 1 tag.

Figure 4-6 ◀
Same heading
as it appears in
different
browsers

You can assign fonts and font sizes to text, just as you do in a word processor, but you should be aware that not all browsers will be able to display the font you choose. Suppose you format text with a Heading 1 tag with a 14-point bold Century Gothic font. If a browser on an operating system without Century Gothic installed retrieves your page, it will use the default font for the style you've assigned rather than Century Gothic. If you designed your page around interesting fonts, you could sell yourself short if the majority of browsers don't have your font.

As a Web page author, you don't have the same kind of control over your page's appearance as you would in creating a word-processed document. Although you can use different fonts and font sizes, the appearance of text is determined by the browser, not by you. Even with these limitations, you can still create interesting and visually attractive documents. And as the Web increases in popularity, new tags will be developed that give Web authors more flexibility and control in creating pages.

In creating your Avalon Books Web page, you'll be using tags with the following document elements:

- paragraphs

- individual characters

- graphic images

Some tags simply contain information about the document. Earlier, when you entered a title for the page, you were actually inserting a tag of this kind into your document. Although these tags do not show up on the page, they do appear in the HTML code. You can see this by viewing the source code, or the actual HTML tags, that define the document.

To view a page's source code:

1. Click **View**, then click **HTML**. The View or Edit HTML window opens. See Figure 4-7. Notice that the title you entered is actually part of a tag. When you enter your page's contents, it will appear between the Body tags.

Figure 4-7 ◀
HTML source code

information about the page

page title within TITLE tag

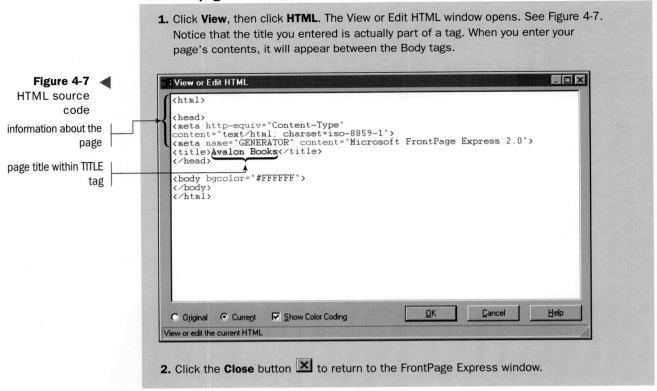

2. Click the **Close** button ⊠ to return to the FrontPage Express window.

Entering and Formatting Text

You are now ready to start formatting the Avalon Books Web page to mirror the appearance of Mark's flyer. As you look over Mark's flyer from Figure 4-2, you identify the following elements:

- Main heading for the title

- Smaller heading listing store's address and phone number

- Heading for each of the two sections of the document

- Bulleted list of activities at the bookstore

- Bolded and italicized weekdays on which Avalon Books has scheduled events

- Indented descriptions of events

- Horizontal line separating headings

- Graphic that makes the page visually attractive

In trying to recreate this flyer on the Web, you will need to apply a tag to each of these elements: headings, bulleted lists, formatted text, indented text, and graphics. FrontPage Express makes it easy for you to choose the appropriate tags for each element. When you want to apply the style to an entire paragraph you choose a paragraph tag. When you want to apply a style to just a phrase, word, or character, you choose a character tag.

To start, you decide to apply the paragraph tags for the headings. HTML offers six different heading tags, labeled H1, H2, H3, and so on through H6. FrontPage Express has assigned a style name to each HTML tag and placed all available style names on a list that is available through the Format toolbar. The HTML tag H1, for example, appears as the Heading 1 style in this list. Figure 4-8 shows how a typical browser might display paragraphs with each of these heading tags applied.

Figure 4-8 ◄
Heading styles
as they appear
in browser

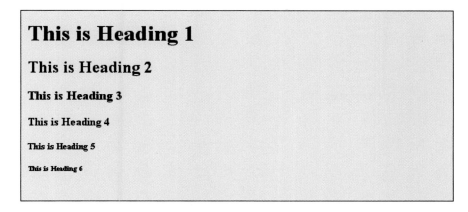

To apply a style to a paragraph, click anywhere in the paragraph and then choose the style you want from the Change Style list. You can apply a style before or after you type the paragraph, and you can apply a different style at any time.

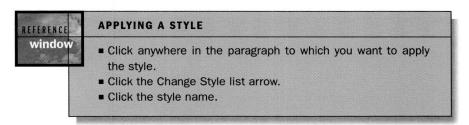

REFERENCE
window

APPLYING A STYLE

- Click anywhere in the paragraph to which you want to apply the style.
- Click the Change Style list arrow.
- Click the style name.

Applying Heading Styles

You decide to use the Heading 1 style (corresponding to the H1 HTML tag) for the page's main heading, "Avalon Books", and the Heading 4 style (corresponding to the H4 HTML tag) for the store's address and phone number.

To enter text and styles for the first two paragraphs:

1. Click the upper-left corner of the document window. The blinking insertion point indicates you are ready to type.

2. Click the **Change Style** list arrow on the Format toolbar. The list of available styles opens. Each style corresponds to an HTML tag. See Figure 4-9.

Figure 4-9
Change Style
list

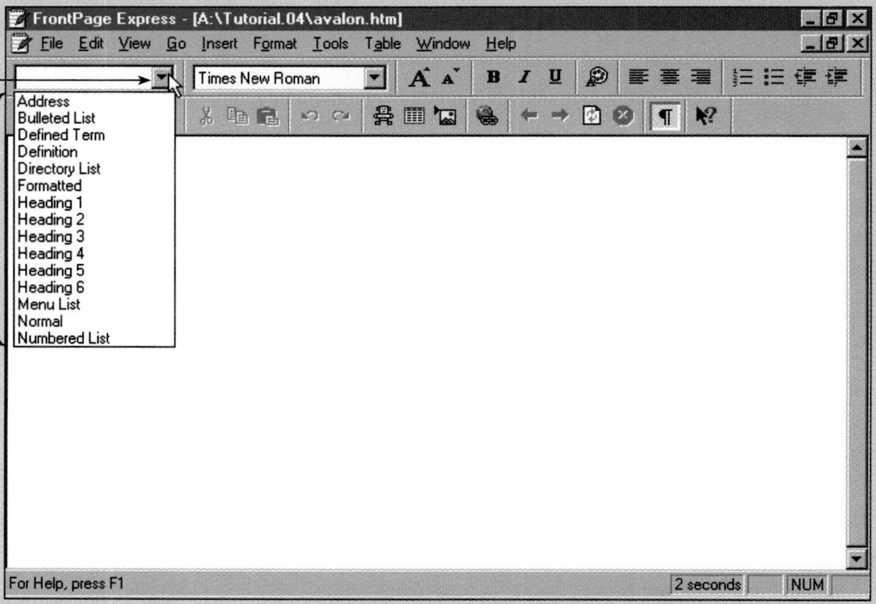

Change Style list
arrow

list of styles

3. Click **Heading 1**.

4. Type **Avalon Books**, then press **Enter**. Now tag and enter the second line.

5. Click the **Change Style** list arrow on the Format toolbar, then click **Heading 4**.

6. Type **341 Gorham Avenue, Lakeside, IL (608) 555-4891**, then press **Enter**. Notice that because you applied a different style to this paragraph, FrontPage Express displays it differently. See Figure 4-10.

Figure 4-10
Entering
headings

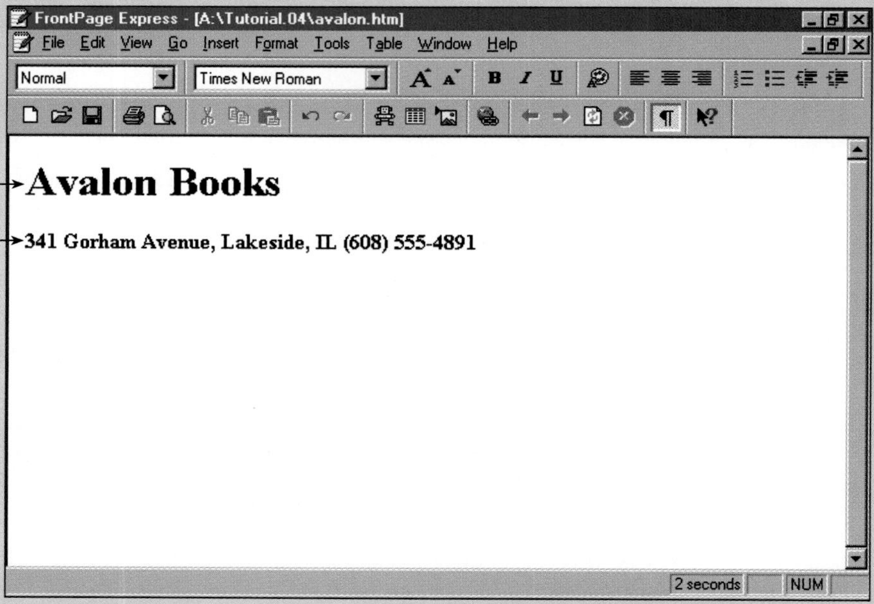

paragraph formatted
with Heading 1 style

paragraph formatted
with Heading 4 style

Within each tag, you can make some additional choices regarding the appearance of text formatted with that tag. These choices are called **properties**. Although tag properties are not as extensive as what you may be accustomed to with word processors, you can still use them to add variety and interest to your text. One such property for a paragraph tag is alignment. Paragraphs can be left-, centered, or right-aligned.

You decide to center the two headings you just created to follow the format of the flyer.

To center the headings on the page:

1. Use the mouse to select the two headings.

   TROUBLE? To select the two headings, drag the mouse with the left mouse button held down from the left side of the first heading to the right side of the second.

2. Click the **Center** button 🗏 on the Format toolbar. Your headings are now centered.

You now add the next two headings to the page. Unlike the first two, they will be aligned with the left edge of the page.

To add additional headings:

1. Click the end of the second line and press **Enter**. The new line is also centered, so you need to set it to left alignment.

   TROUBLE? If you press Enter while the text is still highlighted, all your typing will disappear. Click the Undo button 🗏 and this time make sure you click the end of the second line before pressing Enter, as directed in Step 1.

2. Click the **Align Left** button 🗏 on the Format toolbar.

3. Type **Come to Avalon Books for...**, then press **Enter**.

4. Type **This week's events**, then press **Enter**.

5. Select the two headings you just entered, then click **Heading 2** from the Change Style list. See Figure 4-11.

Figure 4-11 ◀
Applying
Heading 2 style

these paragraphs are
centered

paragraphs formatted
with Heading 2 style

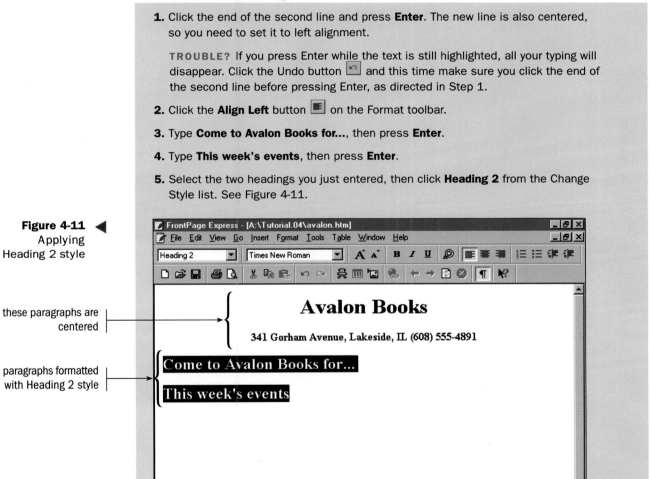

You've entered your headings, and now you want to enter the introductory paragraph on Mark's flyer.

Inserting Text with the Normal Style

Most Web pages include a descriptive paragraph that serves as an introduction to the page, usually in the Normal style. This text can describe the page, its goals, and its resources, or it can give brief instructions about how the page operates.

Unformatted sections of text such as descriptive or informational paragraphs are called **normal text**. You tag normal text with the Normal style. Inserting additional text into a Web page with FrontPage Express works much as it would with a word processor. Move the mouse pointer to the spot on the page where you want the new text to appear, click the left mouse button, press Enter if you want a new line, and then start typing the new text.

Mark's flyer includes a paragraph describing Avalon Books attractions. You are ready to enter this information into your Web page.

To add normal text to a page:

1. Click the end of the line containing Avalon's address and press **Enter**. When you press Enter, FrontPage Express automatically formats the next paragraph with the Normal style, as you can see from the Change Style list box.

2. Click the **Align Left** button ▤ on the Format toolbar.

3. Type the following text into the document window:

    Avalon Books is Lakeside's premier bookstore. Come and curl up next to our cozy fire with a good book and a cup of one of our classic coffees. Meet with an author at one of our discussion sessions, or stop by for live music every Friday and Saturday night. Bring the kids any afternoon for storytime and snacks.

    Your page should now look similar to Figure 4-12, although your text might wrap differently.

Figure 4-12 ◀
Entering normal
text

normal text ⟶

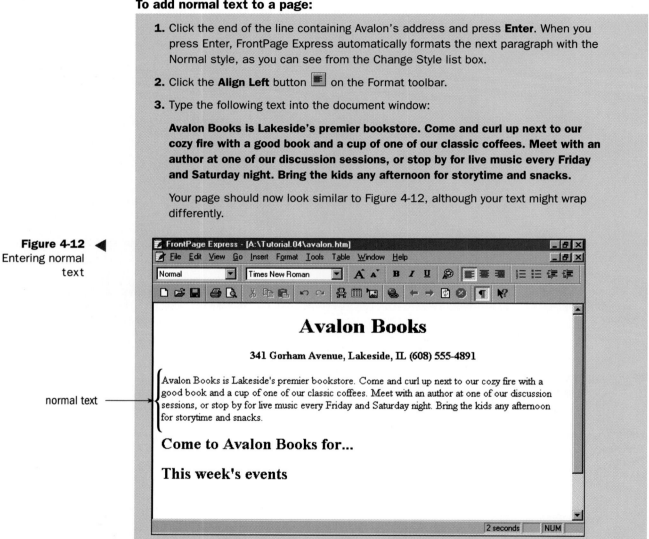

You are satisfied with your page so far. You decide to save your work and then take a break.

To save your changes to the Avalon Books Web page:

1. Click the **Save** button 🖫.

2. Click **File**, then click **Exit**.

Your Web page is well on its way. You've entered a page title, the page's headings, and normal text.

Quick Check

1. What is a WYSIWYG document?

2. Under what circumstances would you want to work offline?

3. The language in which a Web page is written is called _____ .

4. What is the difference between a markup tag and a style?

5. Why might you choose not to use a special font in your page?

6. How does FrontPage Express differ from a word processor like Microsoft Word?

7. What style do you use for unformatted sections of text such as descriptive paragraphs?

SESSION

4.2

In this session you will learn how to enhance the appearance of your documents with numbered and bulleted lists, how to indent text, and how to format text using character formats.

Creating Lists

As you look over Mark's flyer, you notice the next thing you want to add is a list of attractions. You can use FrontPage Express to create two kinds of lists: a numbered list or a bulleted list. Use a numbered list, also called an **ordered list**, when you want to display, for example, chronological information such as a list of the steps needed to complete a task. Use a bulleted list, known as an **unordered list** because the order doesn't matter, to distinguish between items in the list with bullet symbols.

You decide to try both the numbered and bulleted list formats so you can decide how you want the list of Avalon Books attractions to appear on Mark's flyer. First, you must reopen the page you were working on in Session 4.1.

To reopen the Avalon Books page in FrontPage Express:

1. Restart FrontPage Express. You do not have to initiate an Internet connection nor load your home page.

2. Click the **Open** button .

3. If necessary, click the **From File** option button.

4. Click the **Browse** button, click the **Look in** list arrow, then locate and select the drive containing your Student Disk.

5. Open the **Tutorial.04** folder, click **Avalon.htm**, then click the **Open** button.

Creating a Numbered List

You decide to enter the list of Avalon attractions first as a numbered list using the Numbered List style. This style has its own toolbar button that you use instead of the Change Style list.

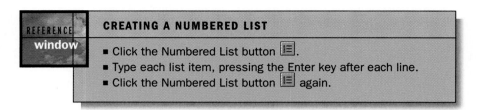

REFERENCE window

CREATING A NUMBERED LIST

■ Click the Numbered List button [icon].
■ Type each list item, pressing the Enter key after each line.
■ Click the Numbered List button [icon] again.

To create a numbered list:

1. Click the end of the **Come to Avalon Books for...** heading, then press **Enter**.

2. Click the **Numbered List** button [icon] on the Format toolbar. The number 1 appears.

3. Type **The largest selection of books in the Midwest**, then press **Enter**.

4. Continue entering the following items in the list, each on its own line:

   Comfortable reading rooms

   Coffee, wines, and delicious desserts as you read

   A computer lab for kids with the best educational software titles

   The Avalon Books page should now appear as shown in Figure 4-13.

   TROUBLE? If you pressed Enter after the last item in the list, press the Backspace key to remove the extra blank line.

Figure 4-13 ◀
Entering a
numbered list

Numbered List button

numbered list

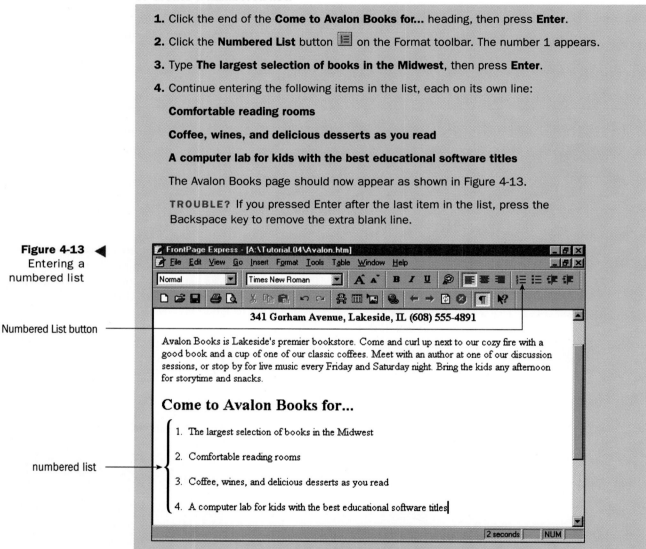

Viewing Your Page in the Browser

You should periodically save your page and open it in your browser to ensure that it looks the way you want it to. Usually it will look the same in the browser as it does in FrontPage Express, but not always. Some Web page creators like to test their pages in several browsers, such as different versions of Internet Explorer and Netscape Navigator, before they publish them so they are sure the page looks good regardless of the browser or version. You can open a page in Internet Explorer even when it is already open in FrontPage Express. If you make changes to your page in FrontPage Express, you can save the page and then use the Refresh button to view the changes in Internet Explorer.

To view the Avalon Books page in the Internet Explorer browser window:

1. Click the **Save** button 🖫 to save your changes to the page.

2. Launch Internet Explorer. You don't have to connect to the Internet to open a page from your disk, so cancel the connection if it is initiated.

3. Click **File**, then click **Open**.

4. Click the **Browse** button and locate the Avalon.htm file in the Tutorial.04 folder of your Student Disk.

5. Click the **Open** button, then click the **OK** button. The page appears in Internet Explorer as shown in Figure 4-14. Notice that the Internet Explorer title bar displays the page's title, Avalon Books. This is how your page will look to other Internet Explorer users, although different browsers might display it differently.

Figure 4-14 ◄
Previewing
page in browser

page title appears in
browser title bar

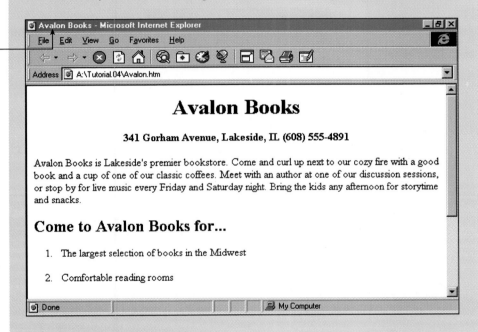

6. Click the **FrontPage Express** button in the taskbar to return to editing your page.

Creating a Bulleted List

A bulleted list uses bullets instead of numbers. Like the numbered list, you apply it using one of the toolbar buttons on the Format toolbar. You decide to format your list as a bulleted list to see how it appears.

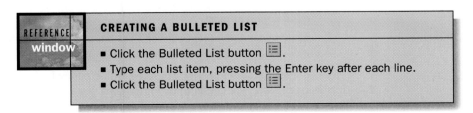

REFERENCE
window

CREATING A BULLETED LIST

- Click the Bulleted List button 📧.
- Type each list item, pressing the Enter key after each line.
- Click the Bulleted List button 📧.

To format a list as a bulleted list:

1. Select the list of attractions by dragging the mouse over all the items in the list.

2. Click the **Bulleted List** button 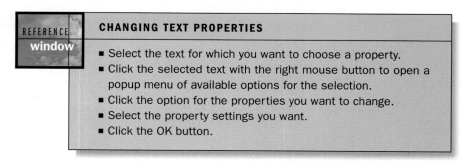 on the Format toolbar. The list changes to a bulleted list of items as shown in Figure 4-15.

Figure 4-15 ◄
Creating a
bulleted list

bullets appear
instead of numbers

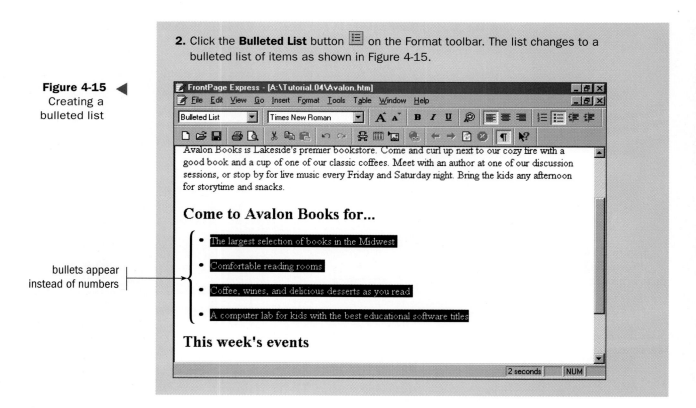

You decide to leave the list as a bulleted list, because it is not in any particular order.

Modifying the Appearance of a List

FrontPage Express allows you to choose a different symbol for bulleted lists or a different numbering format for numbered lists, although you should be aware that not all browsers will properly display the formats you choose, but will instead revert to the standard bulleted or numbered style. The bullet symbol is one of the properties of the bulleted list style. Some properties, such as the alignment property, can be accessed with toolbar buttons, but not all properties have corresponding toolbar buttons; you can access those properties by clicking the selected text with the right mouse button and choosing the appropriate properties option from the popup menu that opens.

REFERENCE window	**CHANGING TEXT PROPERTIES**
	■ Select the text for which you want to choose a property.
	■ Click the selected text with the right mouse button to open a popup menu of available options for the selection.
	■ Click the option for the properties you want to change.
	■ Select the property settings you want.
	■ Click the OK button.

You decide to replace the bullet symbol in your list of attractions with a symbol that more closely approximates the square bullet symbol used in Mark's flyer.

To change the bullet symbol:

1. If necessary, select the bulleted list, then right-click the selection.

2. Click **List Properties** from the popup menu.

3. Click the solid square bullet style from the available styles. See Figure 4-16.

Figure 4-16 ◀
Changing bullet
style

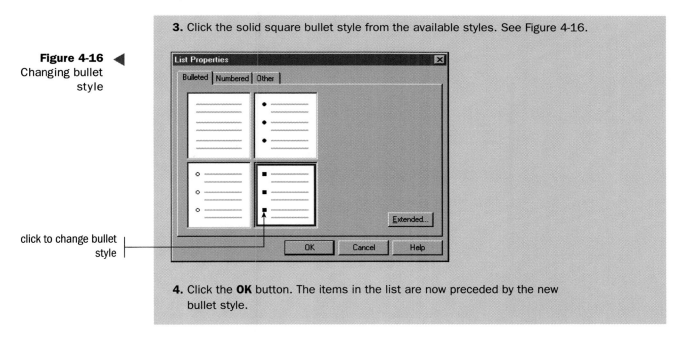

click to change bullet
style

4. Click the **OK** button. The items in the list are now preceded by the new bullet style.

You like the way the bulleted list looks. You're now ready to start entering upcoming events.

Indenting Text

If you want to offset text from the left edge of the page, you can do so by indenting the text using the Indent buttons ⊞ and ⊞ on the toolbar.

Based on Mark's flyer you decide to indent the descriptions of the upcoming events. First you enter the text describing the upcoming events.

To enter the week's events and indent the descriptions:

1. Click the end of the heading "This week's events", then press **Enter**.

TROUBLE? If you can't see this heading, scroll down the document window.

2. Verify that the Normal style is applied by checking the Change Style list box.

TROUBLE? If the style does not appear as Normal, select the Normal style from the Change Style list box.

3. Type **Monday, 10/7**, then press **Enter**.

4. Type the following, then press **Enter**:

Isaac Anderson discusses humor and science fiction and will sign copies of his new book, The Time Traveler's Bar and Grill

5. Continue typing the following information into the document window, pressing **Enter** after each line.

Wednesday, 10/9

The Avalon Reading Club will discuss Maureen Dawson's book, Deconstructing Beethoven

Friday, 10/11

Soft Jazz by Burns, Sutton, and Davis

6. Select the line or lines describing the Isaac Anderson discussion and book signing (do not include the date).

7. Click the **Increase Indent** button 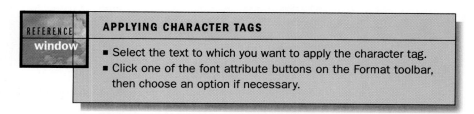 to shift the line to the right.

8. Indent the rest of the event descriptions in the list, leaving the dates unindented. Click the page when you're finished to deselect the text. Your page should look like Figure 4-17.

Figure 4-17 ◀
Indenting text

indented text ⟶

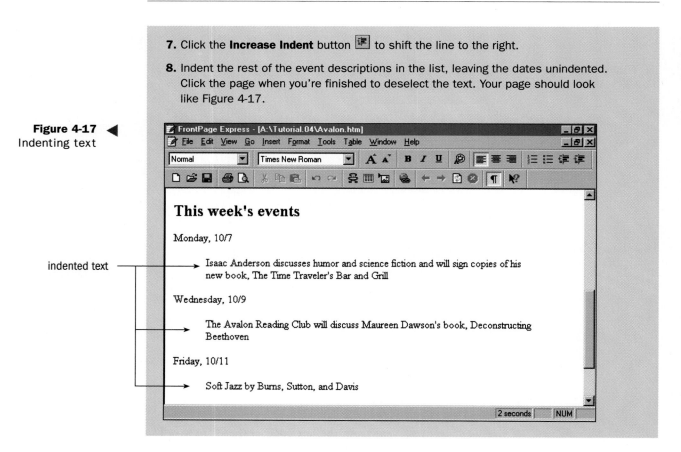

You realize that some of the events include book titles, which need to be italicized. To do this, you need to work with character tags.

Applying Character Tags

Although you can't change the definition of a style like "Heading 1", you can alter the appearance of individual characters. The HTML formats that you can apply to characters are called **character tags**. FrontPage Express allows you to use character tags to italicize your text, bold it, change its font type and size, or display it in a different color.

REFERENCE window	**APPLYING CHARACTER TAGS**
	▪ Select the text to which you want to apply the character tag.
	▪ Click one of the font attribute buttons on the Format toolbar, then choose an option if necessary.

Changing Font Attributes

A **font attribute** is a characteristic of a font that you can change, including its font type, size, color, and whether it is in bold or italics. Font attributes are represented in FrontPage Express by toolbar buttons on the Format toolbar. The descriptions of the upcoming events include book names that should be italicized.

To italicize text in the Avalon Books page:

1. Select the text **The Time Traveler's Bar and Grill** from the description of the Isaac Anderson discussion.

2. Click the **Italic** button 🔲 on the Format toolbar.

3. Select the text **Deconstructing Beethoven** from the description of the Reading Club event.

4. Click 🔲.

To help the dates stand out better on the page, you decide to bold the day of the event by applying the bold character tag.

To bold text in the Avalon Books page:

1. Select the text **Monday** from the list of events.

2. Click the **Bold** button 🔲 on the Format toolbar.

3. Repeat Steps 1 and 2 to bold **Wednesday** and **Friday**. Click a blank part of the page to deselect the text when you are finished. The updated page should appear as shown in Figure 4-18.

Figure 4-18 ◀
Applying
character tags

days are bolded ——

book titles are
italicized

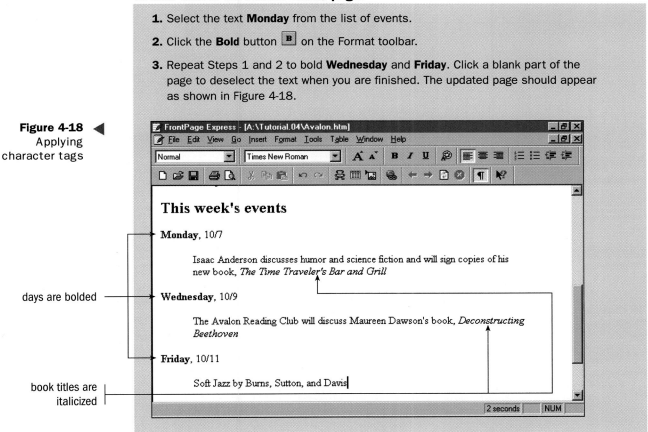

Changing Font Type Size

The type of font and its size are additional font attributes you can change. You have already seen how to change the font size of an entire paragraph by applying one of the heading styles, and individual browsers might change font types based on those headings. To change the font size or type of individual characters, not necessarily entire lines or paragraphs, you use the Font list and the text size buttons on the Format toolbars.

Looking at your page, you decide to increase the size of the Avalon Books heading. At present it is formatted with the Heading 1 tag. You would like the text to be larger, but there isn't another heading tag that will display the text in a larger font, so you will change its text size attribute. You decide not to change the font type, because you don't want your page design to rely on a font that other browsers might not support.

To increase the size of the Avalon Books heading:

1. Scroll to the top of your Web page, then select the text **Avalon Books** from the first line of your page.

2. Click the **Increase Text Size** button $\boxed{A^*}$ on the Format toolbar. The font size is increased accordingly. Figure 4-19 shows the updated page heading.

Figure 4-19 ◀
Increasing font
size

font size is larger ——————

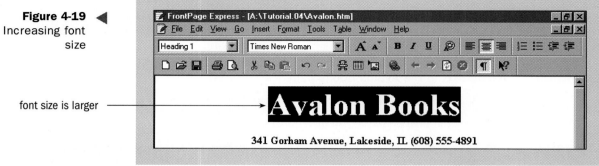

The heading looks better, but you'd like to emphasize it further by using color.

Changing Font Color

Another way of adding emphasis and interest to the text on your page is to use different colors by applying the Text Color character tag to selected text. FrontPage Express allows you to choose colors from a palette of colors. The default color of text in your Web document is black.

You decide to change the color of the first two lines of the page to red to give them greater emphasis.

To change the text color:

1. Select the first two headings on the page.

2. Click the **Text Color** button $\boxed{\mathscr{D}}$ on the Format toolbar.

3. Click the red color shown in Figure 4-20.

Figure 4-20 ◀
Changing font
color

click this color ——————

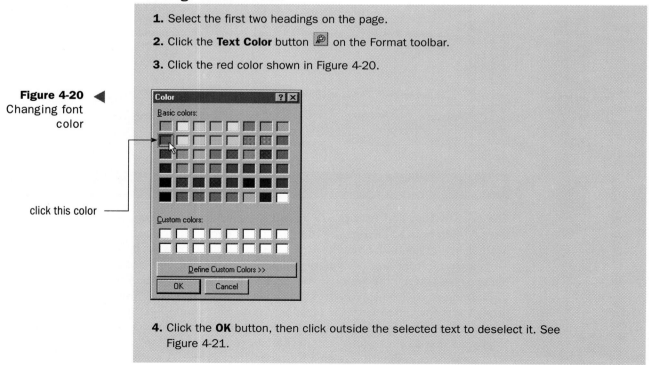

4. Click the **OK** button, then click outside the selected text to deselect it. See Figure 4-21.

Figure 4-21 ◀
New font color

text is now red

The first two headings now appear in red.

Applying Multiple Character Tags

So far you've been changing one character property at a time using the buttons on the Format toolbar. You can apply more than one character tag at a time using the Font dialog box. You open this dialog box the way you open any properties dialog box: by right-clicking the selected text and choosing the appropriate properties option from the popup menu that appears. You then make the selections you want in the property sheets and apply them all at once by clicking the OK button.

Mark stops by and looks at the work you've done. He's pleased with the use of color on the page and would like you to change the color for the two other headings. He thinks they should be italicized as well. You can change the font style, size, and color properties all at the same time.

To apply multiple character tags using the Character Properties sheet:

1. Select the line **Come to Avalon Books for...** .

2. Right-click the selection, then click **Font Properties** from the popup menu.

3. In the Font dialog box, click **Italic**.

4. Click the **Color** list arrow, then click **Blue**, as shown in Figure 4-22.

Figure 4-22 ◀
Setting
character
properties

text will be italicized

new blue color

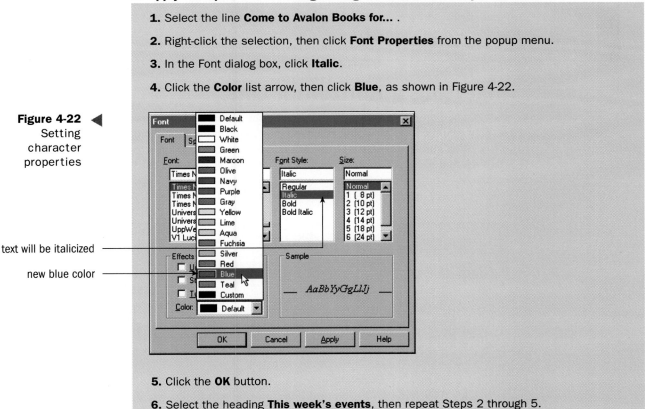

5. Click the **OK** button.

6. Select the heading **This week's events**, then repeat Steps 2 through 5.

You're finished modifying the text on the Avalon Books page. You decide to take a break. Save your changes to the file and close FrontPage Express. In the next session you'll add graphic elements to the page.

To save your changes and then exit FrontPage Express and Internet Explorer:

1. Click the **Save** button 🖫.

2. Click **File**, then click **Exit**. Your Web page is saved to your Student Disk. Close Internet Explorer if necessary.

You've finished entering the text of the Avalon Books Web page, and you've formatted it so that the important parts are most noticeable.

Quick Check

1. How do you change the symbol FrontPage Express uses in bulleted lists?

2. Name three font attributes you can change in FrontPage Express.

3. Why might you decide not to specify a different font, such as Century Gothic, for a heading?

4. How would you change the font size, font color, and appearance for a section of text without opening several dialog boxes?

5. How would you change the color of text on your page to green?

SESSION

4.3

In this session you will learn how to insert graphic elements on your page, including graphical lines, images, and a background. You will also learn how to modify the properties of these graphical elements.

Inserting a Horizontal Line

Part of the popularity of the Web is due to the ability of browsers like Internet Explorer to display graphic objects within the Web page. Graphic objects lend interest to the page and allow Web authors to share visual information. Because graphic objects require more time than normal text for a browser to access, however, you should use graphic objects sparingly.

To give shape to your page, consider adding horizontal lines. Horizontal lines divide the Web page into sections for easy viewing.

REFERENCE
window

INSERTING A HORIZONTAL LINE

- Click the end of the paragraph below which you want to insert the line.
- Click Insert, then click Horizontal Line.
- To change the line's appearance, right-click the horizontal line and click Horizontal Line Properties from the popup menu. Make any changes you want, then click the OK button.

Mark's flyer includes horizontal lines, and he would like his Web page to feature them as well. You decide to add a horizontal line separating the name and address of the bookstore from the rest of the page.

To insert a horizontal line:

1. Restart FrontPage Express and open the Avalon Books page into the FrontPage Express window.

2. Click the end of the heading containing address information for Avalon Books.

3. Click **Insert**, then click **Horizontal Line**. A horizontal line appears on the page.

You can use the Horizontal Line Properties dialog box to change your line's width, height, alignment, and appearance. Figure 4-23 describes the properties you can change.

Figure 4-23 ◀
Line properties

Property	Description
Width	The width of the line is expressed either as a percentage of the window or in the number of pixels, where a pixel is a single dot or point on your monitor's screen. Therefore setting the line width to 100% means the line will stretch the full width of the document window. If you want the line to always stretch across the document window, you should use the percent of window option. If you are trying to define the line width so that it is the same for all browsers, you should use the pixels option.
Height	The height of the line is always expressed in pixels, with a default height of two pixels.
Alignment	Lines can be left-, centered, or right-aligned on the page.
Color	You can specify a color from the color palette.
Shadow	A line can appear with or without shading, which gives the line an illusion of depth.

Figure 4-24 shows several examples of lines whose appearance varies depending on the properties they use.

Figure 4-24 ◀
Examples of
line styles

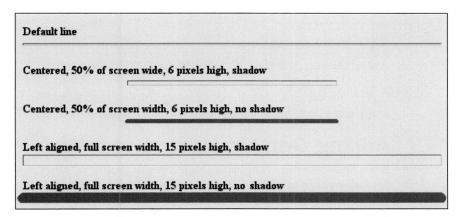

You decide to modify the appearance of the line you just created so it looks more like the one in Mark's flyer.

You might find that your line settings already match these; if that is the case, read the steps without performing them.

To change the properties of a horizontal line:

1. Right-click the horizontal line, then click **Horizontal Line Properties**.

2. Type **325** in the Width box, then click the **Pixels** option button.

TROUBLE? The Width and Height boxes use pin arrows to ease number entry. You can click the up spin arrow or down spin arrow to change the value. Alternately, you can simply click the box and type the new entry.

3. Change the Height box to **3** to set the line's height to three pixels.

4. Verify that the **Center** alignment option button is selected.

5. Make sure the **Solid line (no shading)** check box is deselected. The completed Horizontal Line Properties dialog box should appear as shown in Figure 4-25.

Figure 4-25 ◀
Changing line
properties

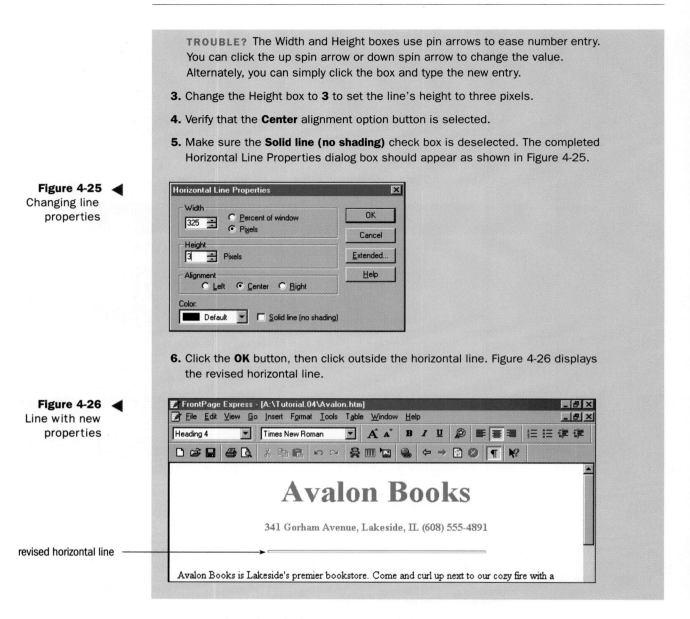

6. Click the **OK** button, then click outside the horizontal line. Figure 4-26 displays the revised horizontal line.

Figure 4-26 ◀
Line with new
properties

revised horizontal line

You are pleased with the appearance of the page so far, and are now ready to add a graphic image to the page so that it matches Mark's flyer.

Adding Graphic Images to a Web Page

Most Web browsers can display two types of graphics: inline images and external images. An **inline image** appears directly on the Web page your browser has accessed. To ensure that your inline image is displayable by most browsers, you should use either the GIF or JPEG graphics file formats. If you have a graphic in a different format, you should convert it to a GIF or a JPEG file to ensure that most browsers can display it.

An **external image** is not displayed on the Web page itself. Instead, a link—either a textual or graphical link—appears on the page that represents the image. Figure 4-27 shows the difference between inline and external images.

Figure 4-27
Inline vs.
external
graphic image

Internet Explorer can't
display files with bmp
extension so it must
start separate
software

inline image appears
on Web page

external image opens
in separate software
or on separate Web
page

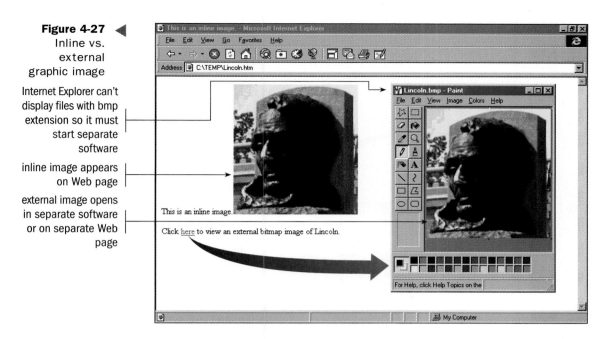

If you have used an external image on your page, a browser accessing that page either displays it on a separate page in the browser or loads software to display the image. Thus, external images have the disadvantage of requiring extra software or linking to an extra Web page, and someone reading your page must activate a link to view the image. But external images are not limited to the GIF or JPEG formats.

GIF File Formats

GIF files come in two formats: interlaced or noninterlaced. When you create your GIF file in your graphics program, you'll need to decide which format you want to use. The difference between the two formats lies in how your browser displays the graphic as it loads the page. With a **noninterlaced** GIF, the image appears one line at a time, starting from the top of the image and working down to the bottom. Figure 4-28 shows this effect. If the graphic is a large one, it might take several minutes for the entire image to appear. People who access your page might find this annoying if the part of the graphic they are interested in is located at the bottom.

Figure 4-28
Noninterlaced
image as
browser
retrieves it

top appears first

image appears one
line at a time

entire image is
retrieved

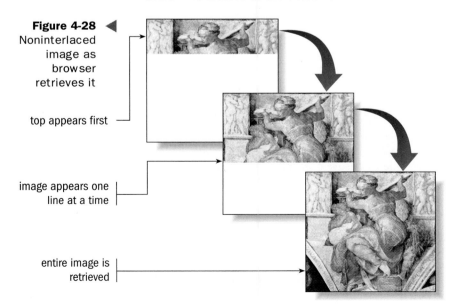

With an **interlaced** GIF, the image appears "stepwise." For example, every fifth line might appear first, followed by every sixth line, and so forth through the remaining rows. As shown in Figure 4-29, the effect of interlacing is that the graphic starts out as a blurry representation of the final image, only gradually coming into focus.

Figure 4-29 ◄
Interlaced image as browser retrieves it

a rough image appears first

image starts to show more detail

final image is crisp and detailed

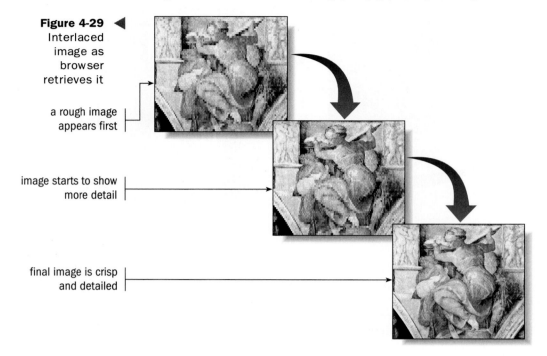

A noninterlaced graphic is always sharp but incomplete while the browser retrieves it. Interlacing is an effective format if you have a large image and want to give users a preview of the final image. They get an idea of what it looks like and can decide whether they want to wait for it to "come into focus." If you are using a graphics package to create GIF images for your Web page, you should determine whether it allows you to save the image as an interlaced GIF.

You can obtain image files from many sources on the Web; the Tutorial Assignments give you the opportunity to download and use images from Microsoft's Web Gallery.

Inserting an Inline Image

Mark has given you the image file he used in the Avalon Books flyer. You have converted it to a GIF file with one of your graphics programs. You are now ready to insert the graphic into the Avalon Books Web page.

REFERENCE window

INSERTING AN INLINE IMAGE

- Click the Insert Image button.
- Click the From File button, click the Browse button, then locate and select the image file. Click the Open button.

You want to place Mark's graphic to the left of the introductory paragraph.

To insert an inline image:

1. Click the beginning of the opening paragraph describing the bookstore to place the insertion point.

2. Click the **Insert Image** button [icon] on the Format toolbar. The Image dialog box opens. Make sure the **From File** option button is selected.

3. Click the **Browse** button, then locate and select the **Book.gif** file located in the Tutorial.04 folder on your Student Disk.

4. Click the **Open** button. The book graphic is inserted onto the page as shown in Figure 4-30.

Figure 4-30 ◀
Inserted
graphic

you want to remove
this unused space

graphic

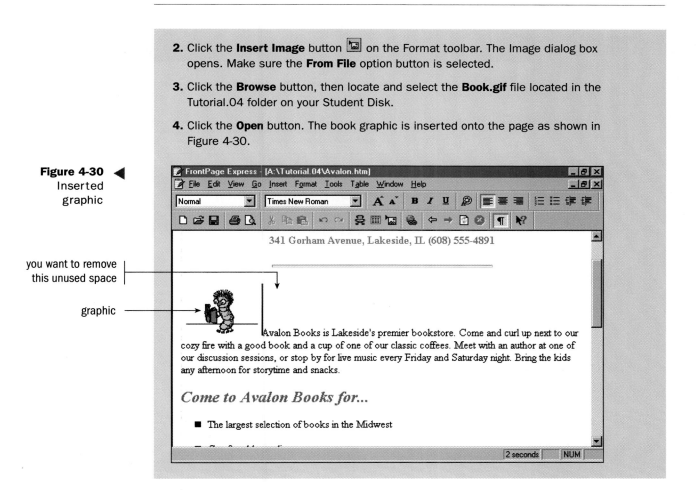

You notice there is a large amount of white space above the paragraph, and you decide to solve that problem.

Setting Image Properties

FrontPage Express gives you some control over how the image appears on your page. You can change the size of the image, add a border, change the distance between the graphic and surrounding text, and modify how the graphic is aligned relative to surrounding text.

Figure 4-31 shows examples of some of the options FrontPage Express provides for aligning the graphic with the surrounding text. Text can appear at the bottom, middle, or top of the graphic, or you can place the image at either the right or left page margin, and have the adjacent text wrap around the image. For larger graphics, you will probably want to choose either of the latter two options, allowing the text to wrap. If the image is small and you want to have it appear as part of the surrounding text, you will probably employ the bottom, middle, or top options.

Figure 4-31 ◄
Examples of
aligned text

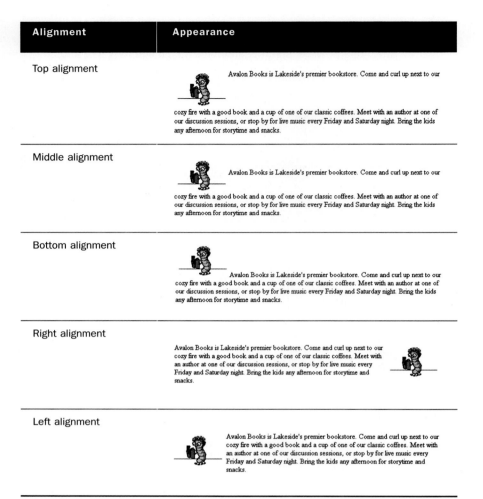

For large graphics you can use FrontPage Express to specify alternative images for the graphic. An **alternative image** is an image that gives users something to look at as they wait for the browser to finish retrieving the larger image from the Web server. You might, for example, want to include a lower-resolution version of the graphic that loads more quickly. You can also specify text that appears as the browser retrieves the graphic image. This is useful for users who are accessing your page with a text browser incapable of displaying the image. In those cases, they can still read your text description.

Another option to consider for your graphic is the space between the graphic and the surrounding text. As shown in Figure 4-32 you can set up your page to have the text closely hugging the graphic or you can add extra space between the image and the text.

Figure 4-32 ◄
Spacing
between image
and text

less space between
graphic and text

more space between
graphic and text

Considering these various options for your graphic, you decide to place the graphic to the left of the paragraph. This will remove much of the blank space between the horizontal line and the start of the paragraph. You also decide to add space between the graphic and the text in the paragraph. Finally, you decide to include a text description of the graphic.

To modify the properties of an inline image:

1. Right-click the inline image, then click **Image Properties**. The Image Properties dialog box opens to the General tab; notice the image is identified as an interlaced GIF.

2. In the Alternative Representations area, click the **Text** box and type **Come to Avalon Books!**

3. Click the **Appearance** tab. In the Layout area, click the **Alignment** list arrow, then click **left**.

4. Set the Horizontal Spacing spin box to **5** to increase the space around the image to five pixels. The completed dialog box should look like Figure 4-33.

Figure 4-33 ◄
Modifying inline
image
properties

select to place image
to left of text

five pixels between
image and space

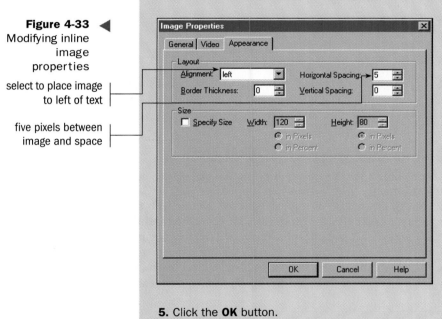

5. Click the **OK** button.

You decide to save your changes and view the page with the Internet Explorer browser to make sure everything looks good.

To view your changes in the browser:

1. Click a blank area of the page to deselect the image, then click the **Save** button 🖫 on the Standard toolbar.

2. Launch Internet Explorer.

3. Open the **Avalon.htm** page in the Internet Explorer browser. Figure 4-34 displays the revised Avalon Books page in the browser.

Figure 4-34 ◄
Inline image
in browser

text is wrapped to
right, five pixels
from graphic

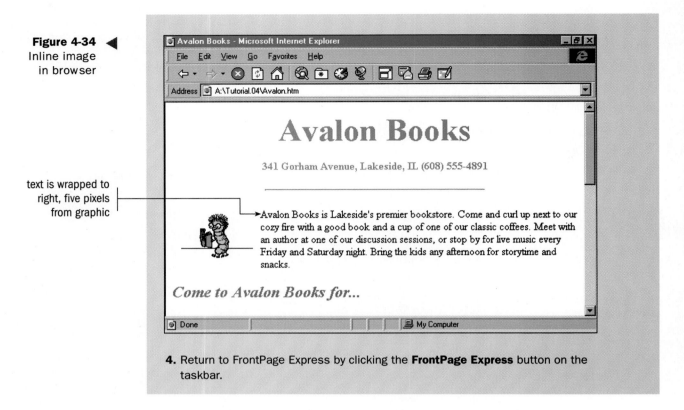

4. Return to FrontPage Express by clicking the **FrontPage Express** button on the taskbar.

Setting Background Properties

FrontPage Express allows you to specify a particular color for your background or a particular background image. When you use a graphic as your background, it appears over and over in a pattern across the document window. Many Web pages employ interesting background images to great effect. You should, however, be careful to minimize the size of the graphic image you use. A large graphic image will cause your page to take much longer to load, causing some users to cancel the page before even getting a chance to view it. Generally, the size of a graphic used for a page background should not exceed 30 kilobytes. You should also be careful not to let the background image overwhelm the text.

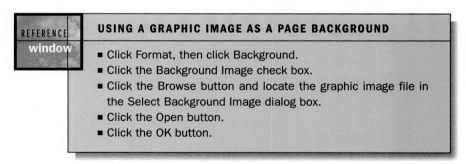

REFERENCE
window

USING A GRAPHIC IMAGE AS A PAGE BACKGROUND

- Click Format, then click Background.
- Click the Background Image check box.
- Click the Browse button and locate the graphic image file in the Select Background Image dialog box.
- Click the Open button.
- Click the OK button.

You've created an image for the Avalon Books background using the store logo. You've been careful to make the image small and unobtrusive.

To change the background of your Web page:

1. Click **Format**, then click **Background**.

2. Click the **Background Image** check box.

3. Click the **Browse** button.

4. On the Other Location tab, make sure the **From File** option button is selected. Click **Browse**, and then locate and select the file **AB.gif** in the Tutorial.04 folder on your Student Disk.

5. Click the **Open** button, then click the **OK** button.

The image background appears throughout the background. Save the page to your Student Disk and view the final version in the Internet Explorer browser.

To view the final version of your work:

1. Click the **Save** button 🔲.

2. Click the Avalon Books–Microsoft Internet Explorer browser button on the taskbar.

3. In Internet Explorer, click the **Refresh** button 🔳 to reload the page. Figure 4-35 displays the final version of the page.

Figure 4-35 ◀
Final Avalon
Books page in
browser
window

background graphic
displayed in pattern

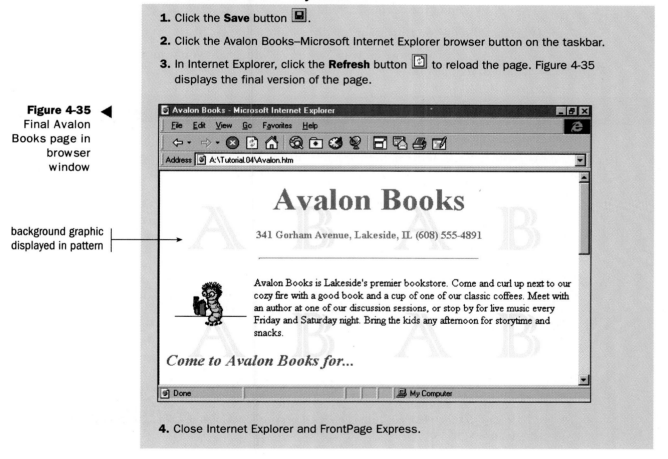

4. Close Internet Explorer and FrontPage Express.

Mark is pleased with the final version of the page and will contact his Internet Service Provider about posting it on the store's Internet account. Because you've done such a good job creating this page, he asks that you be responsible for keeping the page up-to-date. Because creating the page was so easy with FrontPage Express, you quickly agree.

Quick Check

1. Explain the difference between expressing line width in percent of window vs. pixels.

2. What is the difference between an inline graphic and an external graphic?

3. Name two file formats you can use for inline graphics.

4. If you want to use a Windows Bitmap image (file extension bmp) as an inline image on your Web page, what should you do to it first?

5. What is the difference between an interlaced graphic and a noninterlaced graphic?

6. How would you set up a horizontal line so that it is centered on a page and covers 25% of the width of the document window?

7. What should you watch out for when using a graphic image for your page background?

8. If you display a picture on your Web page, why might you want to enter a text description of that picture?

Tutorial Assignments

It's been a week since you created the Avalon Books Web page. Mark approaches you with a list of things he wants to have added and changed on the page. In the upcoming week, the bookstore will host the following events:

Monday, 10/14

A lecture given by Professor Patricia Fuller on *The Art of Maurice Sendak*

Thursday, 10/17

Peter Daynes will sign copies of his new book, *Glencoe Memories*

Friday, 10/18

Classical music by the Lakeside Quartet

Mark asks you to add these events to the page and remove the old event list. He also wants you to include a new item in the bulleted list of Avalon Books attractions: "An impressive collection of used and out-of-print books".

As for the appearance of the page, he wants you to change the color of the activity days so that they match the blue color of the section heading. He also has a new graphic image that he wants you to use in place of the book and quill pen image. He has the image stored in a file called "Book2.gif". When inserting the image he wants you to increase the space between the graphic image and the text in the surrounding paragraph. Finally, you should replace the background image with the new Avalon Books logo, found in the "AB2.gif" file. The final version of this page should appear as shown in Figure 4-36.

Figure 4-36 ◀

Avalon Books

341 Gorham Avenue, Lakeside, IL (608) 555-4891

Avalon Books is Lakeside's premier bookstore. Come and curl up next to our cozy fire with a good book and a cup of one of our classic coffees. Meet with an author at one of our discussion sessions, or stop by for live music every Friday and Saturday night. Bring the kids any afternoon for storytime and snacks.

Come to Avalon Books for...

- The largest selection of books in the Midwest
- Comfortable reading rooms
- Coffe, wines and delicious desserts as you read
- A computer lab for kids with the best educational software titles
- An impressive collection of used and out-of-print books

This week's events

Monday, 10/14

A lecture given by Professor Patricia Fuller on *The Art of Maurice Sendak*

Thursday, 10/17

Peter Daynes will sign copies of his new book, *Glencoe Memories*

Friday 10/18

Classical music by the Lakeside Quartet

To complete this tutorial assignment:

1. Open the "Avalon.htm" file that you created in this tutorial in FrontPage Express.

2. Save the page as "Avalon2" to the TAssign folder on your Student Disk. As you save the page, change the title to "Avalon Books 2".

3. Add the item "An impressive collection of used and out-of-print books" to the end of the bulleted list.

4. Delete the outdated events list and replace it with the new events list. Use the same indentation.

5. Change the color of the day to match the color of the section heading.

6. Replace the "Book.gif" graphic with the "Book2.gif" graphic found in the TAssign folder of the Tutorial.04 folder on your Student Disk. To replace a graphic, right-click the old graphic, click Image Properties, click the Browse button, and then locate and select the new graphic.

7. Change the horizontal spacing around the graphic to 9 pixels but leave the graphic to the left of the paragraph so the text wraps to the right.

8. Replace the "AB.gif" background graphic with the "AB2.gif" graphic in the TAssign folder of the Tutorial.04 folder on your Student Disk.

9. Save the Web page.

10. View the revised page in the Internet Explorer browser.

11. Print a copy of the page for your instructor.

Case Problems

1. Creating a Web Page for the River Bar Seafood Restaurant You work as a manager at the River Bar Seafood Restaurant in Woolworth, Missouri. The owner, Gwen Foucoult, has asked you to create a Web page listing the weekly specials at the restaurant. She shows you a printout of what she wants on the page, shown in Figure 4-37.

Figure 4-37

The River Bar Seafood Restaurant
211 West State St., Woolworth, 555-4532

Stop by the River Bar for the best in seafood, or call us today and order one of our delicious dishes for carryout!

This Week's Specials

Grilled Norwegian Salmon
Grilled salmon topped with Dijon mustard sauce, served with vegetables and roasted red potatoes. $15.95

Grilled Yellowfin Tuna
Grilled and topped with cilantro-lime salsa. Served with roasted red potatoes and vegetables. $15.95

Scallops with Linguine
Jumbo scallops with mushroom and herbs in lemon cream sauce. $14.95

Butterflied Shrimp
Tender shrimp lightly breaded and fried, served with vegetable and rice pilaf. $15.25

Grilled Halibut
Atlantic halibut steak seasoned with lemon and pepper and grilled, served with vegetables and roasted potatoes. $14.95

Using Figure 4-37 as a guide, create the River Bar page.
To complete this case problem:

1. Open FrontPage Express to a blank page.

2. Save the page as "Seafood.htm" to the Cases folder in the Tutorial.04 folder on your Student Disk. Give the page the title, "River Bar Specials".

3. Enter the text shown in Figure 4-37.

4. Format and center the main heading using the Heading 2 style. Then apply an interesting, applicable font to it.

5. Format and center the restaurant address using the Heading 5 style.

6. Insert a horizontal line after the restaurant address. Use the default line style.

7. Enter a brief description of the restaurant in the Normal style.

8. Format and center the heading, "This Week's Specials" with the Heading 3 style.

9. Format and left-align the name of each dish with the Heading 4 style.

10. Indent the description of each dish.

11. Use the graphic file "Fish.gif," located in the Cases folder of the Tutorial.04 folder on your Student Disk, as a background for your page.

12. Save your changes to the page.

13. Print the page for your instructor. On the back of the printed page, write the name of the font you used to format the main heading in Step 4.

2. Displaying a Lecture Outline   You are the teaching assistant for history professor, Clifford Foote. Starting this semester, he is putting his lecture outlines on the Web for students to view. He wants you to create the lecture outline for his September 22 lecture on Abraham Lincoln's life prior to the Civil War.

To create such a page you will have to use numbered lists. With FrontPage Express you specify the symbol used for the list items. You can use Roman Numerals (I, II, III, IV...), capital letters (A,B,C...), numbers (1,2,3...), and so forth. For Professor Foote's lecture outline, you will format major points with the Roman Numerals format. You will also indent minor points, listing them with capital letters.

The professor also has a photo from the Lincoln mausoleum that he wants you to place on the page. The photo has been saved to the file "Lincoln.gif".

The page should include a heading for the history course, the professor's name, and the date of the lecture. The professor also wants you to place the text on a solid blue background. The complete Web page should look like Figure 4-38.

Figure 4-38 ◀

U.S. History 1722 - 1872

Professor: Clifford Foote

Lecture outline from September 22

Life of Lincoln

I. Early Life
   A. Born 1809 in Hodgenville, KY
   B. Moved to Spencer County, IN in 1811
   C. Settled in Macon County, IL in 1831
   D. Worked as a rail splitter and grocery store clerk
   E. Captain in Black Hawk war in 1832
II. Politician and Lawyer
   A. Defeated in run for state legislature in 1832
   B. Elected to state legislature in 1834 as a Whig
   C. Admitted to the bar in 1837 and joined law partnership
   D. Served in U.S. Congress from 1846-1848
III. Rise to national prominence
   A. Campaigned for newly-formed Republican party in 1856
   B. Lincoln-Douglas debates in 1858
   C. House Divided Speech in 1858
   D. Republican presidential nominee in 1860
   E. Elected president in 1860

To complete this case problem:

1. Open a blank document in FrontPage Express.

 2. Set the page background color to Aqua. To do this, use the Background tab on the Page Properties dialog box, click the Background list arrow, and select Aqua.

3. Save the page as "Lincoln.htm" to the Cases folder in the Tutorial.04 folder on your Student Disk and specify "September 22 lecture" as the title.

4. Type the main heading "U.S. History 1722–1872," formatted with the Heading 1 style and centered on the page.

5. Change the color of the main heading to red (second row, first column in the list of basic colors).

6. Type the secondary heading "Professor: Clifford Foote," formatted with the Normal style and centered.

7. Bold the title of professor.

8. Type "Lecture outline from September 22," formatted with the Normal style, italicized, and left-aligned.

9. Type "Life of Lincoln," formatted with the Heading 3 style and left-aligned.

 10. Enter the three main outline heads as a numbered list, and use the Roman Numeral style for the list items. You can change ordered list styles on the Numbered tab of the List Properties dialog box.

 11. Within each main point, enter the subpoints and indent them.

12. Format the indented subpoints as a numbered list using the capital letter style.

13. At the beginning of the line reading "Life of Lincoln" insert the "Lincoln.gif" image, available in the Cases folder of the Tutorial.04 folder on your Student Disk.

14. Format the image so that the image will be placed to the right of the text.

15. Add a 2-pixel horizontal border to the image. Use the Border Thickness spin box.

16. Save your completed page.

17. View the page in the Internet Explorer browser and print the page.

18. Hand in the printout to your instructor.

3. Using Preformatted Text on the Weber State Weather Page You are in charge of a weather page at Weber State University. You use a program that creates temperature charts like the one shown in Figure 4-39.

Figure 4-39 ◀

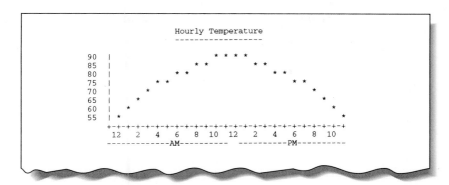

This chart uses a monospace font, which allots the same amount of space to each character. Because it is a monospace font, the characters in the chart are perfectly aligned. The normal font used by most Web browsers, however, is not monospace. Using the normal font would result in a chart that is out of alignment. You can solve this problem by using another of the styles provided with FrontPage Express called "Formatted." The Formatted tag displays text in a monospace font. The temperature chart has been placed in the file "Temp.txt" in the Cases folder of the Tutorial.04 folder on your Student Disk. By copying the temperature chart from the Temp.txt file and pasting it into FrontPage Express, try to create a Web page detailing the previous day's temperature variations.

To complete this case problem:

1. Open FrontPage Express to a blank page.

2. Save the page as "Temp" in the Cases folder in the Tutorial.04 folder on your Student Disk and enter "Weber State Weather Page" as the page title.

3. Return to the document window and type the text "Yesterday's Temperature Chart" at the top of the page.

4. Format the heading with the Heading 1 style and center it on the page.

5. Beneath the heading, type yesterday's date.

6. Center the date and format it with the Heading 5 style.

7. Insert a horizontal line beneath the date.

 8. Start Notepad (click the Start button, point to Programs, point to Accessories, and then click Notepad). Open the file "Temp.txt" in the Cases folder of the Tutorial.04 folder on your Student Disk.

 9. Copy the temperature chart (click Edit, click Select All, click Edit again, and then click Copy).

10. Close Notepad and return to the Temp page.

 11. Insert a new paragraph underneath the horizontal line and format it with the Formatted tag on the Change Style list.

12. Click the Align Left button to align any formatted text with the left edge of the window.

13. Paste the temperature chart into the new line (click Edit, then click Paste).

14. Save the changes you made to the Temp page.

15. View the page in the Internet Explorer browser.

16. Print the page and hand in the printout to your instructor.

4. Creating a Realty Listing You work as a real estate agent for TK Realty. Just recently your company has started putting listings on the World Wide Web. You're responsible for creating your own listing. One of the houses you want to create a Web page for is a lake-front house located at 22 Northshore Drive. The owners have given you this description, which they want placed on the page: "This is a must see. Large waterfront home overlooking Lake Mills. It comes complete with 3 bedrooms, a huge master bedroom, hot tub, family room, large office, and three-car garage. Wood boat ramp. Great condition."
The main points about the house are:

- 2,300 sq. feet
- 15 years old
- Updated electrical and heat
- Asking price: $230,000

You also have a photo of the house, saved as "House.jpg" in the Cases folder on the Tutorial.04 folder on your Student Disk. Using this information, create a page describing the house to interested house-hunters. You may choose any design for the page, but it must include the following elements:

1. A main heading

2. The photo of the house

3. A bulleted list describing the features of the house

4. A paragraph containing the owner's description

5. Information on how to contact you, in italics

Internet
Explorer

You can make your page more interesting by inserting lines or other graphics that you download off the Web. Start Internet Explorer, and connect to the http://www.microsoft.com/gallery page. This page is maintained by Microsoft, and features free graphics, sounds, and other objects useful to Web page designers. Click the Images link and then scroll through the graphics and download a horizontal line and an image or two to include on your page; perhaps as a background. Figure 4-40 shows the Images page.

Figure 4-40 ◀

click any image link to save it to your Student Disk and then insert it in your Web page

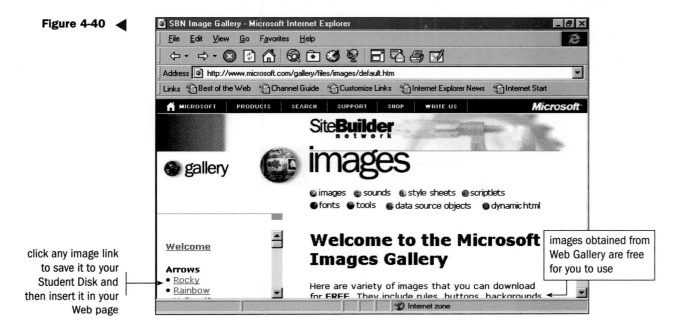

Save the page you create in the Cases folder on the Tutorial.04 folder on your Student Disk with the name "Realty". When you submit the page to your instructor, indicate which graphics or objects you used from the Web Gallery site.

Creating a Hypertext Document

Creating a Web Presentation

In this tutorial you will:

- Create bookmarks within a Web page

- Create hypertext links to bookmarks on the same Web page

- Learn the principles of structuring a Web presentation

- Create links to other Web pages on the same computer

- Create links to bookmarks on other Web pages

- Create links to other Web pages on the Internet

- Create links to e-mail addresses

- Publish a page on the Web

 CASE

The Findlay Farmhouse Bed and Breakfast

Prince Edward Island in Canada is a popular summer vacation spot. The island is known for its natural beauty and peaceful setting. Visitors to the island can choose their lodging from several attractive inns and picturesque bed and breakfasts. One of the most popular bed and breakfasts on the island is the Findlay Farmhouse outside of Summerside. The proprietors, Ian and Fiona Findlay, have owned the inn for many years. Several years ago they bought a computer to help manage their business, and recently they set up an Internet connection. The Findlays want to advertise their bed and breakfast on the Internet in hopes that it will generate new business. Fiona has started creating a page for the Findlay Farmhouse, and she hopes you can help finish it.

Fiona explains that she has organized information about the Findlay Farmhouse and its surroundings into five topics, each with a Heading 2 style heading, with the following titles:

- Your home on Prince Edward Island

- What are they saying about us?

- Area attractions

- How do I get there?

- For more information

Fiona tells you that she has also created two supplementary Web pages, Bio and Events, which contain information on the Findlay family and area events. She would like users to be able to access the Bio and Events pages from the Findlay Farmhouse page. She would also like users to be able to jump to other pages on Prince Edward Island from the Findlay Farmhouse page, as well as to be able to send her e-mail messages. You tell her she can accomplish all this with hypertext links. Then you suggest that she could make her page, which is rather long, more user-friendly by adding links that help users move more easily around the page. Fiona agrees that would be a good idea, so the two of you get to work.

SESSION

5.1

In this session you'll learn how to create bookmarks within a Web page and to create hypertext links to those bookmarks.

Setting Bookmarks

As you've seen by browsing the Web, Web pages contain hypertext, or links that you can select, usually by clicking a mouse, to jump instantly to another location. In addition to making access to other documents easy, hypertext links provide some important organizational benefits.

For example, when your Web page is too long to fit on a single screen, you can help users quickly locate the information they need by providing hypertext links to important points within the page. A typical screen can display only a small section of a long page, and this could be a problem for users in a hurry. Because many Web users glance at a page and then move on, you should make your page's topics as accessible as possible. You can do this by placing links at the beginning that point to the main topics on the page. When readers click the link, they jump to that section of the document.

To create links that jump to a specific point on a Web page, you must first insert a bookmark at the destination location. A **bookmark**, also called an **anchor** or **target**, is a reference point that identifies a specific location on the page. Once you insert a bookmark, you can then refer to that particular location. You create the link and indicate the bookmark to which the link points. Figure 5-1 illustrates how the bookmark you create will work as a reference point for a link.

Figure 5-1 ◀
Link pointing
to bookmark
within the
same Web
document

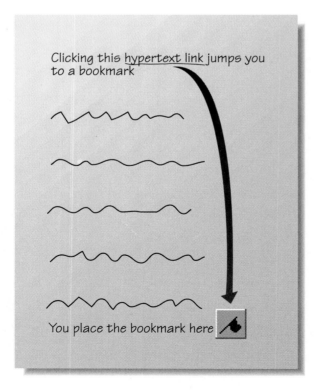

Clicking this <u>hypertext link</u> jumps you
to a bookmark

You place the bookmark here

Bookmarks do not appear in the browser, but you can view them in FrontPage Express.

For the Findlay Web page, you decide to create five bookmarks—one bookmark at each of the five section headings of the document. You can then create links at the beginning of the page that point to each of the five bookmarks. A user can click one of the links to jump to the bookmark it targets without having to scroll through the page to reach it. Figure 5-2 shows the location of the five bookmarks you will create on the Findlay Web page.

Figure 5-2
Bookmarks in
the Findlay
Web page

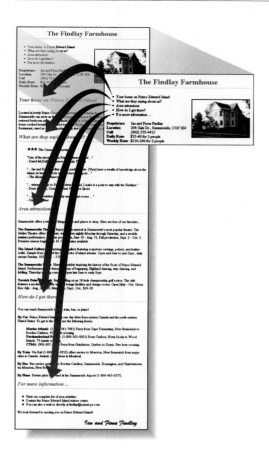

Fiona stored her page as Findlay.htm. You'll open the file and save it with a new name, Findlay2.htm, so you don't alter the contents of the original—just in case.

To open the Findlay.htm file in FrontPage Express and save it with a new name:

1. Launch FrontPage Express and insert your Student Disk in the drive.

2. Click the **Open** button 🖻.

3. Click the **Browse** button, locate and select the **Findlay** file from the Tutorial.05 folder on your Student Disk, and then click the **Open** button.

4. Click **File**, then click **Save As**.

5. Click the **As File** button.

6. Type **Findlay2** in the File name box, then click the **Save** button.

7. Scroll down the entire page to view the location of the five section headings.

First you will create the five bookmarks. FrontPage Express makes it very easy for you to create a bookmark. The first bookmark you create will be for the heading "Your home on Prince Edward Island".

To set a bookmark in your Web page:

1. Scroll the page to the first section heading, "Your home on Prince Edward Island". Make sure you are viewing the section heading, not the bulleted list.

2. Click at the start of the section heading to place the blinking insertion point at the beginning of the line.

TROUBLE? If you click too far to the left of the section heading, you highlight the heading. Make sure the blinking insertion point is just to the left of the heading.

3. Click **Edit**, then click **Bookmark**.

4. Type **Your home** in the Bookmark Name box as shown in Figure 5-3.

Figure 5-3 ◄
Setting a
bookmark

bookmark name ——————

click here to insert
bookmark

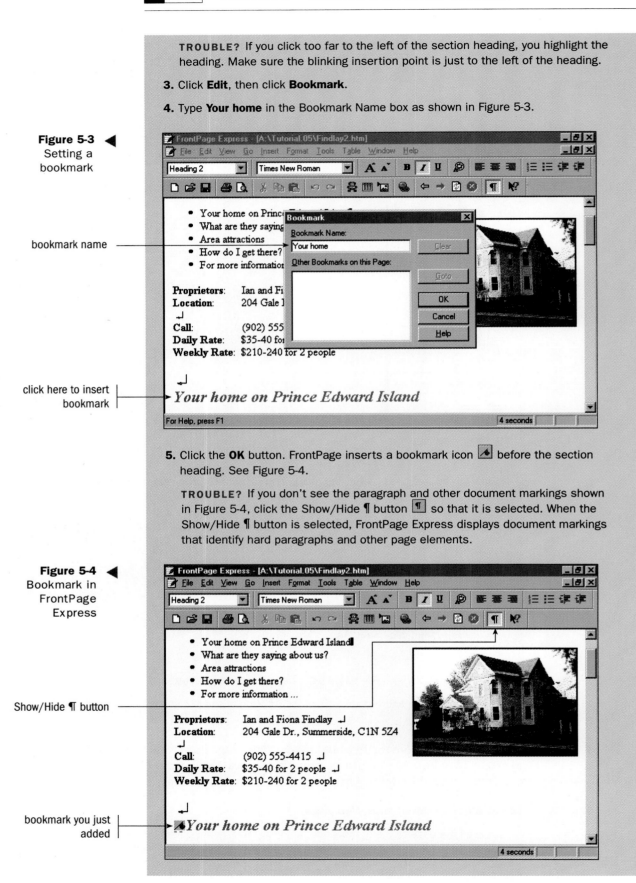

5. Click the **OK** button. FrontPage inserts a bookmark icon before the section heading. See Figure 5-4.

TROUBLE? If you don't see the paragraph and other document markings shown in Figure 5-4, click the Show/Hide ¶ button so that it is selected. When the Show/Hide ¶ button is selected, FrontPage Express displays document markings that identify hard paragraphs and other page elements.

Figure 5-4 ◄
Bookmark in
FrontPage
Express

Show/Hide ¶ button —————

bookmark you just
added

The bookmark icon ▨ indicates the presence of a bookmark on a Web page. This icon appears only in FrontPage Express—not in the browser. If you ever forget the name you gave the bookmark, you can right-click it and click Bookmark Properties to view the bookmark name.

You're ready to add the rest of the bookmarks, one for each section heading. You can type in any characters or blank spaces into the bookmark name. Be sure you pay attention to case. A bookmark named "home" is different from one named "HOME".

To add the other section heading bookmarks:

1. Scroll down to the heading, "What are they saying about us?" then click the left side of the heading.

2. Click **Edit**, click **Bookmark**, type **Reviews**, and then click the **OK** button.

3. Scroll down to the heading, "Area attractions", then click the left side of the heading.

4. Add a bookmark named **Attractions**.

5. Scroll down to the heading, "How do I get there?" then add a bookmark named **Travel**.

6. Scroll down to the heading, "For more information", then add a bookmark named **More Info**.

Now all five bookmarks are in place. You are ready to create hypertext links to the bookmarks.

Creating Hypertext Links to Bookmarks

You can change existing text to a hypertext link by simply selecting the text, then clicking the Create or Edit Hyperlink button ▨ and indicating the bookmark to which you want the link to point.

Creating Links

The Findlay Farmhouse page begins with a bulleted list that corresponds to the five section headings. By changing the items in this list to hypertext links, you enable users to jump directly to a bookmark. You begin by creating the link to the first section heading, which has a bookmark named Your home.

To change the list item to a hypertext link:

1. Scroll to the top of the page.

2. Select **Your home on Prince Edward Island** from the bulleted list.

3. Click the **Create or Edit Hyperlink button** ▨. Make sure the Open Pages tab is selected and the Findlay Farmhouse page is selected.

4. Click the **Bookmark** list arrow.

5. Click **Your home** from the list of named bookmarks in the current document, as shown in Figure 5-5.

Figure 5-5 ◀
Selecting a
bookmark for a
hypertext link

Open Pages tab is
active

bookmark list

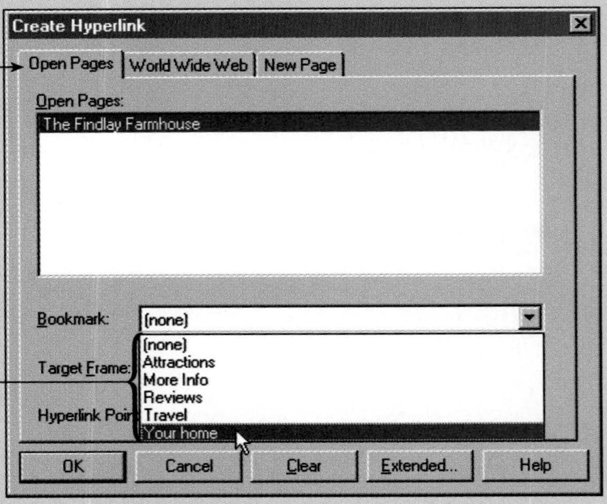

6. Click the **OK** button, then click the page to deselect the link. The text, "Your home on Prince Edward Island", is now underlined and in a different color.

7. Move the mouse pointer over the linked text. Notice the link's target appears in the status bar. See Figure 5-6.

Figure 5-6 ◀
Hypertext link
you just added

move pointer over
hypertext

hypertext link

link's target, the
bookmark Your home,
appears when you
point at link

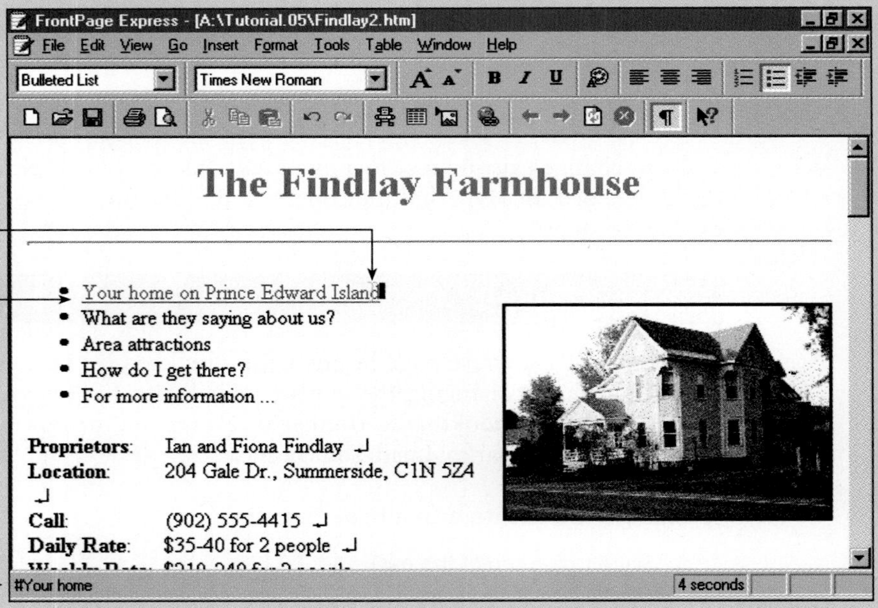

Note that the name of the bookmark is prefaced by a pound sign (#). All bookmark names are prefaced by this symbol to differentiate them from other names such as filenames or document locations.

Using the same technique you just learned, turn the other items in the bulleted list to hypertext links.

To convert the rest of the list to hypertext links:

1. Select **What are they saying about us?** then link the text to the **Reviews** bookmark.

2. Select **Area attractions** then link the text to the **Attractions** bookmark.

3. Select **How do I get there?** then link the text to the **Travel** bookmark.

Internet Explorer

4. Select **For more information...** then link the text to the **More Info** bookmark. Figure 5-7 shows the completed list of hypertext links.

Figure 5-7 ◀
Inserted links

complete list of links ────────▶

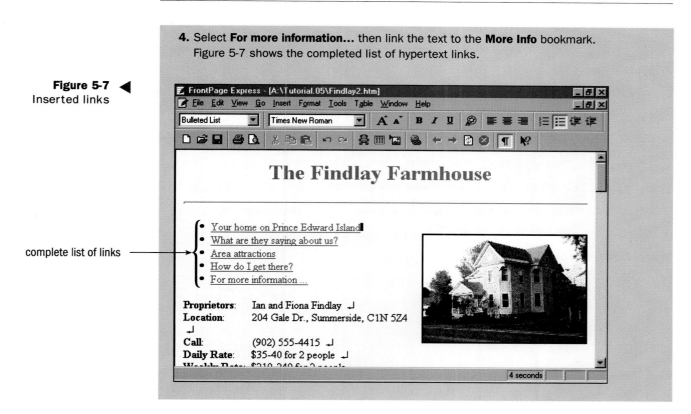

Users can now use the bulleted list to jump to any heading on the Findlay page. You notice that there is no easy way of returning to the top of the Findlay Farmhouse page, aside from scrolling. You realize that it might be helpful to include a hypertext link pointing to the top of the page. This is a common feature of long pages. To create this hypertext link, you first must create a bookmark at the top of the page.

To add a bookmark to the top of the page:

1. If necessary, scroll to the top of the document, then click to the left of the main heading, **The Findlay Farmhouse.**

2. Click **Edit**, then click **Bookmark.**

3. Type **Top** in the Bookmark Name box, then click the **OK** button.

Now you create a new hypertext link at the bottom of the document that points to the bookmark you just created at the top of the page.

To insert a link to the bookmark at the top of the document:

1. Scroll down to the bottom of the page.

2. Click at the end of the line: **We look forward to meeting you on Prince Edward Island!** then press **Enter.**

3. Type **Return to the top of the page**, then select the line you just typed.

4. Click the **Create or Edit Hyperlink button** .

5. On the Open Pages tab, click **Top** from the list of bookmarks.

6. Click the **OK** button. Figure 5-8 displays the linked text that appears on the Web page.

Figure 5-8 ◀
Link to the top
of the page

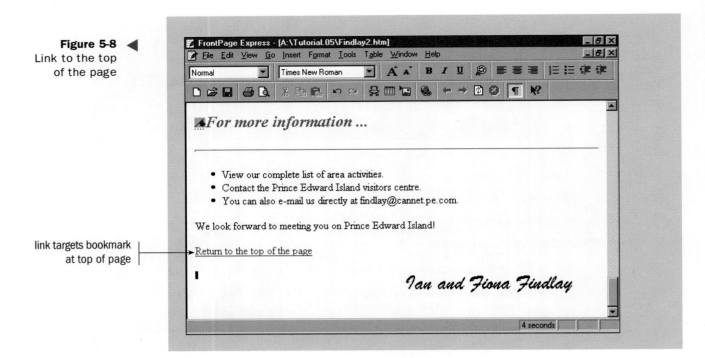

link targets bookmark
at top of page

You are finished adding links that help users navigate the Findlay page.

Testing Links

Once you have entered links into a hypertext document, you should test them in the Internet Explorer browser to make sure they target the correct bookmarks.

To test the links in the Internet Explorer browser:

1. Click the **Save** button 🖫 and then start the Internet Explorer browser and open the Findlay2 page in the Tutorial.05 folder on your Student Disk in the browser. You don't need to connect to the Internet to open this page from your Student Disk. You can now verify that your hypertext links are working correctly.

2. Move the mouse pointer over the list item, **Your home on Prince Edward Island.** The mouse pointer changes to 🖑 and the status bar shows the target. See Figure 5-9.

Figure 5-9 ◀
Testing a link

pointer when you
point at hypertext link

bookmark in status
bar

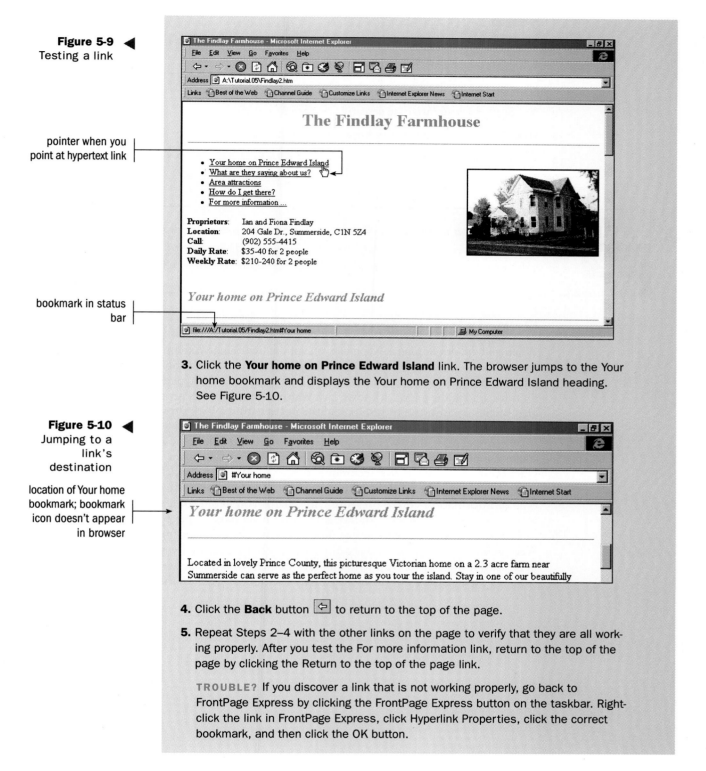

3. Click the **Your home on Prince Edward Island** link. The browser jumps to the Your home bookmark and displays the Your home on Prince Edward Island heading. See Figure 5-10.

Figure 5-10 ◀
Jumping to a
link's
destination

location of Your home
bookmark; bookmark
icon doesn't appear
in browser

4. Click the **Back** button ⇦ to return to the top of the page.

5. Repeat Steps 2–4 with the other links on the page to verify that they are all working properly. After you test the For more information link, return to the top of the page by clicking the Return to the top of the page link.

TROUBLE? If you discover a link that is not working properly, go back to FrontPage Express by clicking the FrontPage Express button on the taskbar. Right-click the link in FrontPage Express, click Hyperlink Properties, click the correct bookmark, and then click the OK button.

You're finished adding hypertext links to the Findlay Web page. Users can now efficiently navigate to different locations on the page. You decide to take a break.

To close all the Internet Explorer windows:

1. Close FrontPage Express.

2. Close Internet Explorer.

Quick Check

1. What is a bookmark? When is it necessary?
2. How do you create a bookmark with FrontPage Express?
3. Are bookmark names case sensitive or case insensitive?
4. How is the presence of a bookmark indicated in a URL?
5. Where do you test links?

SESSION 5.2

In this session you will create a Web presentation that consists of several documents connected together with hypertext links. You'll learn how to control the development of such multidocument structures through the technique of storyboarding.

Principles of Storyboarding

When you are developing a Web page, one of the first things you must ask yourself is whether you intend to develop and include additional pages on related topics. A structure that contains the primary Web page, additional related pages, and the hypertext links that allow users to move among the pages, is known as a **Web presentation**. Web presentations are usually created by the same person or group, and the pages within a Web presentation usually have the same look and feel.

When you plan your Web presentation, you should determine exactly how you want to relate the pages using hypertext links. Charting the relationship between all the pages in your Web presentation is a technique known as **storyboarding**. Storyboarding your Web pages before you create links helps you determine which structure will work best for the type of information you're presenting and helps you avoid some common problems. You want to make sure readers can navigate easily from page to page without getting lost.

Fiona reminds you that she has developed two other pages for the Findlay Farmhouse Web presentation: Bio, a directory of people on the island, and Events, a list of activities and organizations in the area. Fiona would like readers who access her page to be able to reach either of these pages from the main Findlay Farmhouse page, as shown in Figure 5-11.

Figure 5-11 ◀
Findlay
Farmhouse
Web
presentation

Findlay Farmhouse page

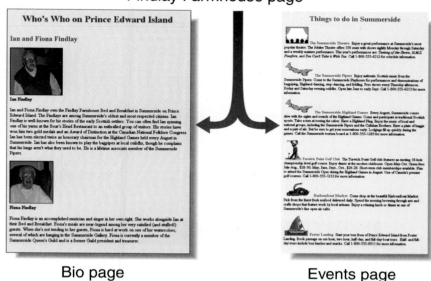

Bio page   Events page

You tell Fiona she should think about the basic principles of structuring Web presentations to decide how to link the three pages together.

Linear Structures

Web presentations can be structured in a number of ways. Examining basic structures can help you decide how to design your Web presentation. Figure 5-12 shows a storyboard for one common structure, the **linear structure**, in which each page is linked to the next and previous pages in an ordered chain of pages.

Figure 5-12 ◀
Linear
structure

in this structure you
can jump only from
one page to the next
or previous page

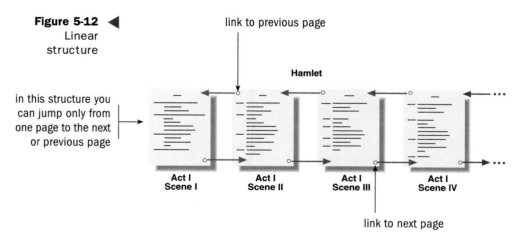

link to previous page

Hamlet

Act I
Scene I

Act I
Scene II

Act I
Scene III

Act I
Scene IV

link to next page

You might use this type of structure in Web pages that have a well-defined order. For example, if you are trying to create a Web presentation of Shakespeare's *Hamlet*, you could create a single Web page for each scene from the play. By using a linear structure, you make it easy for users to progress back and forth through the play. Each hypertext link takes them to either the previous scene or the next scene.

You might, however, want to make it easier for users to return immediately to the opening scene rather than backtrack through several scenes. Figure 5-13 shows how you could include a link in each page that jumps directly back to the first page.

Figure 5-13 ◀
Augmented
linear
structure

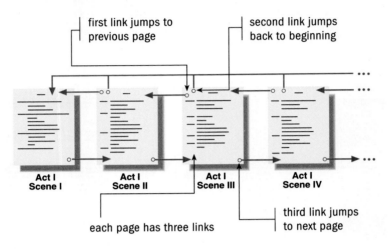

Hierarchical Structures

Another popular structure is the hierarchical structure of Web pages shown in Figure 5-14. A **hierarchical structure** starts with a general topic that includes links to more specific topics. Each specific topic includes links to yet more specialized topics, and so on. In a hierarchical structure, users can move easily from the general to the specific and back again.

Figure 5-14 ◀
Hierarchical
structure

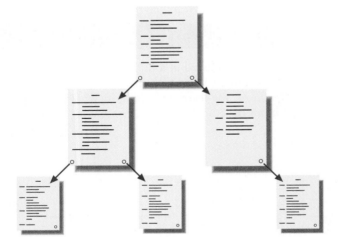

As with the linear structure, including a link to the top of the structure on each page gives users an easy way back to the hierarchy tree. Figure 5-15 shows a storyboard for this kind of Web presentation.

Figure 5-15 ◀
Augmented
hierarchical
structure

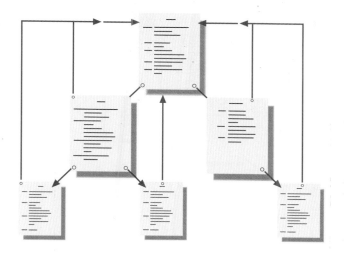

Mixed Structures

You can also combine structures. Figure 5-16 shows a hierarchical structure in which each page level is related in a linear structure. You might use this system for the *Hamlet* Web site to let the user move from scene to scene linearly or from a specific scene to the general act to the overall play.

Figure 5-16 ◀
Combination
of linear and
hierarchical
structures

overall structure is
hierarchical

the scenes

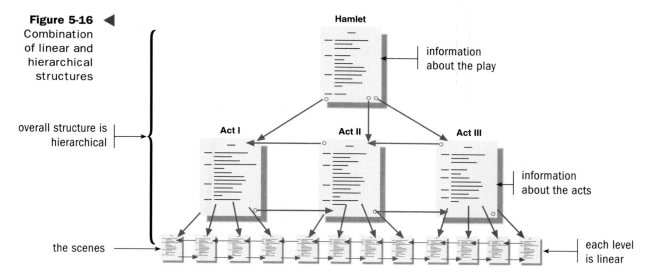

As these examples show, a little foresight can go a long way in making your Web pages easier to use. The best time to organize a structure is when you first start creating multiple pages and those pages are small and easy to manage. If you're not careful, you might end up with a structure like the one shown in Figure 5-17.

Figure 5-17 ◀
Web
presentation
with no
coherent
structure

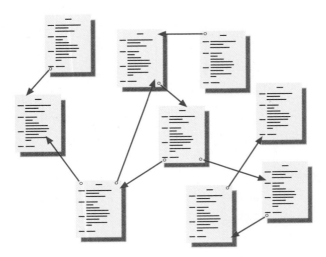

Many of the pages in this Web presentation are isolated from one another, and there is no clear path from one document to another. A user won't know what content to expect when jumping from one link to another. Nor are users ever sure if they have viewed all possible pages.

Creating Links to Other Documents

You and Fiona discuss the type of structure that will work best for the Findlay Farmhouse Web presentation. Fiona wants users to access the Findlay Farmhouse page first, and then both the Bio page and the Events page from the Findlay Farmhouse page. To make navigation easy, she wants hypertext links on both the Bio and Events pages that jump back to the Findlay Farmhouse page. Fiona doesn't see a need to include a hypertext link between the Bio page and the Events page. Based on her recommendations, you draw the storyboard shown in Figure 5-18. Fiona looks it over and agrees that this is what she had in mind.

Figure 5-18 ◀
Structure of
the Findlay
Farmhouse Web
presentation

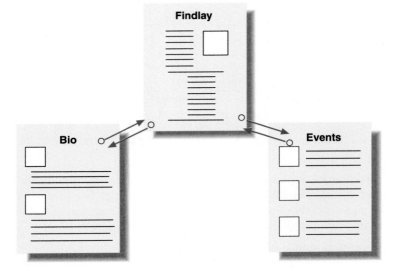

Opening Multiple Documents

Fiona's Web presentation has three pages, and you'd like to be able to work with all of them at once. Like most word processors, with FrontPage Express you can have several documents open at once; you use the Window menu to switch from document to document. You need to open Findlay2 (the page you were working on in Session 5.1), Bio, and Events, and then you need to save Bio as Bio2 and Events as Events2, so you don't alter the original files.

To open and rename the Findlay files:

1. Start FrontPage Express.

2. Click the **Open** button ⬚.

3. Locate and open **Findlay2.htm** in the Tutorial.05 folder on your Student Disk.

4. Locate and open **Bio.htm** from the Tutorial.05 folder on your Student Disk.

   TROUBLE? If the file extension "htm" doesn't appear on your screen, don't worry. Your computer is configured to hide file extensions.

5. Click **File**, click **Save As**, then click the **As File** button.

6. Type **Bio2** in the File name box, then click the **Save** button.

7. Locate and open **Events.htm** from the Tutorial.05 folder on your Student Disk.

8. Save the Events file as **Events2**.

9. Click **Window** on the menu bar. Figure 5-19 shows the Events2 page as the active document, with the other open pages listed on the bottom of the Window menu.

   TROUBLE? If an untitled Normal page is also open, click that window on the Window menu and then close that window before you proceed.

Figure 5-19 ◀
Opening
multiple Web
documents

Findlay Web pages on
Window menu

click to open Findlay2
document

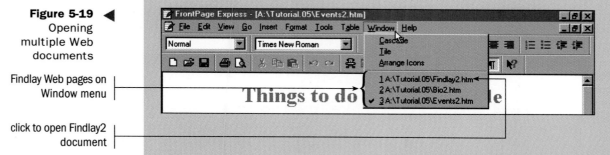

10. Click the **Findlay2** page in the Window menu to make the Findlay Farmhouse page the active document.

Creating a Hypertext Link Between Two Documents

You create a link between two documents in the same way you created a link to a bookmark within the same document—using the Create or Edit Hyperlink button ⬚. Instead of clicking a bookmark, however, you select the document that is the destination of the link. If the document is open, you can use the Open Pages tab, but if the document is not open, use the World Wide Web tab. Fiona's three pages are all open in FrontPage Express. You are ready to create links between the pages. You decide to start by linking the Findlay2 page to the Bio2 page.

To create a hypertext link to the Bio2 page:

1. Locate the Proprietors information just below the bulleted list at the top of the page.

2. Select the text **Ian and Fiona Findlay**.

3. Click the **Create or Edit Hyperlink** button ⬚.

4. On the Open Pages tab, click **Ian and Fiona Findlay**, the title of the Bio2 page. See Figure 5-20.

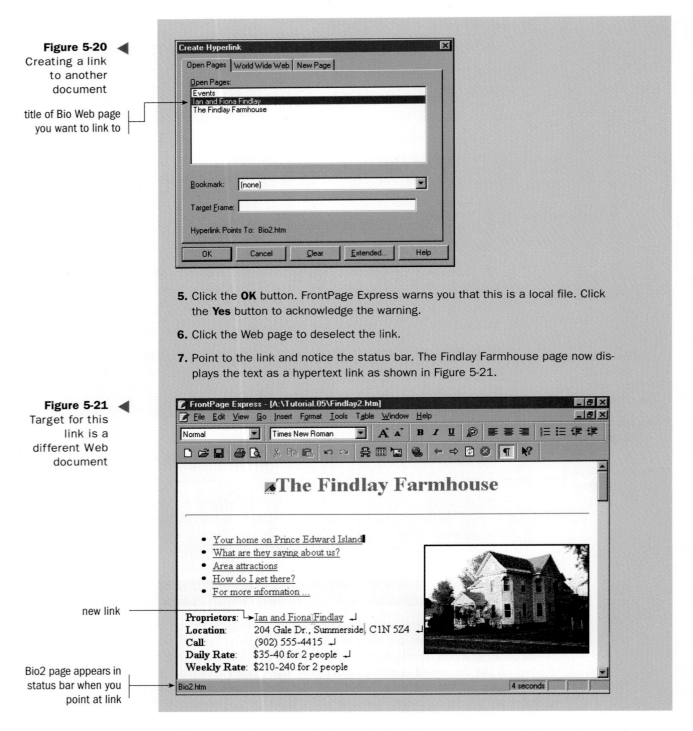

Figure 5-20 ◀
Creating a link
to another
document

title of Bio Web page
you want to link to

5. Click the **OK** button. FrontPage Express warns you that this is a local file. Click the **Yes** button to acknowledge the warning.

6. Click the Web page to deselect the link.

7. Point to the link and notice the status bar. The Findlay Farmhouse page now displays the text as a hypertext link as shown in Figure 5-21.

Figure 5-21 ◀
Target for this
link is a
different Web
document

new link

Bio2 page appears in
status bar when you
point at link

Clicking the link shown in Figure 5-21 will jump you to the Bio2 page in your browser. You'll test this link later. Now you are ready to create a hypertext link to the Events2 page.

To create a hypertext link to the Events2 page:

1. Scroll down the document window to the **For more information...** section.

2. Select the text **View our complete list of area activities**.

3. Click the **Create or Edit Hyperlink** button 🔗.

4. On the Open Pages tab, click **Events**.

5. Click the **OK** button, click the **Yes** button, and then click the Web page to deselect the link. The text referring to area activities should now be converted to hypertext as is displayed in Figure 5-22.

Figure 5-22 ◀
Link to Events2
page

link this text to
Events2 page

page is scrolled to
bottom

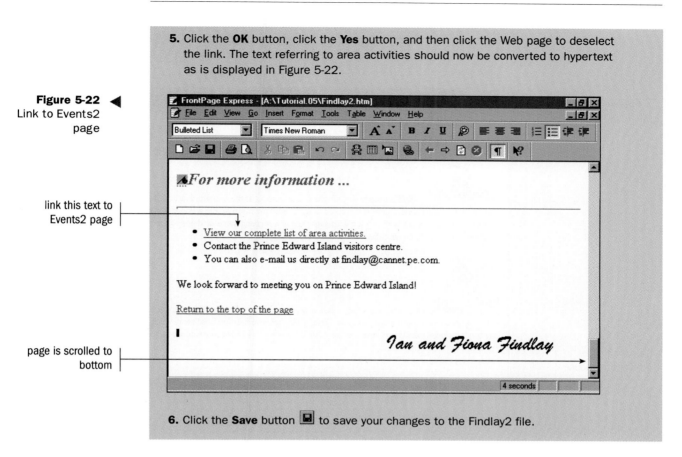

6. Click the **Save** button 🖫 to save your changes to the Findlay2 file.

Now insert links in the Bio2 and Events2 pages that point back to the Findlay2 page. Start with the Bio2 page first.

To create a hypertext link from the Bio2 page to the Findlay2 page:

1. Click **Window**, then click the **Bio2** page.

2. Select the text **Findlay Farmhouse Bed and Breakfast** located in the paragraph below the picture of Ian Findlay.

3. Click the **Create or Edit Hyperlink** button 🖼.

4. On the Open Pages tab, click **The Findlay Farmhouse**. Click the **OK** button, then click the **Yes** button.

5. Click the **Save** button 🖫.

Finally, you need to create the hypertext link from the Events2 page back to the Findlay2 page. Because there is no text on the Events2 page that specifically references the Findlays or their bed and breakfast, you will have to insert new text as the hypertext link.

To create a hypertext link from the Events2 page to the Findlay2 page:

1. Click **Window**, then click **Events2**.

2. Scroll to the bottom of the document window and click to the right of the description of Foster Landing, then press **Enter**.

3. Type **Go to the Findlay Farmhouse page**. Select the text you just typed.

4. Click the **Create or Edit Hyperlink** button 🖼.

5. On the Open Pages tab, click **The Findlay Farmhouse**, click the **OK** button, and then click the **Yes** button. Click outside the link to deselect it. Figure 5-23 shows the page with the newly inserted hypertext link.

Figure 5-23
Link to Findlay
Farmhouse
page

location of link to
Findlay Farmhouse
page

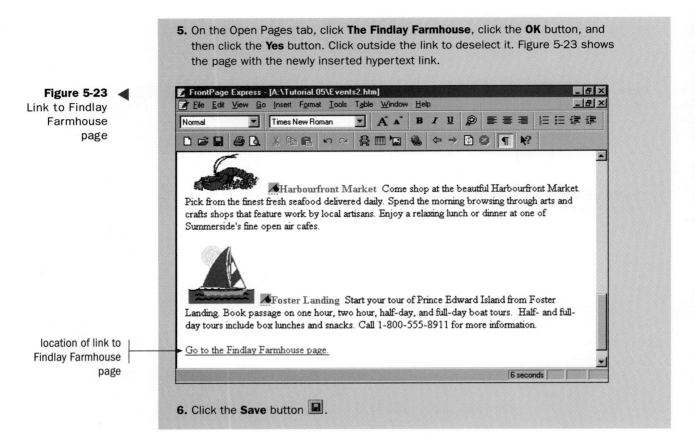

6. Click the **Save** button 🖫.

The hypertext links between the pages in the Findlay Farmhouse Web presentation are now in place.

Testing Hypertext Links to Other Documents

Now that the hypertext links are in place, you should return to the Findlay Farmhouse page in the browser and then test the links among the three pages to verify that they are working properly.

To test your links:

1. Start the Internet Explorer browser and open the Findlay2 page in the browser.

2. Click the hypertext link **Ian and Fiona Findlay**. The Bio2 page opens in the browser.

3. Scroll down the document window and click the hypertext link, **Findlay Farmhouse Bed and Breakfast**. You return to the Findlay Farmhouse page.

4. Click the **For More Information...** hypertext link to jump down the Findlay Farmhouse page to that heading.

5. Click the hypertext link, **View our complete list of area activities**. The Events2 page is displayed in the browser.

6. Scroll to the bottom of the document window and click the hypertext link, **Go to the Findlay Farmhouse page**. You return to the Findlay Farmhouse page.

The links are working properly.

Creating Links to Bookmarks Within Other Documents

You can create links not just to other documents, but also to specific points within documents. The destination point must have a bookmark, and the hypertext link you insert must point to that bookmark. You already know how to link to bookmarks within the same document, but now you'll see how to link to bookmarks in a different document.

You and Fiona discuss creating links from the individual items on the Findlay Farmhouse page that correspond to events on the Events page. You both agree that it would be a good idea. To save you time, the Events page already contains bookmarks for the theatre, bagpiping, golf, and so on. Using those bookmarks, you decide to add links from activities mentioned on the Findlay2 page to the corresponding activity on the Events2 page.

To insert a link to an event on the Events2 page:

1. Return to FrontPage Express and use the Window menu to return to the **Findlay2** page.

2. Scroll to the **Area attractions** section.

3. Select the text **The Summerside Theatre**, then click the **Create or Edit Hyperlink** button ⬛.

4. On the Open Pages tab, click **Events**.

5. Click the **Bookmark** list arrow. A list of bookmarks on the Events2 page appears. See Figure 5-24.

Figure 5-24 ◀
List of bookmarks in Events2 page

name of page to which you are linking

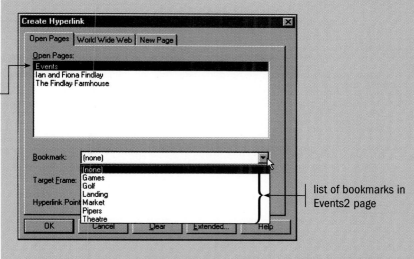

list of bookmarks in Events2 page

6. Click the **Theatre** bookmark. The bookmark name is appended to the filename, separated by a pound sign (#). See Figure 5-25.

Figure 5-25 ◀
Filename and
bookmark

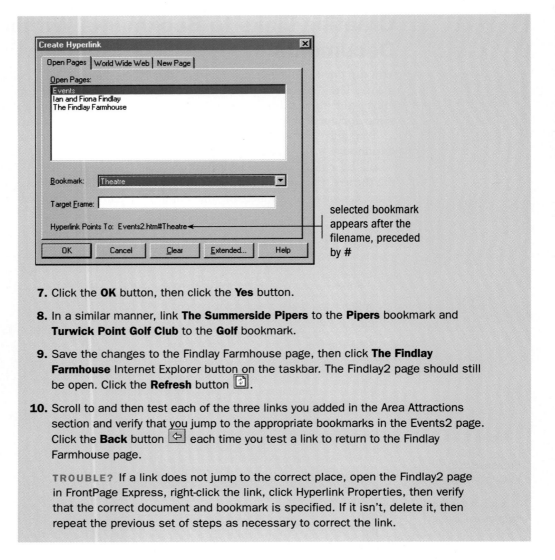

selected bookmark
appears after the
filename, preceded
by #

7. Click the **OK** button, then click the **Yes** button.

8. In a similar manner, link **The Summerside Pipers** to the **Pipers** bookmark and **Turwick Point Golf Club** to the **Golf** bookmark.

9. Save the changes to the Findlay Farmhouse page, then click **The Findlay Farmhouse** Internet Explorer button on the taskbar. The Findlay2 page should still be open. Click the **Refresh** button ⟳.

10. Scroll to and then test each of the three links you added in the Area Attractions section and verify that you jump to the appropriate bookmarks in the Events2 page. Click the **Back** button ⇦ each time you test a link to return to the Findlay Farmhouse page.

   TROUBLE? If a link does not jump to the correct place, open the Findlay2 page in FrontPage Express, right-click the link, click Hyperlink Properties, then verify that the correct document and bookmark is specified. If it isn't, delete it, then repeat the previous set of steps as necessary to correct the link.

You have now inserted links to the Findlays' Web page that make it easy for users to navigate through the presentation. You decide to take a break.

To close all the Internet Explorer windows:

1. Close the browser.

2. Close FrontPage Express.

Quick Check

1. What is storyboarding? Why is it important in creating a Web page presentation?

2. What is a linear structure? Draw a diagram of a linear structure and give an example of how to use it.

3. What is a hierarchical structure? Draw a diagram of a hierarchical structure and give an example of how to use it.

4. How do you create a hypertext link to another open document with FrontPage Express?

5. How do you create a hypertext link to a bookmark in another open document with FrontPage Express?

SESSION

5.3

In this session you will learn how to create hypertext links to Web pages on the Internet and to an e-mail address. Finally, you'll learn to publish your Web presentation.

Linking to Web Pages

Until now you've worked with files all located on the same computer. However, you make use of the real power of the Web when you start linking your document with Web pages on other computers located anywhere from across the hall to across the world. The technique for creating a hypertext link to a Web page on a different computer is very similar to the technique you use to link to documents on your computer, except that instead of specifying the document's filename, you have to specify the page's URL.

As you have seen, a URL is the address of a page on the World Wide Web. If the URL you are targeting includes additional bookmarks within the page, you can add that bookmark to the URL so the link points to a specific location in the document. For example, the URL you might enter for a section of a page on majors at MidWest University might be: http://www.mwu.edu/course/info.html#majors

Figure 5-26 dissects the structure of this URL.

Figure 5-26 ◀
Parts of URL

Parts of URL	Interpretation
http	The communications protocol. Between the protocol and the Internet host name, type a separator, usually a colon followed by a double slash (://).
www.mwu.edu	The Internet host name for the computer storing the Web document.
course	The folder containing the Web document.
info.html	The filename of the Web document.
#majors	The bookmark in the document, preceded by a pound sign (#).

Some Web page URLs, such as http://www.microsoft.com/, do not include the filename section. In cases where the filename is missing, the name of the file is assumed to be index.html, but you don't need to specify that in the URL you enter on your page.

Inserting a Hypertext Link to a Web Page

Fiona would like the Findlay Farmhouse page to include a link that points to a Prince Edward Island information page. The URL for this page is http://www.gov.pe.ca. The text for this link is already in place at the bottom of the page.

To insert a link to a page on another computer:

1. Open **Findlay2** from the Tutorial.05 folder in FrontPage Express.

2. Scroll down to the **For More Information...** section at the bottom of the page.

3. Select the text **Contact the Prince Edward Island visitors centre**.

4. Click the **Create or Edit Hyperlink** button 🖇.

5. If necessary, click the **World Wide Web** tab.

6. Make sure the Hyperlink Type list box displays http. Type **http://www.gov.pe.ca** in the URL box as shown in Figure 5-27.

Figure 5-27 ◀
Specifying a
URL as the link
target

type URL here —

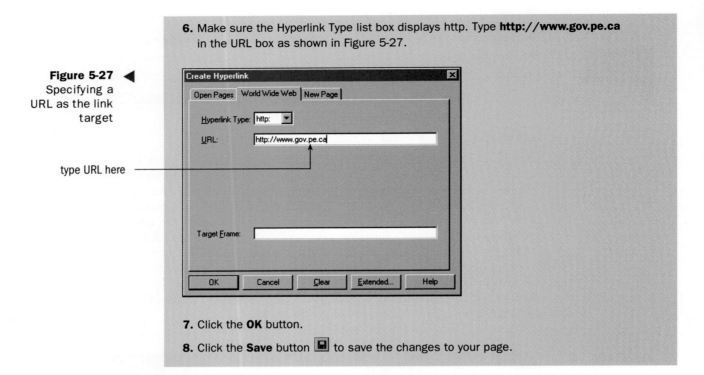

7. Click the **OK** button.

8. Click the **Save** button 🖫 to save the changes to your page.

As usual, you should test your link. To test a link on another computer, you will need to connect to the Internet.

To test this hypertext link:

1. Start Internet Explorer and connect to the Internet.

2. Open Findlay2 in the Internet Explorer browser.

3. Scroll to the bottom of the Findlay Farmhouse page, then click the **Contact the Prince Edward Island visitors centre** hypertext link. The information page appears as shown in Figure 5-28.

   TROUBLE? If the page does not appear, it could be because you are not connected to the Internet or that the Web server that is storing this page is not working. If the page looks different from the one shown in the figure, it could be because the page has changed since the time this tutorial was written. Ask your instructor if you should create a different link.

Figure 5-28 ◀
Prince Edward
Island page

page might have
changed when you
open it

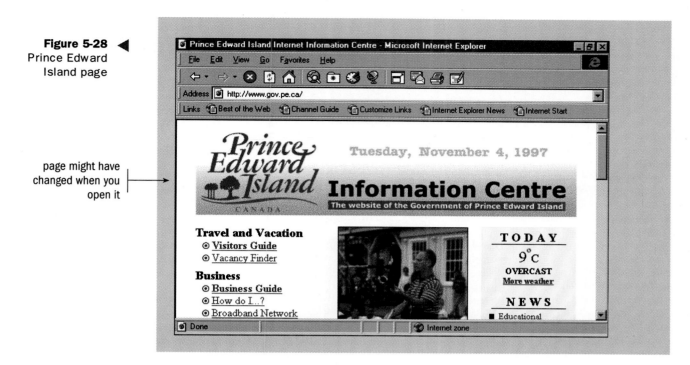

Users of the Findlay page will now be able to access Prince Edward Island information directly.

Creating a Link Using Drag and Drop

FrontPage Express offers an even easier way to add links to your Web page. The **drag and drop** technique involves dragging a hypertext link from the Internet Explorer browser window and dropping it into the FrontPage Express window. This useful technique helps you avoid typing errors, because you don't have to type long and complicated URLs. The Findlays would like a link to a page featuring attractions on the island. The tourism page that you just accessed includes a page with such information. You can drag the link to that page directly into your document.

To create a link through dragging and dropping:

1. Resize the Prince Edward Island Internet Explorer window and The Findlay Farmhouse FrontPage Express window so that you can see both on your desktop.

   TROUBLE? To resize windows, you must first click the Restore button 🗗 on each of the windows. Then drag the lower-right corner until the two windows are about the same size. Drag the title bars to move the windows into place.

2. Click within the FrontPage Express window to make it the active window.

3. Add a new list item in the FrontPage Express window by clicking the end of the item, "Contact the Prince Edward Island visitors centre" at the bottom of the page, then pressing **Enter**. See Figure 5-29.

Figure 5-29 ◄
Positioning the
FrontPage
Express and
Internet
Explorer
windows

FrontPage Express
window

Internet Explorer
window

click this link to locate
link Fiona wants to
insert

you'll drop link here

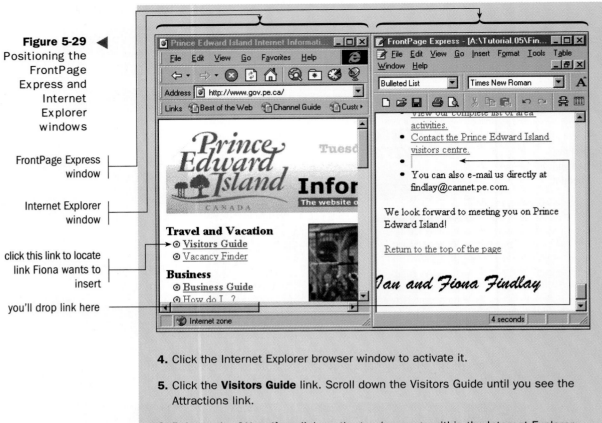

4. Click the Internet Explorer browser window to activate it.

5. Click the **Visitors Guide** link. Scroll down the Visitors Guide until you see the Attractions link.

6. Point to the **Attractions** link on the tourism page within the Internet Explorer window. Then, with the mouse button held down, drag the pointer across to the FrontPage Express window as shown in Figure 5-30.

TROUBLE? If you don't see an Attractions link like the one in Figure 5-30, choose a different link.

TROUBLE? If you click the Attractions link by mistake, click the Back button ⬅, then repeat Step 6.

Figure 5-30 ◄
Inserting a link
using drag and
drop

pointer changes
when you drop a link

you'll drop Attractions
link into FrontPage
Express window

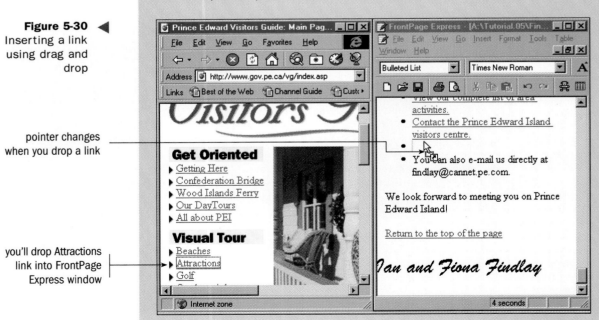

7. Release the mouse button, dropping the link into the space for the new list item you created.

8. Maximize the FrontPage Express window. Figure 5-31 shows the new hypertext link in the list of items.

Figure 5-31 ◀
Inserted link

link you added using
drag and drop

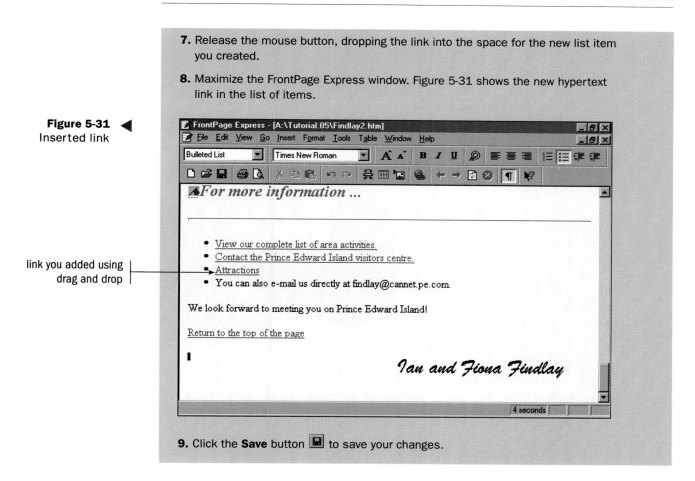

9. Click the **Save** button 🖫 to save your changes.

As usual, you should confirm that the link you just created works.

To check your new hypertext link:

1. Return to the browser and maximize the browser window.

2. Click the **Back** button ⟵ until you return to The Findlay Farmhouse page.

3. Click the **Refresh** button 🖻.

4. Scroll to the bottom of the page, then click the **Attractions** link. The Attractions page appears as shown in Figure 5-32.

TROUBLE? If the page that appears looks different, don't worry. The links and pages at this site might have changed since this book was published.

Figure 5-32 ◀
Target of link
you dragged
and dropped

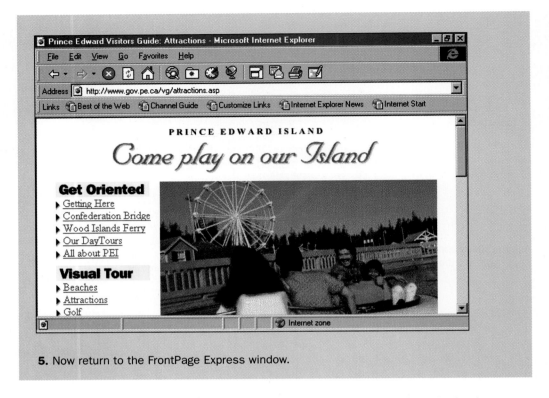

5. Now return to the FrontPage Express window.

You've successfully inserted hyperlinks to two different Prince Edward Island pages.

Linking to an E-mail Address

You can link to other Internet resources besides Web pages, such as FTP servers or e-mail addresses. Many Web authors include their e-mail address on their Web pages so that they can receive direct feedback from people who use the page. The URL for an e-mail address is:

mailto:*e-mail_address*

where *e-mail_address* is the Internet e-mail address of the user. For example, if a user's e-mail address is davis@mwu.edu, the URL for this address is mailto:davis@mwu.edu. When someone reading the page clicks this e-mail address link, the browser starts an e-mail program from which the user can create and send an e-mail message. Not all browsers can work with the e-mail hypertext link.

In order to make it easy for people to contact them, the Findlays have included their e-mail address on their Web page. You suggest that they make this a hypertext link.

To create a link to an e-mail address:

1. In the FrontPage Express window, if necessary, scroll to the bottom of the page. Select the text **findlay@cannet.pe.com** from the For more information... section.

2. Click the **Create or Edit Hyperlink** button 🖼.

3. On the World Wide Web page, click the **Hyperlink Type** list arrow, then click **mailto**.

4. Type **mailto:findlay@cannet.pe.com** in the URL box, as shown in Figure 5-33.

Figure 5-33
Creating an
e-mail link

e-mail link

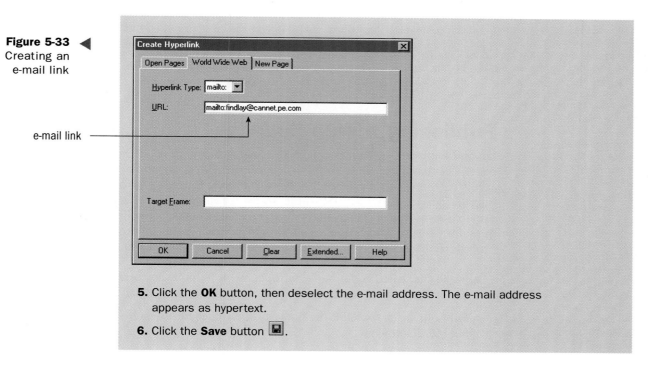

5. Click the **OK** button, then deselect the e-mail address. The e-mail address
appears as hypertext.

6. Click the **Save** button 🖫.

Now you should test this link to verify that it works properly. When you click an e-mail
link, Internet Explorer automatically opens the New Message window: the same one you
used with Outlook Express.

To test your e-mail address link:

1. Open the Internet Explorer browser and click the **Back** button ⬅ until The
Findlay Farmhouse page appears.

2. Click the **Refresh** button 🔃.

3. Scroll to the bottom of the page, if necessary, and click **findlay@cannet.pe.com**.
The New Message window opens and the address you clicked automatically
appears in the To box as shown in Figure 5-34. At this point you could enter a
message and send it off. For now, you should simply exit without sending anything
(the e-mail address is fictional).

Figure 5-34
New Message
window

Findlay e-mail
address automatically
inserted

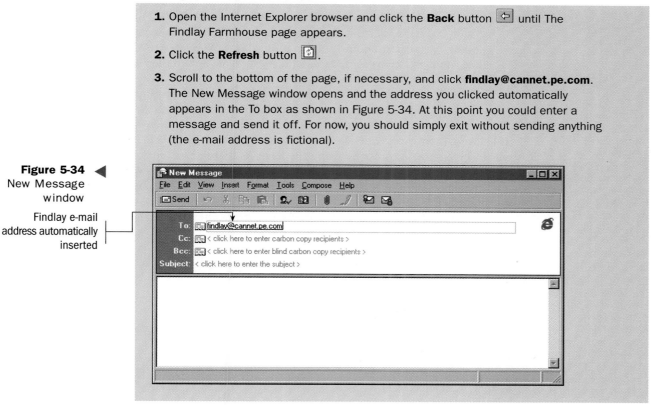

4. Click **File**, then click **Close**. You return to the Internet Explorer window.

5. Close both Internet Explorer and FrontPage Express.

The Findlay Farmhouse home page is now complete.

Publishing a Web Page

Ian and Fiona are very pleased with the final appearance of the Findlay Farmhouse home page. They are now ready to publish it on their Web site so that the general public can access it. To publish a page on the Web, you must first have space on a Web server. Your Internet Service Provider (ISP)—the entity through which you have Internet access—usually has a Web server available for your use. Because each ISP has a different procedure for storing Web pages, you should contact your ISP to learn its policies and procedures. Generally, you should be prepared to do the following:

- Make sure the filenames of your documents exhibit the correct case. For example, if your page refers to "Ian.gif" make sure the filename is Ian.gif, not ian.gif.

- Find out from your ISP the name of the folder into which you'll be placing your HTML documents.

- Work with your ISP to select a name for your site on the Web (such as http://www.findlays.com). Choose a name that will be easy for customers and interested parties to remember and return to.

- If you select a special name for your Web site, register it at http://www.internic.net. Registration is necessary to ensure that any name you give to your site is unique and not already in use by another party.

- Add your site to the indexes of search pages on the Web. This is not required, but it will make it easier for people to find your site. Each search facility has different policies regarding adding information about Web sites to their index. Be aware that some will charge a fee to include your Web site in their list.

The Findlays have already worked with their ISP to acquire and register the name www.findlays.com. They are ready to publish their page on the Web. The Web Publishing Wizard walks you through the steps of publishing your presentation. If you are posting just a single page to your Web server, you can start the Web Publishing Wizard from within FrontPage Express by using the Save As dialog box, entering a page location that includes your server address, and following the prompts. However, if you are publishing multiple pages with hyperlinks between them, as with the Findlay presentation, you cannot publish the entire presentation from FrontPage Express. Instead, you must start the Web Publishing Wizard from Windows Explorer. These steps show you how to publish your Web presentation from Windows Explorer.

You will be able to perform the next sets of steps only if you have space on a Web server.

To publish your Web presentation:

1. Click the **Start** button ![Start], point to **Programs**, and then click **Windows Explorer**.

2. Double-click the **3½ Floppy (A:)** icon in the left pane to display the contents of your Student Disk.

3. Select the **Tutorial.05** folder in the left pane to display the contents of the Tutorial.05 folder.

4. Select the following files in the Tutorial.05 folder: **Bio2.htm**, **Events2.htm**, **Findlay2.htm**, and all the gif graphic files.

TROUBLE? To select multiple files in Windows Explorer, press the Ctrl key while you select each file.

5. Right-click the selected files, point to **Send To**, and then click **Web Publishing Wizard**. See Figure 5-35. The Web Publishing Wizard starts.

Figure 5-35 ◀
Publishing
a Web
presentation
from Windows
Explorer

Web presentation
files are selected

Tutorial.05 folder is
open

click to start Web
Publishing Wizard

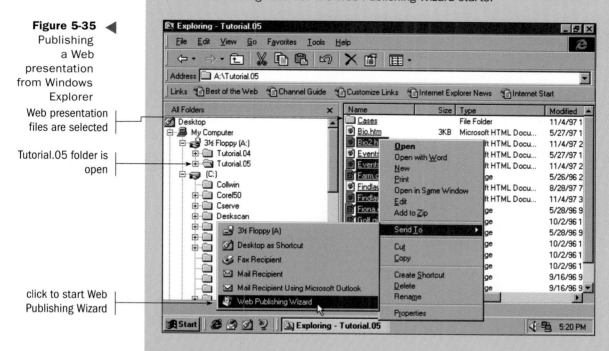

6. Read the information on the opening screen, then click the **Next** button. You are now asked to select a Web server. Click the **Web server** list arrow, click your Web server, and then click the **Next** button.

TROUBLE? If your Web server is not listed or if you are prompted to enter a name for your Web server, ask your instructor or technical resource person for assistance. You can create a new entry in the Web server list by clicking the New button. The Web Publishing Wizard then prompts you for a name for your Web server, a URL or Internet address, the name of your local directory, your user name and password, your server name and directory, and so on. If you have the necessary information, you can proceed through the process of creating a new Web server.

7. Once your Web server is selected, click the **Finish** button. If the Web Publishing Wizard asks for your user name and password, provide that information in the dialog box that opens, shown in Figure 5-36. Wait as the Web Publishing Wizard uploads your files to your Web server.

TROUBLE? If you don't know your user name and password, check with your ISP.

TROUBLE? If the Enter Network Password dialog box appears numerous times, your Web server site might request authentication for each file you transfer. Continue to provide the information until the dialog box no longer appears.

Figure 5-36 Entering user name and password

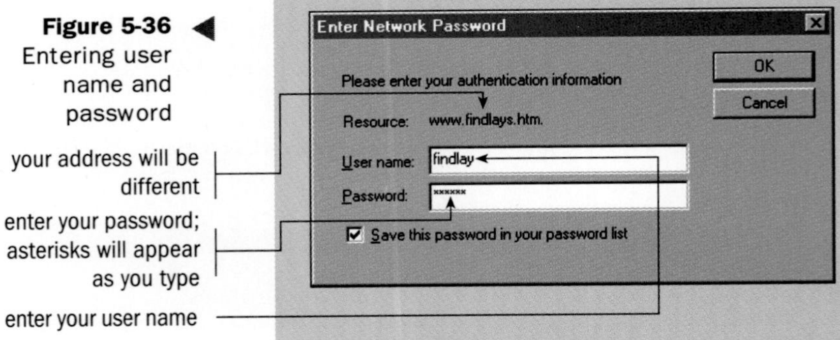
Enter Network Password
OK
Cancel
Please enter your authentication information
Resource: www.findlays.htm.
User name: findlay
Password: ******
Save this password in your password list
your address will be different
enter your password; asterisks will appear as you type
enter your user name

8. Click the **OK** button when informed that the files have been properly transferred.

Once you have published your Web page, you should connect to it on the Web to make sure the graphics appear correctly and the links all work.

To test your Web page:

1. Open Internet Explorer.
2. Type the URL of the Web page you just published in the Address box, then press **Enter**. See Figure 5-37.

Figure 5-37 Findlay page on the Web

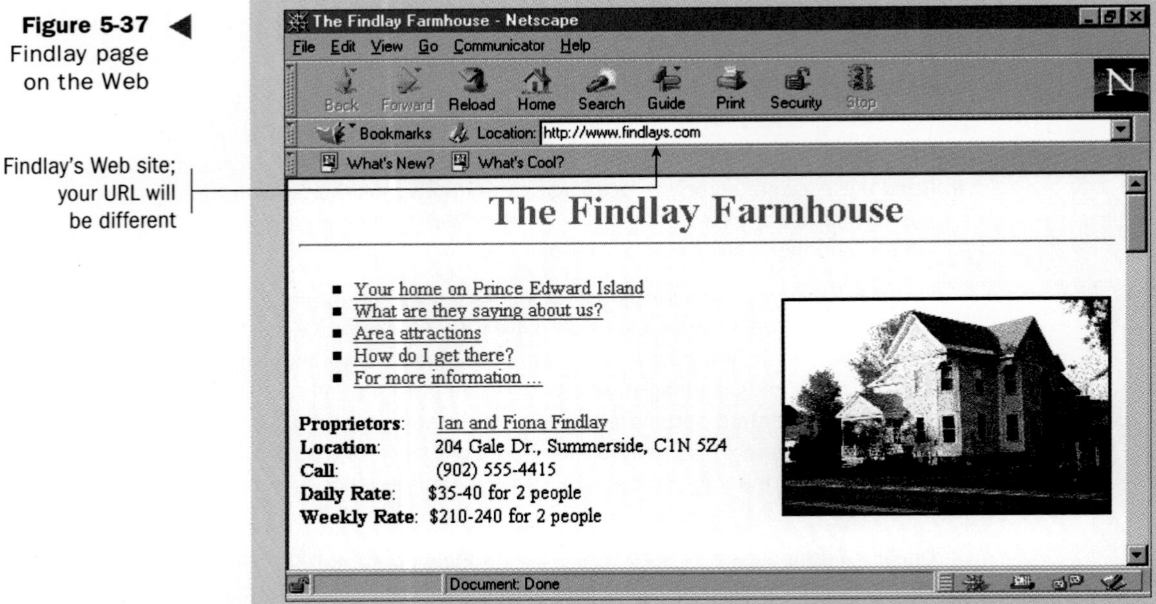
The Findlay Farmhouse - Netscape
File Edit View Go Communicator Help
Back Forward Reload Home Search Guide Print Security Stop
Bookmarks Location: http://www.findlays.com
What's New? What's Cool?
The Findlay Farmhouse
Your home on Prince Edward Island
What are they saying about us?
Area attractions
How do I get there?
For more information ...
Proprietors: Ian and Fiona Findlay
Location: 204 Gale Dr., Summerside, C1N 5Z4
Call: (902) 555-4415
Daily Rate: $35-40 for 2 people
Weekly Rate: $210-240 for 2 people
Document: Done
Findlay's Web site; your URL will be different

3. Test all the links by clicking them and using the navigation buttons.
4. Click **File**, then click **Close**.

Ian and Fiona thank you for all your help. They decide to work with the page for a few days and get customer feedback. Then they'll let you know if they need any more help.

Quick Check

1. What is the URL for a bookmark named #petunia in a file named info.htm located in the /flowers/inventory folder of the Web server whose host name is www.ftd.com?

2. If you are connecting to the site http://www.cinemagreats.com, what is the name of the html file you will most likely see?

3. If you are connected to a page containing a link that you'd like to include on your page, how can you easily create such a link?

4. What is the advantage of using drag and drop to add a link to your page?

5. If you want to include a link to your e-mail address, what URL should you enter?

6. You have just published your Web page, but when you test it you notice a graphic doesn't appear properly. What might you suspect? Give two possibilities.

7. True or false: Adding your Web page to Web indexes is always free.

Tutorial Assignments

Ian and Fiona have had a chance to work with the page you created. They would like you to make the following changes:

- Add a link to the Events2 page that takes the user from the bottom of the page to the top.

- On the Events2 page, include a note that Ian Findlay is honorary chairman of the Highland Games. Include a link to the Bio2 page.

- Include a link on the Events2 page that points to the official Prince Edward Island list of events and attractions located at http://www.gov.pe.ca/vg/attractions.asp.

To complete this tutorial assignment:

1. Open the Events2.htm file in FrontPage Express.

2. Insert a bookmark named "Top" at the beginning of the main heading.

3. Scroll to the bottom of the page and add a new line, "Return to the top of the page".

4. Link the text to the bookmark named "Top" that you just created.

5. Scroll up to the description of the Summerside Highland Games. Add the following text to the end of the paragraph:
   You can also contact Ian Findlay, this year's honorary chairman, care of the Findlay Farmhouse Bed and Breakfast.

6. Open the Bio2 page, return to Events2, and select the text "Ian Findlay" from the sentence you just entered. Link the sentence to the Bio2 page in the Tutorial.05 folder.

7. Scroll down to the bottom of page and add a new line:

   "For more events and attractions, go to the Prince Edward Island list of current attractions".

8. Select the text "Prince Edward Island list of current attractions" and link it to the URL http://www.gov.pe.ca/vg/attractions.asp.

9. Save your changes to the "Events2.htm" file.

10. Open the Events2 page in the browser and confirm that the links are working properly.

11. Print the page.

12. If you are able, publish the Events2 page. You might be prompted to replace the existing page on your Web site. Check that all links are still working properly.

13. Hand in the printout to your instructor.

Case Problems

1. The Author Series at Avalon Books Avalon Books is adding a new set of pages to their home page that will include biographical information for authors making appearances at the bookstore. They've asked you to set up the hypertext links between the bookstore's home page and the biographical pages.

To complete this case problem:

1. Start FrontPage Express and open the file "Avalon3.htm", located in the Cases folder in the Tutorial.05 folder on your Student Disk.

2. Save the file as "Avalon4" in the Cases folder.

3. Scroll down to the list of the coming week's events.

4. Select the text "Sandy Davis" and create a hypertext link to the file "Sd.htm", located in the Cases folder in the Tutorial.05 folder on your Student Disk. *Hint:* When you link to a file that is not open in FrontPage Express, use the World Wide Web tab and choose File as the Hyperlink Type. Then enter the file path and filename.

5. Select the text "John Sheridan" and create a hypertext link to the file "Js.htm" in the Cases folder in the Tutorial.05 folder on your Student Disk.

6. Save your changes to the Avalon4 file.

7. Open the file in the Internet Explorer browser and confirm that the links are working correctly.

8. Print the Avalon4 page.

9. Hand in the printout to your instructor.

2. Creating a List of Movie Reviewers You want to create a Web page for the Film School that lists pages containing reviews and synopses of major movies. You've received a list of existing pages and their URLs from your instructor. See Figure 5-38.

Figure 5-38 ◀

Page Name	URL
America Cinema	http://www.geocities.com/Hollywood/2171/
Washington Post Reviews	http://www.washingtonpost.com/wp-srv/searches/movies.htm
All-Movie Guide	http://www.allmovie.com/amg/movie_Root.html
Roger Ebert on Movies	http://www.suntimes.com/ebert/ebert.html
The A-List Movie Reviews	http://www.geocities.com/Hollywood/Hills/1197/a-list.html
The Best Video Guide	http://www.99lives.com/
BoxOffice Online	http://www.boxoff.com/

Create a Web page of this list. Format the list as a bulleted list. Make each page name a hypertext link to the appropriate Web page. Add the title "Movie Review Pages" at the top of the Web page, and then publish the page when you are finished.

To complete this case problem:

1. Open a blank document in FrontPage Express.

2. Save the page as "Movie.htm" in the Cases folder in the Tutorial.05 folder on your Student Disk, with a title of Movie Review Pages.

3. Type the main heading "Movie Review Pages", formatted with the Heading 1 style and centered on the page.

4. Create a bulleted list of the page names shown in Figure 5-38.

5. Select each item in the list and link the entire text in the item to the URL specified in Figure 5-38.

6. Save your changes to the file.

7. View the file in the Internet Explorer browser and confirm that each link is working correctly.

8. Create a printout of your Web page.

9. If possible, publish your page and ensure that you can connect to it once it is published.

10. Hand in the printout to your instructor.

3. Personnel Pages at First City Bank The systems manager at First City Bank is creating Web pages listing company employees and their positions. Figure 5-39 shows one such page, which details the bank's loan officers.

Figure 5-39 ◀

First City Bank

Loan Officers

Loan Officer, Linda Keller

Loan Officer, Laura Flint

Assistant Loan Officer, Mary Taylor

Each photo on the page is linked to another page that gives more detail about the employee. The three employee pages are located on your Student Disk in the Cases folder in the Tutorial.05 folder with the filenames Keller.htm, Flint.htm, and Taylor.htm. Create the page shown in Figure 5-39, including the hypertext links to these three files.
   To complete this case problem:

1. Open a blank document in FrontPage Express.

2. Save the page as "Bank.htm" in the Cases folder in the Tutorial.05 folder on your Student Disk, with First City Bank Loan Officers as the page title.

3. Type the main heading "First City Bank", formatted with the Heading 1 style and centered on the page.

4. Insert a horizontal line after the main heading that covers the width of the page.

5. Type the title "Loan Officers", formatted with the Heading 2 style and left-aligned on the page.

6. Insert the graphic image file "Keller.gif" on the first line below the Loan Officers heading.

7. Type "Loan Officer, Linda Keller" to the right of her photo.

8. Insert the graphic image file "Flint.gif" on the next line.

9. Type "Loan Officer, Laura Flint" to the right of her photo.

10. Insert the graphic image file "Taylor.gif" on the next line.

11. Type "Assistant Loan Officer, Mary Taylor" to the right of her photo.

12. Select each of the three photos, and using the Create or Edit Hyperlink button, link the photos to the files Keller.htm, Flint.htm, and Taylor.htm. *Hint:* When you link to a file that is not open in FrontPage Express, use the World Wide Web tab and choose file as the Hyperlink Type. Then enter the file path and filename.

13. Save your changes to the file.

14. Open the "Bank.htm" file in the Internet Explorer browser and verify that the links are working properly.

15. If possible, publish the page and verify that the links are functioning.

16. Print a copy of your page.

17. Hand in your printout to your instructor.

4. Create Your Own Web Presentation Create a Web presentation about yourself. There should be three pages in the presentation. The first page should deal with your interests. Include an ordered list of your top-ten favorite Web pages. The second page should deal with your coursework. Include a bulleted list detailing your previous courses. The third page should be a résumé page that you could submit to an employer. Include short summaries of your work experience and educational background. Create hypertext links between the three pages including links to specific points within each page using bookmarks. The appearance of the page is up to you. Use whatever colors, page backgrounds, or inline images you think are appropriate. Publish the page on your Web server when you are finished and provide the URL of your page to your instructor.

Answers to Quick Check Questions

SESSION 4.1

1 "What you see is what you get" allows you to see how the final document will appear as you develop your page.

2 when you don't need to be connected to the Internet, such as when you are developing a Web page

3 HTML

4 A markup tag is an HTML label within angle brackets. A style is a name assigned by FrontPage Express to a tag that appears in the Change Style list on the Format toolbar.

5 Not all browsers will be able to view it.

6 It allows only options supported by HTML.

7 Normal

SESSION 4.2

1 Select the list items and right-click the selection. Click List Properties, then click the bullet from the list of available styles. Click OK.

2 Italics, bold, font type, font size, and font color

3 Not all browsers will be able to display the font.

4 Select the text, right-click the selection, click Font Properties, change the properties, then click OK.

5 Select the text, click the Text Color button, click green, then click OK.

SESSION 4.3

1 Percent of window indicates what percentage of the window the line will extend across; pixels indicates the number of pixels the line will occupy.

2 Browser displays inline graphic on the page while a separate application must start to display an external graphic.

3 GIF and JPEG

4 Convert it to GIF or JPEG format.

5 A non-interlaced graphic appears one line at a time, starting from the top of the image and working down. In an interlaced graphic, the image appears stepwise with the image coming gradually into focus.

6 Right-click the line, click Horizontal Line Properties, enter 25 in the Width box and choose Percent of window as the width option. Click OK.

7 That the graphic is not so large that it makes the page take longer to display and that it is not too distracting from the main text on the page

8 So users know the picture's content without having to view the image itself.

SESSION 5.1

1 A bookmark is a reference point on a page that identifies a specific location; it is necessary when you want to link to that location.

2 Click where you want the bookmark or highlight the text you want to use as the bookmark, click Edit, and then click Bookmark.

3 Case sensitive.

4 With a pound sign #.

5 In the Internet Explorer browser.

SESSION 5.2

1 Storyboarding is the technique of creating a graphical representation of the pages and links in a Web presentation. Storyboarding is important in creating a coherent and user-friendly structure.

2 A linear structure is one in which Web pages are linked from one to another in a direct chain. Users can go to the previous page or to the next page in the chain, but not to a page in a different section of the chain.

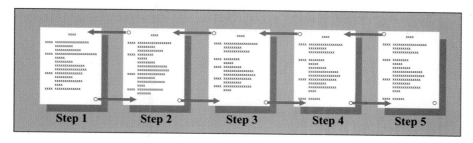

You could use a linear structure in a Web page presentation that included a series of steps that the user must follow, such as in a recipe or instructions to complete a task.

3 A hierarchical structure is one in which Web pages are linked from general to specific topics. Users can move up and down the hierarchy tree.

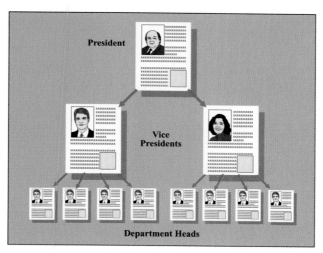

A company might use such a structure to describe the management organization.

4 Click the Create or Edit Hyperlink button, click the Open Pages tab, click the page you want to link to, click OK, then click Yes.

5 Click the Create or Edit Hyperlink button, click the Open Pages tab, click the page you want to link to, click the Bookmark list arrow, click the bookmark you want to link to, click OK, then click Yes.

SESSION 5.3

1 http://www.ftd.com/flowers/inventory/info.htm#petunia

2 index.html

3   Drag the link onto your Web page.

4   You are less likely to make a typographical error.

5   mailto:*e-mail address* where *e-mail address* is the Internet e-mail address of the user

6   The graphic filename might have the wrong case or might be in the wrong folder.

7   False.

Downloading and Installing a New Version of Internet Explorer

Downloading the Internet Explorer Software

You can download the Internet Explorer software, new versions of the Internet Explorer software, and other software available through Microsoft Corporation, from Microsoft's Web site. First connect to Microsoft's Web site, then locate the Download page for the product you need. Microsoft constantly updates its Web site, and the steps you need to take to locate this page might change. If you use these steps as a general guide and you read the Microsoft pages for information, you should be able to locate the software successfully. Once you connect to the Microsoft site and locate the Download page, you then need to specify which version of Internet Explorer you want, depending on your operating system. You might also need to provide some additional information.

To locate the Download page and provide the necessary information:

1. Start your browser.

2. Enter **http://www.microsoft.com** in the Address box, then press **Enter**.

3. Click the **Products** link, which appears somewhere on the Microsoft home page (probably on a band across the top). The Products page should offer several ways to select the product you're interested in, either by product group or product name. See Figure A-1.

Figure A-1 ◀
Microsoft's
Products page

Products link

you can also locate a
specific product by
linking to a
product group

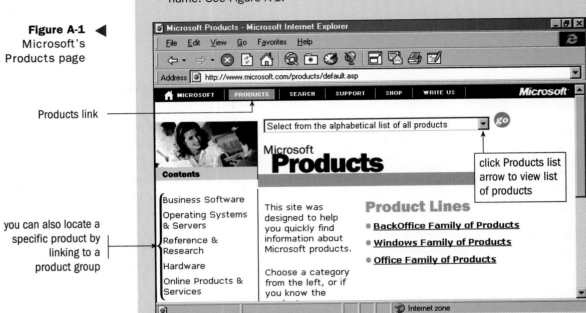

4. Locate the Internet Explorer software page. You can probably do this quickest by clicking the Products list arrow and selecting **Internet Explorer 4.0** (or whatever version you need) from that list, then clicking a button such as **Go**, as shown in Figure A-2. Alternatively, you could locate Internet Explorer by selecting it from a group such as "Online Products and Services." If the Security Alert dialog box opens warning you that you are sending information over the Internet, click the **Yes** button (this could happen more than once).

Figure A-2 ◀
Selecting the
Internet
Explorer
version you
want to
download

click once you have
selected the product
you want

products list

click to download
Internet Explorer
version 4.0; you
might need to
download a different
version

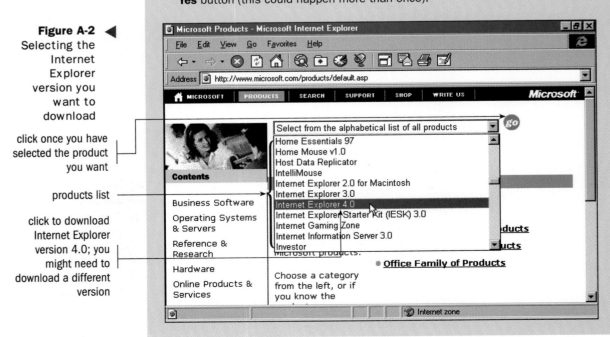

5. If you reach an Overview page, you might need to click a link targeting specific product information, such as "Click here for in-depth information about Internet Explorer."

6. Click **Download** (you might need to click more than one Download link, such as Download for Free). Figure A-3 shows the Download page for Internet Explorer version 4.0 for Windows 95/NT 4.0.

Figure A-3 ◄
Locating the
Setup
program's
download site

Download page for
Internet Explorer
version 4.0

information about the
version and operating
system

click to download
software

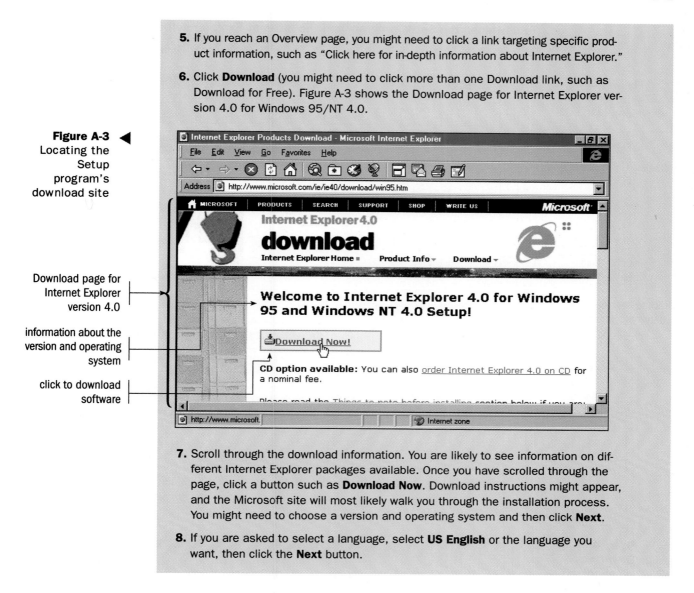

7. Scroll through the download information. You are likely to see information on different Internet Explorer packages available. Once you have scrolled through the page, click a button such as **Download Now**. Download instructions might appear, and the Microsoft site will most likely walk you through the installation process. You might need to choose a version and operating system and then click **Next**.

8. If you are asked to select a language, select **US English** or the language you want, then click the **Next** button.

You have now made all the choices you need to make about the software. The next phase of the download process involves choosing a site from which to download the executable file that contains the Setup program. The File Download dialog box then appears, giving you two options for handling this file:

- Run this program from its current location

- Save this program to disk

If you choose to run the program from its current location, your computer creates a temporary folder on your hard disk into which it places the Setup program. The Setup program, however, is not saved permanently on your computer. For this reason, the steps instruct you to save the program to your hard disk so you can run the Setup program at any time, can install different options when you want, and can reinstall the software if necessary.

You also need to decide where you want to store the Setup file. Many users store program files in a directory they have created for the purpose of storing downloaded software, or in the Windows Program Files directory.

To download the Setup program and the Internet Explorer software:

1. Click the **Install setup** link for the site you have chosen. See Figure A-4.

Figure A-4 ◀
Choosing a
download site

download instructions
might appear

list of available
download sites

click to download the
Setup program from
the adjacent site

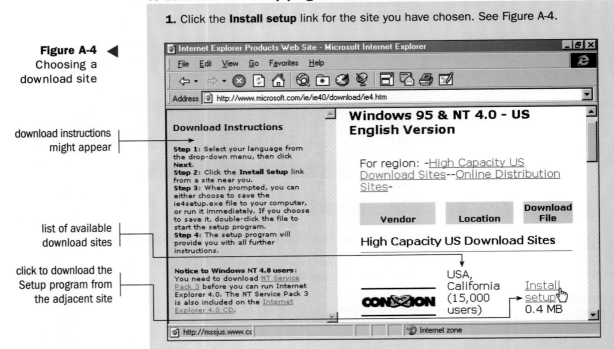

2. When the File Download dialog box opens, which gives you the choice to either run the software or save it to disk, click the **Save this program to disk** option button. See Figure A-5.

   TROUBLE? If you are using a browser other than a recent version of Internet Explorer, the download options might be different. Choose the option that enables you to save the Setup program to your hard disk. This same warning applies to Steps 3–4; follow whatever prompts appear on your screen to specify a location for the saved files.

Figure A-5 ◀
File Download
options

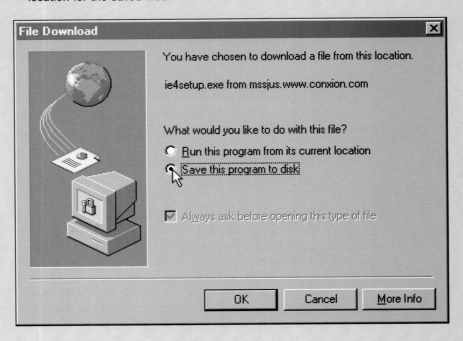

3. Click the **OK** button. When the Save As dialog box opens, select the drive and folder into which you want to place the program you are downloading.

> **TROUBLE?** If you want to store the Setup program file in a folder you create, first select the drive and folder in which you want to create the new folder in the Save As dialog box. Then click the Create New Folder button ⌐. Type a name for the folder, then click the Open button. Now proceed with Step 4.

4. Click the **Save** button. The File Download dialog box, shown in Figure A-6, now shows the download progress. Note the Download to: line, which shows the folder into which you are downloading the software. This dialog box informs you of the download progress. When the download finishes, the dialog box will close.

> **TROUBLE?** If the Saving Location dialog box does not appear, there might be a delay in connecting to the server. After waiting a reasonable amount of time, you might need to repeat Steps 5–8.

Figure A-6 ◀
Downloading
the Setup
program

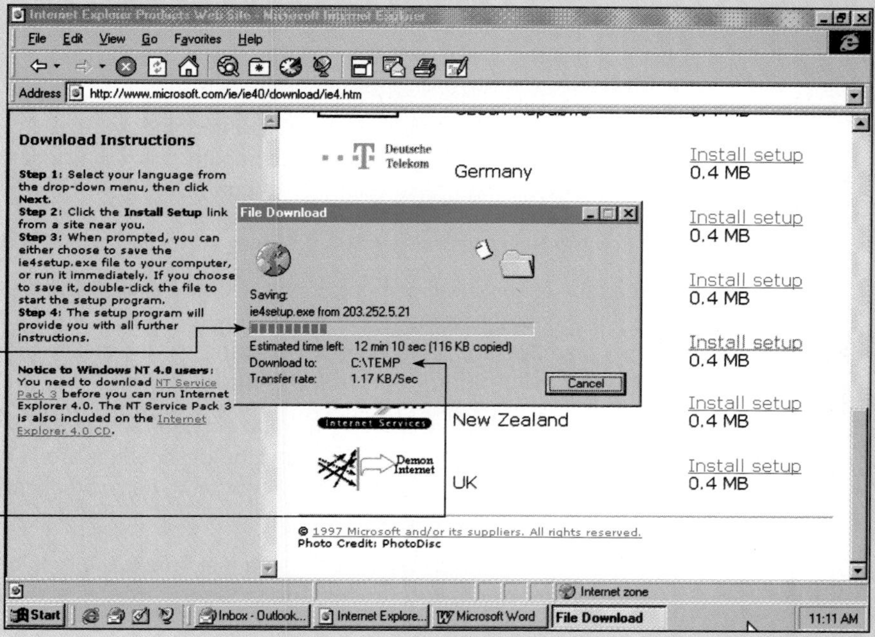

download progress ────

folder into which you
are downloading the
Setup program; yours
might be different

5. Click the **OK** button when the Download complete message appears.

6. Exit your browser.

The download is complete and the Internet Explorer Setup program file is stored on your hard disk.

Installing Internet Explorer

Once you have downloaded the Internet Explorer Setup program, you are ready to install Internet Explorer. When you run the program, it first uses a self-extraction program to extract the Setup files. Then the Setup program starts automatically and completes the installation process.

Depending on the version of Internet Explorer you are installing, it is possible these steps will vary somewhat. If that is the case, read through the steps because they are likely to be similar to what you see on your screen. Then proceed through the installation process and read the Setup windows carefully. They should guide you through a smooth installation.

To initialize the Setup program:

1. Close all open windows and programs.

2. Click the **Start** button, then click **Run**.

3. Enter the path of the file you just downloaded by either typing it or using the Browse button to locate it. You will need to include the folder and the filename. Figure A-6 shows where you can find the folder information. Figure A-7 shows the Run dialog box for a computer whose program file was saved in a folder on drive C named TEMP.

Figure A-7 ◀
Saving the
Setup program
to disk

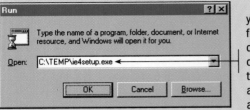

your path and
filename might be
different, depending
on where you stored
the Setup program
and what version you
are installing

4. Click the **OK** button.

TROUBLE? If a message box appears informing you that a previous version of Internet Explorer is already on your computer, click the Update installation from the Internet button, then click the OK button.

5. When the Internet Explorer Setup Wizard starts, click the **Next** button to continue.

6. Read the licensing agreement, then click the **I accept the agreement** option button to accept the terms of the licensing agreement. Click the **Next** button. The Download Options dialog box opens, giving you the choice to install now or download and install later. Click the **Install** option button.

7. Click the **Next** button. You now need to choose the type of installation you want: Browser Only, Standard, or Full. Read the descriptions. You can click each option and then read the description of that option to help you decide. Click the option you want, then click the **Next** button.

8. When asked to select which active channel broadcaster region you want, click the appropriate region, such as the United States. Then click the **Next** button.

9. When the destination folder appears, click the **Next** button to accept the default folder, which in Figure A-8 is C:\Program Files\Internet Explorer.

Figure A-8 ◀
Setup program
determining the
destination
folder

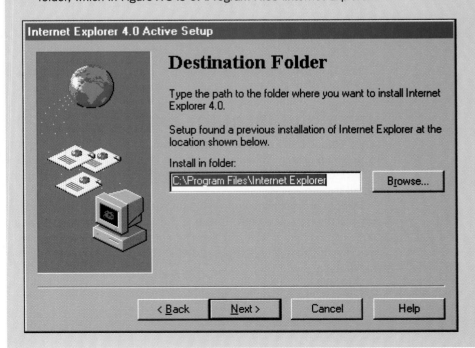

> **TROUBLE?** If you want to change this location, click the Browse button and then click a new location.
>
> **10.** Finally, you need to choose the site from which you want to download the Internet Explorer software. Click the site you want, then click the **Next** button. The download begins. If additional dialog boxes appear, read them carefully and provide the requested information as necessary.

Once the files are downloaded, the Setup program proceeds to install Internet Explorer. The Setup program guides you through the process with a set of easy-to-read dialog boxes.

To install Internet Explorer with the Setup program:

> **1.** When the download procedure is finished, it asks if you want to view the README file, which informs you of licensing and release note issues. Click the **Yes** button to view the README file.
>
> **2.** When you are finished reading it, click the **Close** button ☒. You are informed that Setup is complete.
>
> **3.** Click the **OK** button. You are informed that Setup must restart your computer. Click the **Yes** button, unless you have other programs running, in which case you should close them first before you restart your computer.
>
> **4.** Click the **OK** button.
>
> **TROUBLE?** If your computer doesn't restart, you might have to restart it manually. Exit Windows, then turn the computer off and on again.

Your computer restarts. You are now ready to launch Internet Explorer. Proceed to the first tutorial in this book. You can read the next section in this appendix for information on adding components to your version of Internet Explorer or installing add-on software.

Adding Components

Depending on how you installed Internet Explorer (Browser Only, Standard, or Full), you might not have all the components to the full product. You can easily add components by re-running the Setup program as described in the previous section. If you have already installed the most current version of all the components, Setup displays the dialog box shown in Figure A-9.

Figure A-9 ◀
Determining
that
components
are all updated

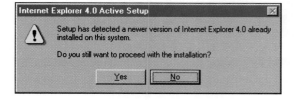

If you don't have the most recent version of all components, Setup automatically detects which components you haven't installed on your computer and walks you through the process of adding new components by connecting you to Microsoft's Component Download page, which analyzes your system and displays a list of all available components and their status on your computer. You can then choose to download and install any components that are revised or new.

You can also access Microsoft's Component Download page directly from your browser without running Setup; the steps follow this method.

To access the Component Download page:

1. Link to the product page for the current version of Internet Explorer for your operating system.

2. Click the **Download** list arrow, then click the link or menu choice targeting components for the version of Internet Explorer you want. Figure A-10 shows the menu of available choices.

Figure A-10 ◀
Selecting the components page from the Internet Explorer product page

Download list arrow

click to view components for Internet explorer 4.0; you might need to choose a different version

3. Read the information on the Internet Explorer Suite Components and Add-Ons page and locate a link that takes you to the components list for the version of Internet Explorer you want. Click that link. Internet Explorer runs the Setup program, then asks if it can analyze your system and determine which Internet Explorer components are already installed.

4. Click the **Yes** button. Once the analysis is complete, the Component Download page displays a list of components and informs you which are already installed on your computer, which components have available upgrades, and which components are not installed. See Figure A-11.

Figure A-11 ◀
Viewing the results of the component analysis for your system

status of each component

list of components; select the ones you want to upgrade

click once you've made your selections

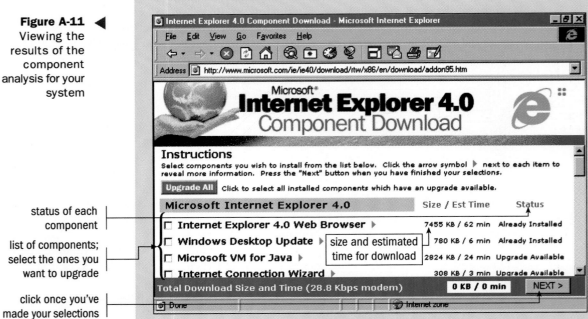

5. Click the check boxes preceding the components you want, then click the **Next** button.

6. Select a download site and scroll down to view the list of components you chose, then click the **Install Now** button. See Figure A-12.

Figure A-12 ◀
Initializing the component download

click to view list of available download sites

click to install components you've chosen

list of components you've selected (yours might be different)

size and estimated download time for components you've chosen

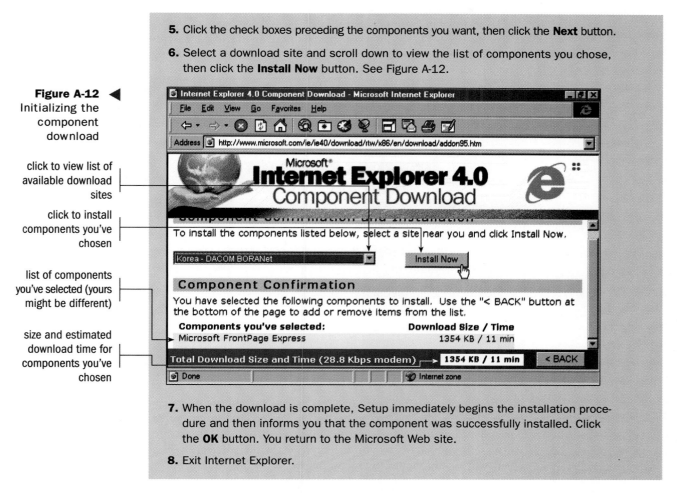

7. When the download is complete, Setup immediately begins the installation procedure and then informs you that the component was successfully installed. Click the **OK** button. You return to the Microsoft Web site.

8. Exit Internet Explorer.

Internet Explorer **add-ons**, also called **plug-ins**, are software programs that extend the capabilities of Internet Explorer and its components. Some add-ons are developed by Microsoft; others come from third-party (non-Microsoft) companies who develop add-ons and make them available through the Microsoft Web site. You can often download trial versions of add-ons for free.

Figure A-13 shows the add-on categories Microsoft maintains. It's possible that Microsoft has added or removed add-on categories since this book was printed.

Figure A-13 ◀
Add-on categories

Category	Description
Microsoft Internet Explorer 4.0	Internet Explorer browser, Windows Desktop Update, Microsoft VM for Java, and Internet Connection Wizard
Communication Components	NetMeeting, Outlook Express, and Chat
Multimedia Components	NetShow, Interactive Music Control, VRML Viewer, DirectShow, VDOLive Player, Agent, Macromedia Shockwave Director, Macromedia Shockwave Flash, and RealPlayer by Progressive Networks
Authoring Components	FrontPage Express, Web Publishing Wizard, Data Components for Internet Explorer
Additional Explorer Enhancements	Wallet, Supplemental Web Fonts, Internet Explorer Sound Pack, Task Scheduler
Multi-Language Support	Language support for numerous languages

The add-ons in Figure A-13 are available from the same Component Download page you saw in Figure A-11. Figure A-14 shows a portion of this page, with the Communication and Multimedia components visible. Microsoft might have since changed this list.

Figure A-14 ◄
Partial list of
components on
Microsoft's
Component
Download page

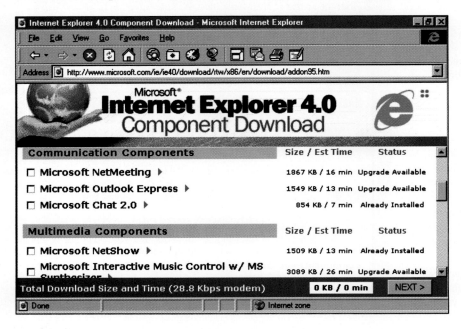

When you are connecting to Web pages that require add-ons to be viewed, you might get a message that warns you that you need additional software to display the page correctly. Sometimes the message gives you the opportunity to download the required software immediately, or you usually can get the software you need by connecting to the Microsoft Component Download page.

Appendix A Assignments

1. Microsoft, like most software companies, makes product information available to the public on the Web. Some of it you can download directly from the Web site but some you must order using more traditional means. Connect to Microsoft's Products page and select a different category of products, such as business software or games. Research several products and note whether you can download them directly or whether you must purchase them separately. Print a product information sheet for one of the products you've researched and write a paragraph on the back of your printout that summarizes your findings for at least three products. Figure A-15 shows, for example, the Excel product information sheet, along with current pricing information. Notice, however, that you can't download the Excel software over the Web; you must purchase it retail.

Figure A-15 ◄

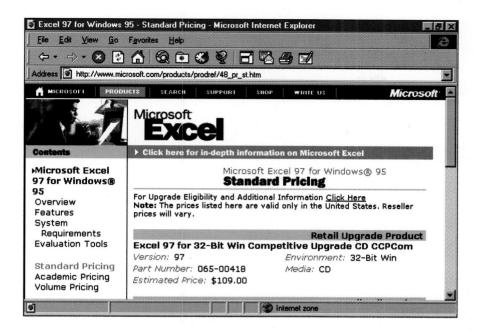

2. Internet Explorer, at the time this book was written, was a free product (hence the link "Download for Free"). However, most of the time software companies must charge for their products, and so must most companies selling goods over the Web. When goods are sold over the Web, how are they most often paid for? What security issues are raised by Internet sales? Use Web Search tools or your library to research the sale of items over the Web, and write a page-long report on how companies are resolving consumer concerns. Summarize your report by indicating whether or not you would be willing to purchase a product over the Web.

3. When you download software over the Web, it can take quite a long time, depending on the size of the software files. When your Internet service comes through your school or institution, you usually have a fast connection that you don't have to pay for, but when you connect to the Internet from home, you usually use a modem and must pay for a dial-up connection to a local Internet Service Provider (ISP). Some ISPs charge by the minute, regardless of whether or not you are calling long-distance, and some offer unlimited connection time for a flat rate fee. If you plan to spend much time on the Internet (and those who regularly download Internet software do), you will need to research ISP dial-up plans. Research at least three of the ISPs in your area and write a page-long report comparing rates, service plans, and technical support. Of the companies you researched, which would you chose?

Bringing the Internet to the Desktop

In this appendix you will learn to:

- Understand push technology

- Enable Active Desktop

- Subscribe to channels

- Use a Web page as background wallpaper

Creating an Active Desktop

Internet Explorer is more than just a suite of Web communications soft-ware. When you install the Internet Explorer program on your computer, it modifies the Windows desktop in an attempt to bring together the two worlds of your computer and the Web. Until recently, the only way to expe-rience the Web was by means of a browser. Internet Explorer version 4.0 and higher, however, merges the Web and your desktop. In this appendix you'll explore how you can use Internet Explorer to design a desktop that functions as your own personal Web page.

Push Technology

When you use the Internet Explorer browser to find information on the Web, you search for information and then "pull" the information from the Web onto your computer by clicking a hypertext link, entering a URL, or choosing a particular page from a menu. More recent Web technology, however, has made it possible for you to request that information be delivered automatically, just as a newspaper is to your front doorstep, without requiring you to go search for it. Users indicate the type of information they want and how often they want it delivered, and special software will go onto the Web, locate the information, and "push" it to the user's computer. Figure B-1 illustrates the difference between the pulling and pushing of information.

Figure B-1 ◀
Pulling vs. pushing

Pull technology

Web server

with the Internet Explorer browser, you pull information to your computer

Push technology

Channel

with push technology, channel pushes information to your computer

With **push technology**, providers of information broadcast their content to the Web users who have requested it. You subscribe to a **channel**, or a Web site, whose contents can be delivered automatically to a subscriber's computer. You can indicate how often you want to receive the updated information. An organization such as CNN or Newsweek might maintain a Web channel to push late-breaking news to subscribers who can then simply check their desktops at regular intervals to get a quick look at the news. As push technology becomes more common it is likely that channels will increase in frequency just as Web pages have done.

Active Desktop

Internet Explorer uses **Active Desktop** technology to alter your operating system's desktop so that it can receive the information broadcast by channel Web sites and display it on your computer without requiring extra communications software. Once Active Desktop is enabled, you are ready to subscribe to the information you want.

To enable Active Desktop:

1. Right-click a blank area of the desktop.

2. Point to **Active Desktop**.

3. If no checkmark precedes the View As Web Page option, click **View As Web Page**.

With Active Desktop enabled, you can subscribe to a channel and place a Web component on your desktop in a resizable, moveable window. A **Web component** is a desktop object such as a weather map, an investor ticker, or a news service that you can set to update automatically via your Web connection. Figure B-2 shows a Windows desktop with several such Web components.

Figure B-2 ◄
Web
components on
the desktop

news service ⟶

financial news service ⟶

weather map ⟶

investor ticker ⟶

Every morning when this user checks her desktop, each component will have been automatically updated (if, that is, she has set the update schedules that way). The weather map will show the morning's weather instead of weather from the night before, her news service will display the most recent news, and the other Web components will update in a similar fashion. If she wants a more detailed look at, for example, the news, she can select and enlarge one of the Web component windows, as shown in Figure B-3.

Figure B-3 ◄
Enlarged Web
component

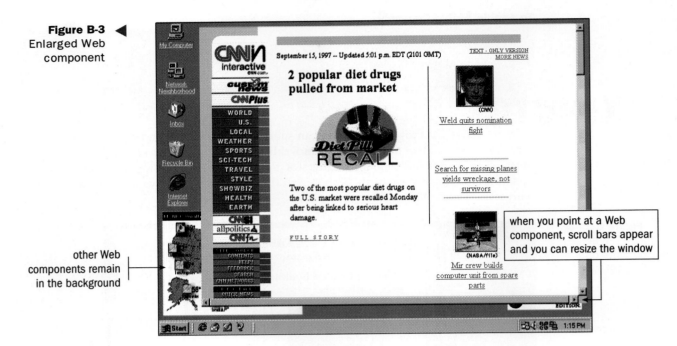

other Web
components remain
in the background

when you point at a Web
component, scroll bars appear
and you can resize the window

There are three ways to add Web components to the Windows desktop: the Active Desktop Gallery, the Active Channel service, and through subscriptions that you initiate from other channels independently of the Active Channel service.

In a student lab it's likely that your lab managers have disabled channel delivery because students often don't have the rights to receive information on the hard disk. For this reason, you might only be able to read these next several sections without performing the steps.

Active Desktop Gallery

The **Active Desktop Gallery,** available from Microsoft's Web site, offers a set of useful Web components, including the weather map, investment ticker, clock, and so on. Try placing one of these Web components on your desktop.

To place an Active Desktop Gallery component on your desktop:

1. Right-click the desktop.

2. Point to **Active Desktop**.

3. Click **Customize my Desktop**. The Display Properties dialog box opens.

4. Click the **Web** tab. A list of current Web components appears. See Figure B-4.

Internet Explorer

Figure B-4 ◄
Current Web
components

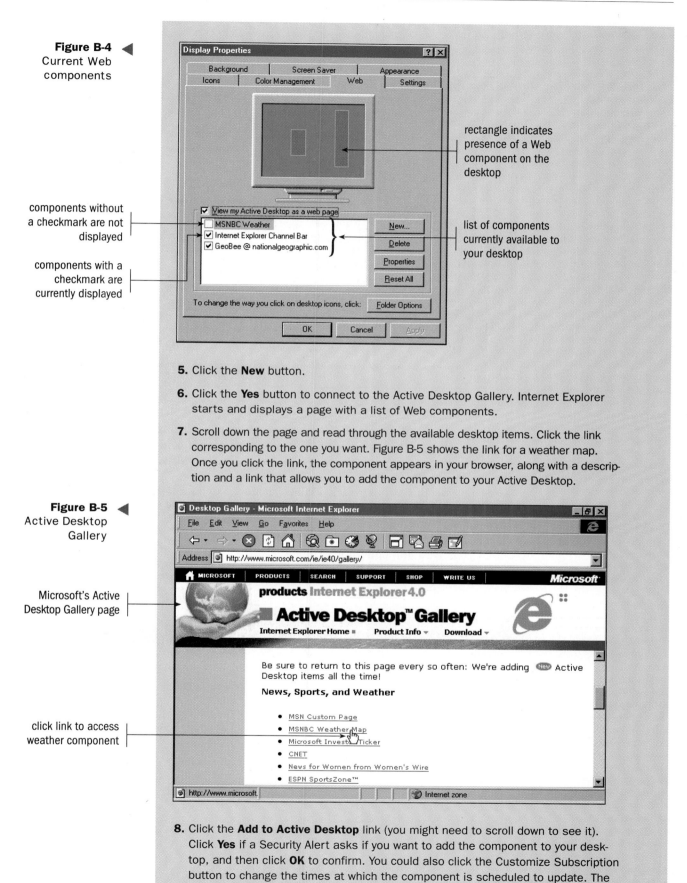

rectangle indicates
presence of a Web
component on the
desktop

components without
a checkmark are not
displayed

components with a
checkmark are
currently displayed

list of components
currently available to
your desktop

5. Click the **New** button.

6. Click the **Yes** button to connect to the Active Desktop Gallery. Internet Explorer starts and displays a page with a list of Web components.

7. Scroll down the page and read through the available desktop items. Click the link corresponding to the one you want. Figure B-5 shows the link for a weather map. Once you click the link, the component appears in your browser, along with a description and a link that allows you to add the component to your Active Desktop.

Figure B-5 ◄
Active Desktop
Gallery

Microsoft's Active
Desktop Gallery page

click link to access
weather component

8. Click the **Add to Active Desktop** link (you might need to scroll down to see it). Click **Yes** if a Security Alert asks if you want to add the component to your desktop, and then click **OK** to confirm. You could also click the Customize Subscription button to change the times at which the component is scheduled to update. The subscription downloads to your computer.

9. Close the Internet Explorer browser. The Web component now appears on your desktop. See Figure B-6.

Figure B-6 ◄
Weather map downloaded from Active Desktop Gallery

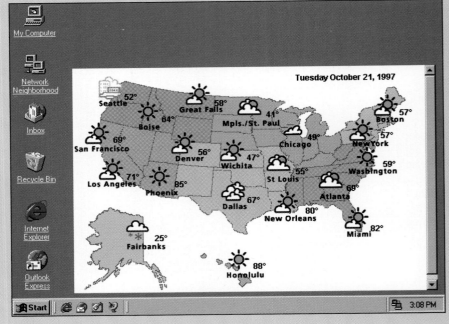

Once you place a Web component on your desktop, a rectangular block appears that seems to be a part of the background. When you select that component, however, a window border appears that you can resize and move as you would any Windows window, as you saw in Figure B-3.

Depending on this component's settings, it might update itself automatically or you might need to update it manually. You can check a component's settings from the Display Properties dialog box.

To check your Web component's settings:

1. Right-click the desktop, point to **Active Desktop**, then click **Customize my Desktop**.

2. Click the **Web** tab.

3. Click the component whose settings you want to view, then click the **Properties** button. The Subscription tab shows the current settings for the component. See Figure B-7. The Receiving tab lets you set options for how you receive the information, and the Schedule tab allows you to change the schedule or to choose to update the component manually.

Figure B-7
Viewing Web
component
properties

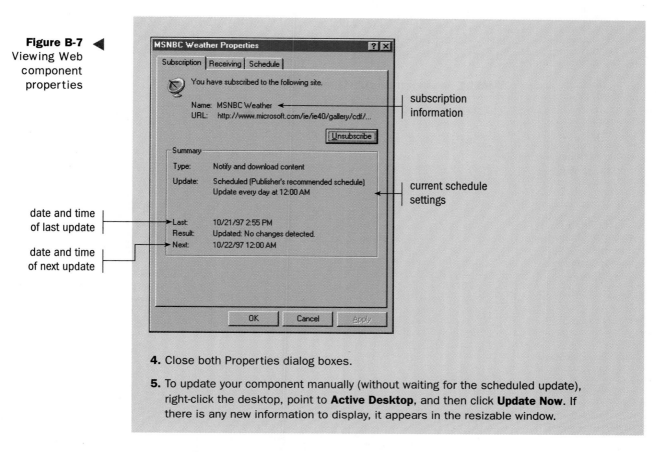

subscription
information

current schedule
settings

date and time
of last update

date and time
of next update

4. Close both Properties dialog boxes.

5. To update your component manually (without waiting for the scheduled update), right-click the desktop, point to **Active Desktop**, and then click **Update Now**. If there is any new information to display, it appears in the resizable window.

If you decide you no longer want to subscribe to the component on your desktop, you can either temporarily disable it or remove it completely.

To disable and then remove a Web component:

1. Right-click the desktop, point to **Active Desktop**, then click **Customize my Desktop**.

2. Click the **Web** tab.

3. To disable the component, click the check box preceding the component so that no checkmark occurs. Click the **OK** button. The Display Properties dialog box closes and the component disappears from the desktop.

4. To remove the component completely, reopen the Display Properties dialog box to the Web tab. Click the component you want to remove, then click the **Delete** button. If a message box asks if you are sure, click the **Yes** button.

Once a component is disabled or removed it no longer broadcasts information to your system. If you simply disabled it, you can re-enable it by selecting it on the Web tab, but if you removed it, you need to resubscribe to it before you can begin receiving information from it again.

Active Channel Service

You can also subscribe to channels created by companies that have agreements with Microsoft to broadcast information directly to the desktops of those who subscribe to the Active Channel service. Active Channels are available through the Internet Explorer Channel Bar. This bar appears automatically on the desktop when Internet Explorer is installed, but it's possible that it has been removed from your desktop. You'll need to restore it before you subscribe to a channel.

The Channel Bar shows channels selected by Microsoft as well as channels that you have added to the Channel Bar. You can use Microsoft's Active Channel Guide to view and subscribe to additional channels.

To add a channel from the Channel Bar:

1. Open the Display Properties dialog box to the Web tab, then click the check box preceding the Internet Explorer Channel Bar component to check it. Click the **OK** button. The Channel Bar appears on your desktop as in Figure B-8.

Figure B-8 ◀
Channel Bar

click to open Active Channel Guide and view more channels

individual channel sites to which you can subscribe instantly

channel categories within the Active Channel Guide

click to view additional channels or channel categories

Channel Bar

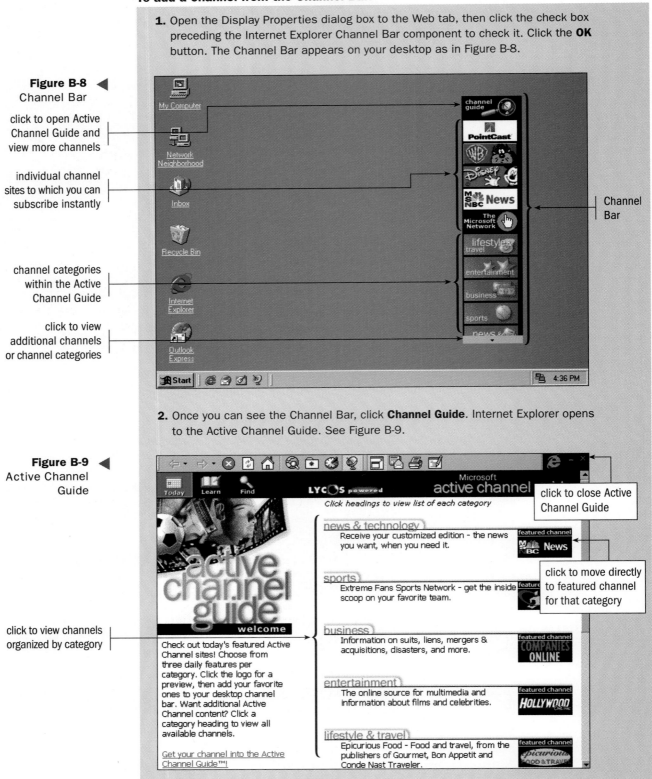

2. Once you can see the Channel Bar, click **Channel Guide**. Internet Explorer opens to the Active Channel Guide. See Figure B-9.

Figure B-9 ◀
Active Channel Guide

click to close Active Channel Guide

click to move directly to featured channel for that category

click to view channels organized by category

3. Click the category you want. A list of available channels appears. Click the channel to which you want to subscribe.

   TROUBLE? If Microsoft has changed the organization of the Active Channel Guide, you might need to navigate additional links. Follow the prompts on the screen.

4. Click **Add Active Channel** to add the channel to your Channel Bar, or click **Add to Active Desktop** to add the component to your desktop. The prompts you see are similar to those you saw when adding a component from the Active Desktop Gallery, so follow the prompts to complete the procedure.

5. Close the Active Channel Guide when the download is complete. You can modify the schedule and other properties of this component by returning to the Display Properties dialog box, clicking the Web tab, clicking the channel you want to modify, and then clicking the Properties button, but you won't do that now.

6. To leave a clean desktop for the next user, re-open the Display Properties dialog box to the Web tab and remove any Web components you subscribed to.

Subscribing to Other Channels

You can add your own Web components by subscribing to channel sites that don't appear on the Channel Bar or in the Active Channel Guide. In most cases, you do this by connecting to the site with your browser. Sites that support channel delivery include a link that asks if you want to subscribe to the site or add the site as a channel. Click the link and follow the prompts; they vary from site to site.

Using a Web Page as Background Wallpaper

Before Internet Explorer 4.0, you might have experimented with the look of your desktop by changing the color or pattern of the default background wallpaper. Then you were limited to using image files as your background wallpaper. Trying to create a desktop background that integrated text and images and other objects was impossible. Active Desktop, however, extends your control over your desktop's background by allowing you to use Web pages as wallpaper so that your desktop background can feature text, images, links, and multimedia objects. You can use the Web page authoring tool that comes with the Full version of Internet Explorer, FrontPage Express, to create such a background. Alternatively, you can use the Internet Explorer browser to save an existing Web page as an HTML file and then use that as your wallpaper.

To designate a Web page as your wallpaper:

1. Right-click the desktop.

2. Click **Properties**.

3. Click the **Background** tab.

4. Click the **Browse** button.

5. Locate and select the HTML file you want to use, then click the **Open** button. See Figure B-10.

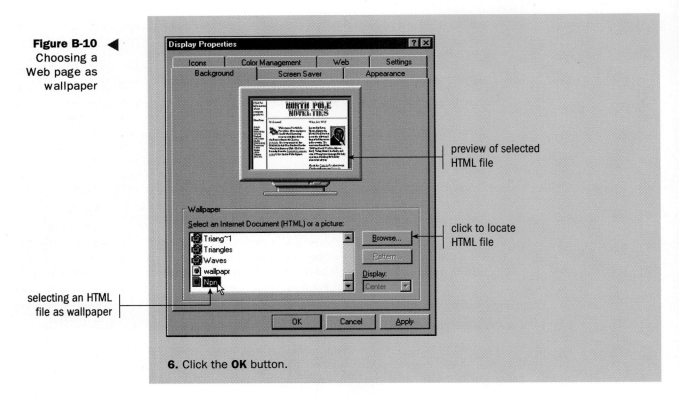

selecting an HTML
file as wallpaper

preview of selected
HTML file

click to locate
HTML file

6. Click the **OK** button.

The added control Internet Explorer 4.0 gives you over background wallpaper makes it possible to make the desktop a launch-pad for your most important projects. A corporation, for example, might create an HTML file that contains important company information, an updateable company calendar, links to company documents, a sound clip welcoming new employees to the company, and so on.

Figure B-11 shows a sample desktop that might appear on the computers of a gift shop chain's main headquarters.

Figure B-11 ◀
Web page
wallpaper

updateable
information

links to company
product information

video clip

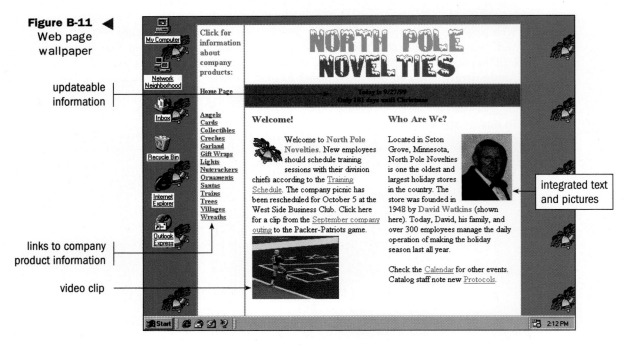

integrated text
and pictures

This company created a wallpaper that includes links to product groups, information about the company, a video clip of a recent company outing, links to current events, company protocols, and training procedures.

Internet Explorer brings the Web to your computer in other ways too: by allowing you to add links to your taskbar, by making your Favorites folder available through the Start menu, and by modifying the My Computer and Windows Explorer windows so you can use them to view Web pages as easily as you view your hard disk. You can explore these options on your own.

Appendix B Assignments

1. Connect to Microsoft's Active Desktop Gallery and scroll through the categories that are currently available. Make a list of the categories and research a few of the components for each category that interests you. If you had the ability to subscribe to Web components, which components would you choose and why? Write a page-long report that lists the current categories and then itemize three components you chose. Summarize the content they provide and indicate why you would choose to place that information on your desktop. Figure B-12, for example, shows the current Entertainment components. The list of categories and available components will probably have changed since this book was published.

Figure B-12 ◀

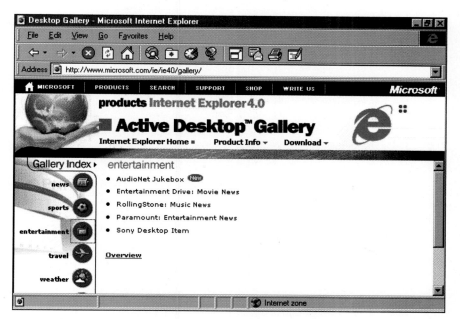

2. If you have the ability to subscribe to a Web component, choose one from either the Active Desktop Gallery or the Active Channel Guide. Once the component is active on your desktop, explore its current scheduling status.

   a. Right-click a blank area of the desktop, point to Active Desktop, and then click Customize my Desktop.
   b. On the Web tab, click the component you just added.
   c. Click Properties.
   d. Examine the settings on each tab (Subscription, Receiving, and Schedule) and write a two-paragraph report that summarizes the default settings for that component.
   e. If you wanted to change the schedule so that the component updated, for example, every hour, how would you do so? Write a set of steps documenting the procedure you would use.

3. If you could create an HTML file for your own computer's wallpaper, what would you include on it? Draw a sketch of your desktop and then draw a picture of how you want the HTML file to look. Indicate links by underlining them, and indicate what other content you would include. Write two paragraphs describing your wallpaper and how the wallpaper you would create would increase your efficiency.

Microsoft Internet Explorer 4 **Task Reference**

TASK	PAGE #	RECOMMENDED METHOD
Address Book entries, delete	IE 3.24	Click Tools, click Address Book, right-click entry you want to delete, click Delete
Address Book, add entry to	IE 3.11	See "Adding an Entry to the Address Book"
Address Book, create group	IE 3.13	Click 📖, type name, click Select Members, click Name and click Select, repeat until all names are entered, click OK twice
Address Book, use address from	IE 3.14	Click 📖, click 📧, click recipient, click To:, click OK
Attached file, view	IE 3.15	See "Viewing an Attached File"
Audio clip, play	IE 2.6	Click audio file link, click Open this file from its current location, click OK
Background, set	IE 4.32	See "Using a Graphic Image as a Page Background"
Bookmark, set	IE 5.3	Click Edit, click Bookmark, type bookmark name, click OK
Bullet symbol, change	IE 4.18	Select the bulleted list, right-click the selection, click List Properties, click bullet style, click OK
Bulleted list, create	IE 4.17	See "Creating a Bulleted List"
E-mail, check for messages	IE 3.8	Click 📧, type password if necessary, click Inbox
E-mail, configure preferences	IE 3.2	Click Tools, click Accounts, click Mail tab, click account with your name, click Properties button
E-mail, create folder for	IE 3.17	See "Creating a Message Folder"
E-mail, delete message or message folder	IE 3.23	Right-click message, click Delete
E-mail, file	IE 3.18	See "Filing a Message"
E-mail, forward	IE 3.22	Click message, click 📧
E-mail, print	IE 3.11	Click message, click File, click Print, click OK
E-mail, read	IE 3.9	Click message in Inbox folder
E-mail, reply to	IE 3.10	Click message, click 📧, enter message, click 📧 Send
E-mail, save to a text file	IE 3.21	Click message, click File, click Save As, enter location, click Save
E-mail, send	IE 3.6	See "Sending an E-mail Message"
E-mail, send to multiple recipients	IE 3.14	Click 📖, click 📧, click recipient, click To:, click additional recipient, click To: or Cc:; or click group name and then click To:, click OK, enter message, click Send
E-mail folder, delete	IE 3.23	Right-click folder, click Delete
E-mail message folder, create	IE 3.17	See "Creating a Message Folder"
Excite, search using	IE 2.25	Click 🔍, click Choose provider list arrow, click Excite, type query in box, click Search
Explorer bar, hide	IE 1.15	Click View, point to Explorer Bar, click None

Microsoft Internet Explorer 4 **Task Reference**

TASK	PAGE #	RECOMMENDED METHOD

Explorer bar, use History	IE 2.11	See "Locating a Visited Page"
Explorer bar, use Favorite	IE 2.17	Click 🔳, click page or folder
Explorer bar, use Search	IE 2.24	Click 🔳, click Choose provider list arrow, click provider, conduct search
Favorite page, delete	IE 2.19	See "Deleting Pages or Folders from the Favorites Folder"
Favorite Web page, access	IE 2.15	Click 🔳, click folder in Explorer bar if necessary, click page
Favorites folder, add page to	IE 2.14	Connect to page, click Favorites, click Add to Favorites, click OK. To add to sub-folder, click Favorites, click Add to Favorites, click Create in, click folder, click OK
Favorites folder, create	IE 2.16	See "Creating a Folder for Favorite Pages"
File, attach to e-mail message	IE 3.20	See "Attaching a File to an E-mail Message"
File, download	IE 2.31	Right-click link to file, click Save Target As, enter a location, click Save
File associations, check	IE 2.3	In My Computer, click View, click Folder Options, click File Types tab, click file type
Font size, increase	IE 4.22	Select text, click 🅰
FrontPage Express, start	IE 4.6	See "Starting FrontPage Express"
Help, access	IE 1.32	Click Help, click Contents and Index
Image, insert inline	IE 4.28	See "Inserting an Inline Image"
Image, modify properties	IE 4.31	Right-click image, click Image Properties, change properties, click OK
Image, save from a Web page	IE 2.30	See "Saving an Image from a Web Page"
Image, view individually	IE 1.31	Right-click image icon 🖼, click Show Picture
Images, load automatically	IE 1.30	See "Viewing Images on Demand"
Infoseek, search using	IE 2.24	Click 🔳, click Choose provider list arrow, click Infoseek, type query, click seek
Internet Explorer, exit	IE 1.24	Click ❎
Internet Explorer, start	IE 1.11	Connect to Internet account, click 🏁Start, point to Programs, point to Internet Explorer, click Internet Explorer
Line, change properties	IE 4.25	Right-click horizontal line, click Horizontal Line Properties, change proper-ties, click OK
Line, insert	IE 4.24	See "Inserting a Horizontal Line"
Link, abort	IE 1.20	Click ❎
Link, activate	IE 1.18	Click the link
Link, create to bookmark within open document	IE 5.5	Select text, click 🔳, click Open Pages tab, click Bookmark list arrow, click bookmark, click OK
Link, create to e-mail address	IE 5.26	Select text, click 🔳, click World Wide Web tab, type mailto:*e-mail address* in URL box, where *e-mail address* is address you are linking to, click OK
Link, create to open file	IE 5.15	Select text, click 🔳, click Open Pages tab, click file, click OK

Microsoft Internet Explorer 4 **Task Reference**

Microsoft Internet Explorer 4 **Task Reference**

TASK	PAGE #	RECOMMENDED METHOD
Text, format	IE 4.20	See "Applying Character Tags"
Text, indent	IE 4.19	Click within paragraph you want to indent, then click ⊞ to shift text to right or ⊞ to shift text to left
Text, italicize	IE 4.20	Select text, click ⬛
Text file, open in Internet Explorer	IE 2.29	See "Opening a Text File"
Toolbar, move	IE 1.15	Drag toolbar up, down, left, or right
Toolbar, resize	IE 1.15	Point at vertical bar preceding toolbar and drag left or right
Toolbar, view or hide	IE 1.14	Click View, point to Toolbars, click toolbar you want to view or hide
Toolbars, customize FrontPage Express	IE 4.7	Click View, then select the toolbar options you want
URL, connect to	IE 1.26	See "Opening a Location"
Web page, open in Internet Explorer	IE 1.16	See "Opening a Web Page into the Internet Explorer Browser"
Web page, print	IE 1.33	Click File, click Print, click OK
Web page, publish multiple pages	IE 5.28	Start Windows Explorer, select files you want to publish, including all html, graphic, and accompanying files, right-click selection, point to Send To, click Web Publishing Wizard, follow prompts
Web page, publish single page	IE 5.28	Click File, click Save As, enter page location that includes server address, then follow prompts
Web page, save as file	IE 4.7	Click File, click Save As, click As File button, click Save in list arrow, select drive and folder, type name in File name box, click Save
Web page, save as text file	IE 2.28	See "Saving a Web Page as Text"
Web page, store location of	IE 2.14	Click Favorites, click Add to Favorites, click OK
Web page, view in full screen	IE 1.23	Click ⬛
Web pages, navigate	IE 1.28	Click ⬅ to move to previous page, ➡ to revisit page, ⌂ to return to home page
Web pages, navigate with Back and Forward lists	IE 2.12	See "Searching the Back and Forward Lists"
Web pages, navigate with File menu	IE 2.9	Click File, click page you want to access
Web pages, navigate with History Explorer bar	IE 2.10	See "Locating a Visited Page"
Yahoo, search using	IE 2.26	Click ⬛, click Choose provider list arrow, click Yahoo, click subject link